STUFF YOU SHOULD KNOW

AN INCOMPLETE COMPENDIUM OF ~~VERY~~ *MOSTLY* INTERESTING THINGS

JOSH CLARK and CHUCK BRYANT
with NILS PARKER

STUFF
YOU
SHOULD
READ

An
iHeart
Book

FLATIRON
BOOKS
NEW YORK

CONTENTS

PREFACE

Hey and welcome to the book everybody. We're Josh Clark and Charles W. "Chuck" Bryant. And this is *An Incomplete Compendium of Mostly Interesting Things.*

Here's the first interesting thing: we've been podcasting since 2008, and we've talked about writing an SYSK book for a long time now, but there came a point a while back when we thought it would never happen and we kind of stopped thinking about it, so we're just tickled that it has all finally come together in this book you are holding or listening to right now. Actually, we're not exactly sure what's interesting about that little bit of personal trivia, to be honest. We know there's got to be something, though, because we feel like there's something interesting about everything.

Understanding this idea—that there's something interesting about everything—is one of the core beliefs that make up the fabric of the entire *Stuff You Should Know* universe, and this book is no exception. It has had a profound effect on us as podcasters, as writers, and as humans in the world. And it has informed everything we do, most directly by supercharging a very specific trait we both possess: curiosity.

The belief that there is something interesting about everything has opened our eyes, our ears, and our minds to the world around us in ways we never could have expected before we started working together all those years ago. From the odd to the mundane, from the overlooked to the underappreciated, from the infinite to the infinitesimal; whether it involved a person, place, or thing, whether it was an idea or an event, a process or a system, real or imagined, every day we found something that made us sit up, take notice, and say "huh, *that's* interesting . . . we should talk about that."[1]

Twelve years and 1,300 podcast episodes later, we decided to take the same approach with a book. *This* book. We said, how about Josh picks thirteen random topics that we've been curious about recently, and Chuck picks fourteen; we'll see what kind of interesting stuff we can find, and then write about it.[2, 3]

The results, if you are a fan of the show already, will hopefully feel familiar. That was the idea, at least. There's lots of stuff you should know; there's

---

[1] And in a few cases, when we really had to dig, we said, "We *will* find what's interesting about this."

[2] Note from Josh: thirteen has always been a fortunate number for me and my wife, Umi, so here's hoping some of that lucky thirteen rubs off on you, dear reader!

[3] Note from Chuck: I don't believe in luck, but me and Josh still manage to work together.

some weirdness and some humor; there are some counterintuitive explanations, some unexpected realizations, some accidental puns, more than a few awesome band names, a heaping helping of dad jokes, tons of dives down little rabbit holes,[4] and several dozen illustrations by an artist named Carly Monardo that we are totally in love with (the illustrations, not Carly, though she is wonderful and a total badass).

We also worked with a co-writer, a great guy named Nils Parker, who helped us tremendously with research, writing, and generally guiding us through what's what with publishing a book. Having a hired gun to help us out was a tough pill to swallow at first, both of us being writers, but as the book project unfolded in earnest, all of our illusions (delusions, really) quickly fell away and we were grateful for Nils's help right out of the gate. Had he not been around, you might be picking this book up in 2030 rather than 2020. Nils has gotten the SYSK vibe so thoroughly that he's become as much a part of the SYSK gang as Jeri and Frank the Chair, so be sure to add him to your holiday card list.

Together, like a Voltron of edutainment, we pounded out and honed this book into a sword of wisdom for you to wield at the water cooler and at cocktail parties, anywhere you feel like impressing people. Use it wisely.

Oh, and it just so happens that sword analogy is also a really great segue for our next point.

In *The Book of Five Rings*, the seventeenth-century samurai Miyamoto Musashi wrote, "from one thing, know ten thousand things." Musashi was a master swordsman and he knew that discipline fully. But he didn't *only* know that. He also learned metallurgy to understand how to make the strongest sword; physiology and anatomy to understand the physical vulnerabilities of his opponents; human psychology to understand their mental vulnerabilities; geometry to understand angles of attack; physics to understand leverage. The list almost certainly goes on.

What Musashi was saying is that if you master one thing completely, it will teach you about so many other things in the process. And while we agree with the great samurai and are very grateful that we never faced the slashing end of his fury, we have respectfully chosen to take the opposite approach to knowledge. From the very beginning of *Stuff You Should Know*, we've had one overarching goal: to teach people as much as we can about the world, one topic at a time. What we learned writing this book is that from ten thousand things (or in this case, twenty-seven things), you can

---

[4] They take the form of footnotes . . . like this one.

know one thing. And that is, when you look closely enough, everything is connected, one way or another.[5]

Just as with everything else in the world, there is a deep interconnectedness to the randomness within the twenty-seven chapters of this book. You can read it front to back, back to front, or jump around;[6] whichever reading adventure you choose, what you will find are connection points and narrative threads that join them. That's why each chapter can stand on its own or be read in any order. It just kind of happened that way, and we are pleased as punch that it did.

The first thing you'll notice is the first thing we noticed: just how many podcast episodes we've done related to topics that we only touch on in each chapter. These connections back to the show are denoted by a microphone icon 🎙 and indicate a relevant podcast episode whose title we have listed in the appendix.

What you might then notice is how wide and far these connections go as we move through the chapters and through the world. We go back in time millions of years with prehistoric wildebeest and elephants to learn about water dowsing. We travel trillions of miles into space to better grasp the magnitude and proportion of massive personal wealth. We travel the globe to meet common criminals in Britain, brilliant distillers in Mexico, Benjamin Button mice in Massachusetts, and extraordinary figures from the islands of the South Pacific. You've got in your hands a guided tour of interconnected time and space, and for a pretty fair price when you consider it like that.

Our hope is that in reading this book you feel more connected to the world around you: to the person next to you on the train and the stranger on the opposite side of the world, to the beginning of human history and to the end of eras you weren't alive for, to places you may never go and people you will probably never meet. More than anything, we hope you learn some new stuff along the way. That would be pretty cool, too.

Okay, well, that's probably enough setup, let's start the book already!

Josh Clark & Chuck Bryant
Atlanta, Georgia
Summer 2020

---

[5] This is, of course, the whole premise of the Six Degrees of Kevin Bacon game. That game alone gives The Great Interconnectedness of All Things an important purpose.

[6] You can also jump up, jump up, and get down if you like.

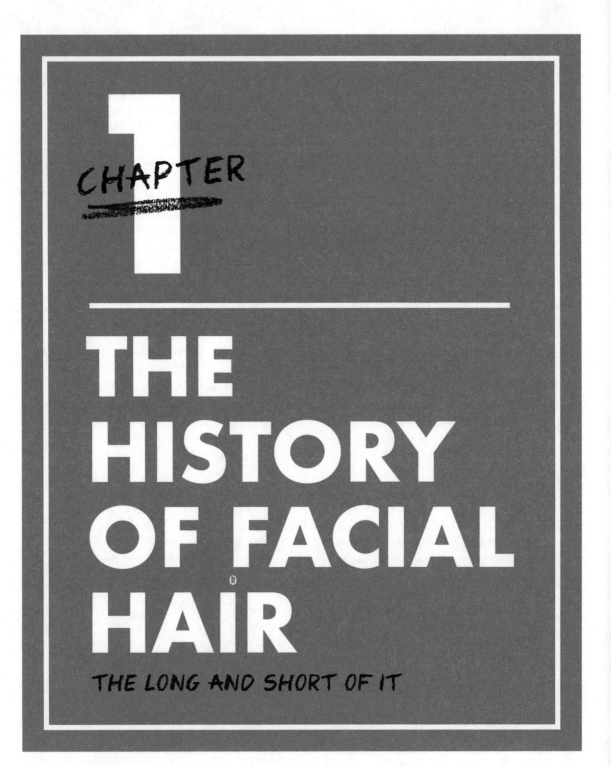

CHAPTER

1

THE HISTORY OF FACIAL HAIR

THE LONG AND SHORT OF IT

There are really only two types of facial hair: beards and mustaches. Every style of facial hair you've ever seen is one of these two, or a combination of both.

Think about it like part of a Linnaean taxonomy of human traits that we just made up but totally makes sense, where facial hair is a Family, beards and mustaches are each a Genus, and their many varieties are individual species that could interbreed, as it were, to create hybrid subspecies like the duck-billed platypus 🔊 of the facial hair Family, the soul patch.

This might seem self-evident when you take a second to think about it, but then why would you be thinking about this at all unless you work in the relatively booming beard care industry or you're a pogonophile—a lover of beards and the bearded. The *Economist* wrote about that very philia in a 2015 article about the growing trend of beardedness while reporting from the National Beard and Mustache Championship that was taking place in Brooklyn that year . . . obviously.[1]

If you are breathing right now, then you must be aware that the beards the *Economist* reported on were part of more than just a passing trend. Facial hair grew more popular over the rest of the decade until it became a full-blown phenomenon of twenty-first-century maleness. It even had a cameo in the novel coronavirus pandemic that started to spread around the globe in early 2020. Media outlets stumbled on a 2017 infographic from our friends at the Centers for Disease Control right here in our hometown of Atlanta. It showed which facial hair styles were okay with a standard face mask and which styles were less ideal because they "crossed the seal," allowing all manner of nasty little things access to your wide-open mouth.[2]

Infographics are neat, especially the unintentionally interesting ones, and this particular one got our attention. It shows thirty-six distinct styles:

....

[1] A year earlier, in February 2014, the *New York Post* ran a story about men in Brooklyn paying as much as $8,500 for facial hair transplants in order to grow better beards.

[2] Sleep tight, don't let the beard bugs bite.

Fourteen mustaches, twelve beards, nine beard-mustache hybrids, and a clean-shaven option. When we noticed that more than two-thirds of these styles were less than optimal for proper mask usage, the chart revealed something we hadn't thought of before: facial hair doesn't seem particularly functional, at least not in the way we typically think about functionality in the high-tech, go-go, N-95 mask wearing world of today.[3] And if that's true, then the question is: why do we have facial hair at all?

It's here that we found, to our great excitement, that scientists aren't exactly sure. But they have come up with a best evolutionary guess that makes a lot of sense, if you take a step back to see the forest for the trees—or the beard for the whiskers, as it were.

PUTTING THE "FUN" IN FUNCTIONAL

As it turns out, facial hair is not a functional physical human trait in the way we thought it was for many years. It's an ornamental one. In fact, of all the physical features on the human body—including other kinds of hair—facial hair is the only one that is purely or primarily ornamental. That is, it doesn't actually *do* anything or perform any kind of specific physiological function. Just take a look at what the rest of our hair does for us:

- Body hair helps with thermoregulation.

- Head hair protects your scalp from the beating sun, but also traps heat in if you're in a cold weather climate.[4]

- Eyelashes are like screen doors for the eyes, keeping bugs and dust and little debris particles out whenever they're open.

- Eyebrows impede sweat from getting in your eyes.

- Armpit hair (the technical term is "axillary" hair, which we are pretty sure we've talked about before, maybe in the body odor episode?) 🎧 collects and disseminates pheromones while acting like the WD-40 of body

---

[3] Our sincere hope is that this reference becomes dated and future readers are entirely confused by it.

[4] This is particularly true of helmet hair.

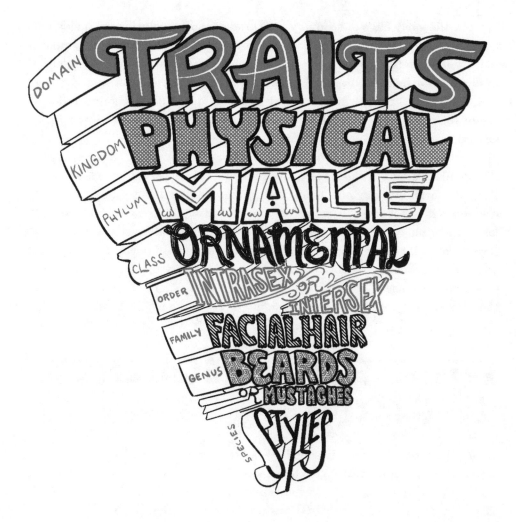

hair, reducing friction between skin on the underside of the arm and skin on the side of the chest as we walk and swing our arms.[5]

- Pubic hair also helps reduce friction, as well as provides a layer of protection from bacteria and other pathogens.

But facial hair? You will notice it doesn't appear on that handy list of adaptive hairy traits.

....

[5] Learning this has made us feel bad about the bare underarm beauty ideal that women in the West have traditionally been expected to follow.

In the early days of studying this kind of stuff, evolutionary biologists thought it might serve thermoregulatory or prophylactic purposes similar to body hair and pubic hair.[6] Beards and mustaches are around the mouth, after all, and the mouth takes in food and other particles that might carry disease. Beards and mustaches are also on the face, which is connected to the head, which loses a lot of heat out of its top if it isn't covered by hair. It all makes sense when you look at it that way.

Except there's a problem with this theory: it leaves out 50 percent of the population, i.e., *females*. Natural selection is ruthless, and it has sent A LOT of species the way of the dodo—for instance, the dodo[7]—but rarely, if ever, does it select for a trait in a species like that and leave half the population hanging, especially the half that makes all the babies (i.e., the most important half). If facial hair were meant to perform important functions, it would be present across both sexes. Instead, thick, mature facial hair is present almost exclusively on the male half of the species, and its only job is to sit there on the face of its wearer as a signal to everyone who crosses his path.

WHAT'S THE FREQUENCY, KENNETH?

What signal does facial hair send? Well, here's where it gets a little complicated, as ornamental traits go. University of New Mexico professor Geoffrey Miller, one of the preeminent evolutionary psychologists in the field, put it this way: "the two main explanations for male facial hair are intersexual attraction (attracting females) and intrasexual competition (intimidating rival males)." Basically, facial hair signals one thing to potential partners

---

[6] Beard and mustache wearers do get some of these benefits, but they are secondary and incidental to their primary purpose. For instance, clean-shaven men are three times more likely to carry MRSA on their faces, but it's not because beards protect you better from the bacteria. It's that shaving abrades the skin and leaves small, open wounds that are much better at collecting pathogens. [Josh shudders.]

[7] Nature is an extinction machine; something to think about next Earth Day. We want to save the big blue marble, but it doesn't care one way or the other if we slide right off. In fact, more than 99 percent of all species that have ever lived in the entire history of Earth (about 5 billion of them) have gone extinct.

(namely virility and sexual maturity, hubba hubba-type stuff) and something else to potential rivals (formidability and wisdom or godliness[8]). Taken together, these signals confer their own brand of elevated status to the men with the most majestic mustaches or the biggest, burliest beards.[9]

The signal that facial hair sends also tends to be stronger and more reliable between males, who are more commonly rivals, than it is between males and females, who are more commonly partners. In fact, evolutionary biologists will tell you (if you ask them) that while some females really like facial hair, and some don't, and some couldn't care less, more often than not attraction has as much to do with beard density as anything else. That is, if you're in a place where there are a lot of beards—say, a lumberjack convention—then a clean-shaven face is more appealing, but if you're surrounded by bare faces, then a beard is best.[10]

In evolutionary genetics, this is called "negative frequency dependence" (NFD), which is science-speak for the idea that when a trait is rare within a population it tends to have an advantage. In guppies, for example, males with a unique combination of colored spots mate more often and are preyed upon less. This is a huge competitive advantage. It's like going to Vegas expecting to lose $1,000 but hoping to break even, only to end up winning $1,000 instead. That's a $2,000 swing! It's the same thing for a trait with NFD selection. The trait goes from fighting for its life to being the life of the party. The downside is that the competitive advantage can result in overpopulation of others with the same trait very quickly, because of all the getting it on the very interesting-looking guppy does—which means it loses its rarity and becomes common. Not to worry, nature has a solution for that: as more guppies bear that same trait, it leads to a decrease in interest from mates and an increase in attention from predators. What was once the hot new guppy thing becomes old news, in other words.

This yo-yoing back and forth between common and uncommon doesn't just explain the variability in the attractiveness of facial hair from

8 Maybe this is why we always depict God with a beard? Something else to think about next Earth Day.

9 Just ask Chuck, he'll tell you!

10 This is one of the big reasons special forces operators have developed such outsized reputations— they get to sport facial hair amidst a sea of regular soldiers who must be clean shaven at all times.

population to population; it also explains why the dominant theory for the evolution of facial hair has begun to resolve around intersexual competition. Because it's not enough simply to be attractive: you also have to be more attractive than the people around you, and in enough of the right ways to stand out. This goes a long way toward understanding the ebb and flow in the popularity of facial hair across time. Sporting a killer 'stache or a bushy beard is only effective, evolutionarily, as long as it still makes you part of the hot new guppy thing around the pond. When it makes you old news, shaving becomes the more effective choice.

HEY MAN, I (DON'T) LIKE YOUR STYLE

Throughout history, people have donned facial hair or shaved it as a response to the choices of their enemies and rivals. The ancient Romans went clean shaven for four-hundred years because the ancient Greeks, their rivals during the Hellenistic Period, celebrated beards as symbols of elevated status and high-mindedness.[11] For the 270 years the English lived under threat of Viking invasion (and, in some parts, actually lived under Viking rule), a period from 793 to 1066 CE tellingly called "The Viking Age of Invasion," Englishmen went clean shaven as a cultural reaction to their bearded Viking invaders. During the Protestant Reformation, many Protestants grew out their beards in protest against Catholicism, whose priests were typically clean shaven.

What's even more fascinating is how great an impact rulers and other high-status individuals have had on facial hair trends. The emperor Hadrian brought beards back to Rome in the second century CE and the

---

[11] Interestingly, it was Greece's own warrior-king, Alexander the Great, who seems to have kicked off this beardless trend. Legend has it that Alexander and his men shaved prior to the final battle against the Persians for control of Asia because he realized the enemy could grab them by their beards during close quarters fighting. The reality is that Alexander shaved because he was trying to fashion himself after the young, beardless Heracles (Hercules, to the Romans) from mythology, and he wanted his men to draw strength and inspiration from his embodiment of demigodliness. No ego there.

entire leadership class of the Roman Empire followed suit, including a number of Hadrian's successors. In the Middle Ages, Henry V was the first king of England to go clean shaven, and because he was such a great monarch English society and the subsequent seven kings followed in his beardless footsteps. It wasn't until Henry VIII came along, in all his egotistical, profligate, murderous glory (we need to do an episode on him), that the beard made a comeback, undoubtedly as a way for him to distinguish himself from his predecessors.

It's not just facial hair, yea or nay, where the choices of rulers and other high-status people have impacted the choices of those around them and for generations to come. You can see it in the evolution of specific facial hairstyles as well. Remember that chart of facial hairstyles issued by the CDC in 2017? Each style has a name. Nine of them—a full 25 percent—are named after influential figures, mostly in the arts. A few of the styles have normal names, but are so obviously connected to the one or two prominent people who made them famous that you're more likely to identify the popularizer than you are the "official" name.

STUFF YOU SHOULD KNOW . . .
About Political Philosophy

The Great Man theory of history, advanced by a nineteenth-century Scottish philosopher named Thomas Carlyle, held that leaders and rulers have an outsized impact on the direction of the story of humanity. Others say it just seems that way because those are the people whose deeds are more likely to be recorded—history is written by the victors, after all—and as such, they are the ones who are still reported on centuries later. In the realm of facial hair, however, it really does seem to be the case that leaders and rulers had an outsized impact on trends, since they were frequently the social influencers of their day. And what's more social than a nice beard/mustache combination?

Beards and Mustaches of Today and Yesteryear

DALI

Salvador Dali, twentieth-century Spanish surrealist painter known for his melting clocks and insanely long formal name, Salvador Domingo Felipe Jacinto Dalí i Domènech.

FU MANCHU

Fu Manchu, controversial mid-twentieth-century fictional villain.

ZORRO

Zorro, fictional early twentieth-century masked vigilante who sported a Cordovan hat, a rapier, and a cape for good measure. Zorro is the Spanish Lone Ranger; that, or the Lone Ranger is the American Zorro, take your pick. Either way, the Lone Ranger didn't have any facial hair.

WALRUS

Popular in the late nineteenth century, thanks to men like Mark Twain and Teddy Roosevelt, when most modern-day observers see The Walrus, their first thought is of Sam Elliott.

ZAPPA

Frank Zappa, 1960s counterculture musician known for his involvement in the freak scene and for having four kids with super-cool names (Moon Unit, who recorded the hit song "Valley Girls," which we discussed in the "Vocal Fry" episode, 🎙 Dweezil, Ahmet Emuukha, and Diva Muffin).

VAN DYKE

Anthony van Dyck, eighteenth-century Flemish painter known primarily for portraiture.

CHEVRON

They call it The Chevron, but really, they should just call it the Magnum P.I. and get it over with, because Tom Selleck is the man who almost singlehandedly made mustaches popular again in the 1980s.

BALBO

Italo Balbo, marshal of the Italian Air Force under Mussolini. Bet you didn't know that one.

GARIBALDI

Giuseppe Garibaldi, nineteenth-century Italian folk hero best known for his role in the unification of Italy.

VERDI

Giuseppe Verdi, nineteenth-century Italian composer best known for his operas *La Traviata* and *Aida*. Giuseppes are well-represented in this list, turns out.

BANDHOLZ

Eric Bandholz, twenty-first-century beard-related entrepreneur and founder of an online magazine called "Urban Beardsman." You can also call this one "The Chuckers."

TOOTHBRUSH

The Toothbrush, that's what we're calling this? Really? Okay, well we all know which short, charismatic figure from the 1930s this style actually reminds us of, so we don't even need to say it.[12]

CHIN CURTAIN

It is a travesty that the Chin Curtain is not called the C. Everett Koop.

----

[12] That's right: Charlie Chaplin.

HOW TO START OR END A FACIAL HAIR TREND

Changing tastes and the influence of high-status men in competitive environments are all well and good, but nothing moves the needle one way or another on the popularity of facial hair like a good crisis. Indeed, it was the coronavirus pandemic that brought the amazing CDC chart to our attention, and not in the most positive way. London's *Daily Mail* published a piece about it under the headline: "Could your facial hair put you at risk for coronavirus?"[13] This is not the first time facial hair has fallen under scrutiny in the midst of a disease outbreak. In a 1916 piece in *McClure's* magazine, one doctor managed to blame facial hair for the spread of nearly every communicable disease known to humanity. "There is no way of computing the number of bacteria and noxious germs that may lurk in the Amazonian jungles of a well-whiskered face," he said, "but their number must be legion." With more column inches, who knows what other ailments the good doctor would have tied to beards. Reporting like this tends to generate a rising tide of clean-shaven faces.

Then sometimes, a crisis goes the other way and leads to a period of increasing beardedness. A period like the one that produced the 2015 *Economist* article about pogonophilia, the CDC facial hair chart in 2017, and the expansion of the National Beard and Mustache Championship in 2019 from eighteen categories to *forty-seven*. The crisis that created this increased facial hair growth? The 2008 global financial crisis.

As banks failed, facial hair grew. As 401Ks got smaller, beards got bigger. Why is that? Well, those same evolutionary psychologists who will tell you about the attractiveness of facial hair will also tell you that there is no more important time to signal your fitness to rivals and potential partners

---

[13] Pro tip: anytime you see a news headline that ends with a question mark, the answer is almost always NO.

than during times of crisis.[14] Because if things are going bad and resources are scarce, and facial hair is a reliable signal of formidability and wisdom, then all other things being equal, may the best beard win.

So what happens to facial hair when a health crisis meets a political or an economic crisis? Your guess is as good as ours, but if and when it happens, you can be pretty sure it's going to look funny.

....

[14] Makes you wonder what was going on in the guppy world when those colored spots became the hot new thing.

CHAPTER

2

MR.
POTATO
HEAD

AMERICA'S TOY

We love toys. New toys, old toys, big toys, small toys.[1] Toys that need batteries, toys that only require your imagination. It doesn't matter to us. We love toys the way Brick loves lamp.

We talk to each other about toys more than any other topic besides maybe those Nazi SOBs and earth science.

So far, we've done episodes on Etch-A-Sketch, Silly Putty, Play-Doh, action figures, Slinky, Barbie®, Rubik's Cube, Easy-Bake Ovens, ET the video game, and probably a whole lot of others we're forgetting right now. 🎙 Like sugary cereal and puppies, even when a toy is bad, it's still great. Yet somehow, we have never talked about Mr. Potato Head.[2]

Those of us who were raised in America are all probably familiar with the same basic version of Mr. Potato Head: the smiling, quasi-legless Russet potato that, when fully assembled, looks like a Portland mixologist, if mixologists were allowed to smile in Portland.[3]

But he didn't always look like that. For the first decade or so of his life, Mr. Potato Head wasn't even really a potato. He was barely even a mister. He was an oddly configured, thirty-piece "funny face man" kit that cost 98 cents and required buyers to provide their own potato—an *actual* potato—to use as the head. Potato in hand, a kid could commence to attach said funny face and build said man.

And if they didn't have a potato? Not to worry: "ANY FRUIT OR VEGETABLE MAKES A FUNNY FACE MAN." Or so said the manufacturer, Hassenfeld Bros Inc., who printed those words on the top of every Mr. Potato Head box as a way to market the toy's versatility.

....

[1] See especially: our longstanding Great G.I. Joe Size Debate

[2] For reasons that remain unclear, articles about Mr. Potato Head are riper for wordplay than naming a boat. So, unlike the authors of nearly every Mr. Potato Head profile we read in preparation for this chapter, we are going to do our very best not to make any potato-based puns. Wish us luck.

[3] We suspect this joke will be a bit like a time capsule of information on early twenty-first-century hipsterism in the future.

The Original Mr. Potato Head Parts List

OF COURSE THAT'S IN THERE	OKAY, WELL THAT'S INTERESTING	WAIT, AM I MISSING SOMETHING?
Eyes (2 pairs)	Hats (3)	Yeah . . .
Ears	Eyeglasses	A FRIGGIN' HEAD!
Nose (4)	Tobacco Pipe	
Mouth (2)	Facial Hair (8!)	
Hands		
Feet		
Body		

It worked too. The Rhode Island-based company sold more than a million units their first full year in production, making it Hassenfeld Bros' first major success in the toy business and drawing them ever deeper into the industry. Eventually they condensed their name and became Hasbro—the largest toymaker in the world. And we can assume the potato farmers of America appreciated their efforts.

This very food-focused approach might have been the end of the brothers if they had gone for it only a few years earlier. It nearly proved to be for Mr. Potato Head's inventor, George Lerner, when he first went out looking for a buyer. Lerner originally called his invention "Funny Face Man"—hence the tagline on the side of the original Mr. Potato Head box—and spent the better part of the next three years struggling to gin up interest from toy companies. This proved to be a Herculean task because, at that time, the average American looked at using a potato for a toy as a shameful waste of food.

It's weird to think of a world where Mr. Potato Head never existed, because you could make a pretty strong case that Mr. Potato Head is *the* toy of the American century. In fact, we'll just say it: Mr. Potato Head is *the* toy of the American century. That's right. A legless plastic potato person, who started out as a collection of disembodied plastic parts and accessories with pins attached to them so kids could stab them into the sides of an actual potato, isn't just some disposable, forgettable childhood distraction. It turns out he is a reflection of America's recent history and cultural evolution. As Mr. Potato Head went, so went the country (or vice versa, but let's not split hairs). You could even say Mr. Potato Head *is* America.

Our theory might sound a little half-baked,[4] but the timeline of events says otherwise. Get a load of this:

1949

George Lerner invents "Funny Face Man" and it nearly dies on the vine because people are still worried, or at least conscientious, about the availability of food. Keep in mind, this is only four years after the end of World War II. Parents of young children still have memories of severe food rationing fresh in their minds. This is also the year the Cold War really kicks into gear. It is true that the United States *did* win World War II and that life in America is good by this time, but it isn't "turn your root vegetables into toys" good. If an adult is going to give a potato to their child in 1949, it's going in his or her mouth, not in their toybox.

1951

Lerner finally finds a buyer: a cereal company that wants to give the "funny face" kits away as prizes in their boxes of cereal. And, really, what kid doesn't look at a box of yummy breakfast cereal and think "I want to play with a potato!"?

But the partnership doesn't materialize. Before the cereal company can put any prize-filled boxes on store shelves, Lerner meets with the Hassenfeld brothers up in Pawtucket, Rhode Island. The Hassenfelds had made all their money to this point by producing things like pencil cases

....

[4] This was an unintentional pun that we fought bitterly with the publishers over removing. We lost.

and toy medical kits that let kids play doctor. They see the potential of this "Funny Face Man" so they buy the idea back from the cereal company, rename it Mr. Potato Head, and give George Lerner a royalty for every sale.

1952

Now the landscape really starts to shift. TV begins to invade American homes. Whereas fewer than half a million television sets were purchased the year Mr. Potato Head was invented just three years earlier, 26 million homes have a TV by the end of 1952. And they couldn't have come at a better time either. The polio  outbreak this year is the worst in the country's history, driving most of America's kids indoors, particularly during the summer months when polio is thought to be at its most virulent.[5]

Recognizing an opportunity, Hassenfeld Brothers decides to run TV ads for Mr. Potato Head. Not only is Mr. Potato Head the very first toy to be advertised on television, the Hassenfelds simultaneously pioneer the strategy of advertising directly to children, urging them to beg their parents to buy the toy for them. It's a phenomenon that will become so widespread that psychologists give it a name: "nag factor."[6]

1953

The Hassenfeld brothers, who by this time have started using Hasbro on their packaging, decide that Mr. Potato Head needs to settle down. So he marries Mrs. Potato Head and they honeymoon in Boise, Idaho (which, for potatoes, is like Branson, Missouri; Honolulu; and Las Vegas all mashed into one). It's not long before they have a couple of kids, a boy and a girl named Spud and Yam. It's a fitting, starchy, all-American choice—Mr. and Mrs.

---

[5] Polio is a type of virus that can attack the neurons in the central nervous system, killing them off and sometimes causing paralysis. Kids used to come down with it from swimming in lakes, water holes, and less-than-clean swimming pools. When outbreaks began, terrified parents would keep their kids indoors and away from other kids.

[6] In the UK, it's called "pester power." Even their term for kids being annoying sounds more refined.

Head, married with two kids, ready to set down roots[7]—for two reasons: 1) we're smack in the middle of the Baby Boom, and 2) America's new favorite toy couple now mirrors America's favorite TV couple, Lucy and Ricky Ricardo, who start the year by having a baby in an episode of *I Love Lucy*. The episode is watched by nearly three-quarters of all homes that have TVs.[8]

EARLY 1960s

Eventually the 1960s arrive, as most people expected them to. It is a decade defined, at least in part, by terms like "consumerism," "materialism," and "conspicuous consumption." The early sixties are the most hedonistic and

....

[7] It happened again.

[8] In an amazing life-imitating-art moment, the episode that filmed in the fall of 1952 airs the same day (January 19, 1953) that Lucille Ball gives birth to her second child in real life; this one a boy, named Desi Arnaz Jr., after his father and Lucy's co-star, whose real name is Desi Arnaz III, which actually makes their son Desi Arnaz IV. So that's not confusing at all.

indulgent of all. These are the *Mad Men* martinis-for-lunch years. And what are Mr. and Mrs. Potato Head doing? In addition, we presume, to drinking martinis and Rob Roys in the middle of the day, every day, they're buying lots of *stuff*, just like every other upwardly mobile middle-class American family. They buy a boat. Then a plane, a train, and an automobile. It's like something out of a movie![9]

MID-TO-LATE 1960s

It takes twelve years, but Hasbro finally leaves behind its draconian "no potato head in the Mr. Potato Head box" policy and starts producing separate plastic heads and bodies with prefabricated holes for the body parts and accessories to plug into. It's the first step toward creating the Mr. Potato Head we know today.

The decision to move toward plastic is due partly to complaints from a generation of parents tired of finding moldy potatoes under sofas and beds and inside drawers, and partly to an increased awareness (finally) of child safety.[10] The small body parts that came standard before 1964, when Hasbro makes the first plastic head and body, are considered a choking hazard, and the sharp pins on their backs are considered a stabbing hazard. So Hasbro solves their safety problems all at once with one word: plastics.

1970s

By the time the seventies roll around and things get truly groovy, concern for child safety has turned into full-blown legislation. In an amazing display of responsibility for its tiniest constituents, Congress passes the Child Protection Act of 1966, and the Child Protection and Toy Safety Act in 1969 (a.k.a. the Summer of Love and Child Safety). These new laws mean Hasbro

---

[9] Specifically, *Planes, Trains and Automobiles*.

[10] Or of safety in general for that matter. Seatbelts didn't become mandatory in all cars until 1968, and only then because of our hero Ralph Nader's incessant nagging.

has to combine the separate body and head pieces of Mr. Potato Head into one single, large body. This new version will be impossible for a small child to swallow unless that child can also detach their jaw like a reticulated python.[11] Unfortunately, this is Hasbro's first crack at a combined body form, and they kinda screw it up big time. This bulbous version, while close to the form we recognize today, looks more like someone took a butternut squash and charred it in a campfire. In other words, not good.

To make matters worse, they replace all the holes in the body with tabbed slots that only accept the pieces that belong in those specific spots: the mouth where the mouth goes, the ears where the ears go, and so on. By doing this, Hasbro takes an interactive toy that's been untapping children's imaginations for more than twenty years and sucks every bit of the magic out of it. Instead, they turn it into the world's easiest, creepiest puzzle. Who does an easy puzzle more than once? Maybe people who strongly dislike themselves and also maybe people with anterograde amnesia. Definitely not kids, though, that's for sure. Oh, and they forgot to give him arms, which was unfortunate considering they made sure he kept his pipe. Good luck packing that pipe, mister. You can't do it!

The seventies are clearly rough for Mr. Potato Head.

....

[11] Which would be something to see!

1980s–1990s

The next thirty years bring the reign of the Mr. Potato Head we all know and love. It's the version of Mr. Potato Head who finally transcends his place next to all the other toys in Toyland and begins to participate in, and affect, the culture. He even gets into politics and activism.

In 1985, Mr. Potato Head returns to Boise, where he and the missus honeymooned all those years ago and runs for mayor. Two years later, in 1987, he participates in the American Cancer Association's Eleventh Great American Smokeout and agrees to quit smoking for good. He gives up his pipe to none other than C. Everett Koop, the US Surgeon General with the greatest chin curtain of all time, in the hopes of inspiring others who are struggling to quit. As far as we know, he has not relapsed.

In the nineties, Mr. and Mrs. Potato Head sponsor the League of Women Voters' "Get Out the Vote" campaign. At the same time, Mr. Potato Head continues his health kick, this time trying to get kids to be more active and not be such couch potatoes, accepting an award in the process, from the chairman of the President's Council on Physical Fitness and Sports—Arnold Schwarzenegger—in a ceremony on the White House lawn.[12]

PRESENT-DAY POTATO

If, by now, Mr. Potato Head isn't forever cemented as a pop culture icon, his role in the *Toy Story* films, beginning in 1995, does the trick. Of all the toys in the movies, he is the one who is the most immediately recognizable and the least changed—since the 1970s, anyway. If three generations of family sat down tomorrow to watch *Toy Story* for the first time, all three would probably be like, "Aww, Mr. Potato Head!" That is the universality and ubiquity of Hasbro's Mr. Potato Head; that, and nostalgia is a powerful force.[13]

....

[12] This is one of the '80s-est sentences ever captured in a book.

[13] And definitely not the "most toxic impulse," despite what our friend John Hodgman thinks.

Ipso facto, our theory that Mr. Potato Head is the toy of the American century remains sound.

The *New York Times* writer N.R. Kleinfeld hit the nail on the head when he wrote back in 1987 that "Hasbro was one of the first companies to recognize the value in endowing a toy with a fantasy life, a practice that has become increasingly commonplace." Mr. Potato Head was first and is still the best at it. Just consider how often we use the words "he" and "his" in this chapter. You don't have to actually count, we can just tell you, it's a lot.[14] And we're not alone. Almost everyone who has ever written about Mr. Potato Head has called him, well, a *him* and not an *it*.

We don't think about Mr. Potato Head as an object the way we do other toys. We anthropomorphize him, treating him like a person. That's because an entire generation grew up with him on their TVs and in their living rooms. The Baby Boomer generation and Mr. Potato Head basically came of age together. And as the Baby Boomers got older, raised families, started running companies and cities, and began making decisions that affected millions of people, Mr. Potato Head always seemed to be right there, first as a reflection of the times, then as a player in the changing of the times. Just look at where he's shown up for the kids and grandkids of his first Boomer fans, dressing up like various members of the Star Wars and Marvel universes as part of crossover promotions[15]—two of the most popular and lucrative franchises in film history.

When you sit back and think about Mr. Potato Head, it's hard not to smile at least a little bit. And if you're like Mr. Potato Head, you can put that smile almost anywhere you please.[16]

....

[14] Let's just keep it at that, shall we?

[15] If you don't own Darth Tater or the full collection of Agents of S.P.U.D., then you're not doing fun right.

[16] Thanks to a design innovation by Hasbro in 1974, Mr. Potato Head can put his smile and every other body part in a storage compartment right where his butt would be. Kids, do NOT try that at home!

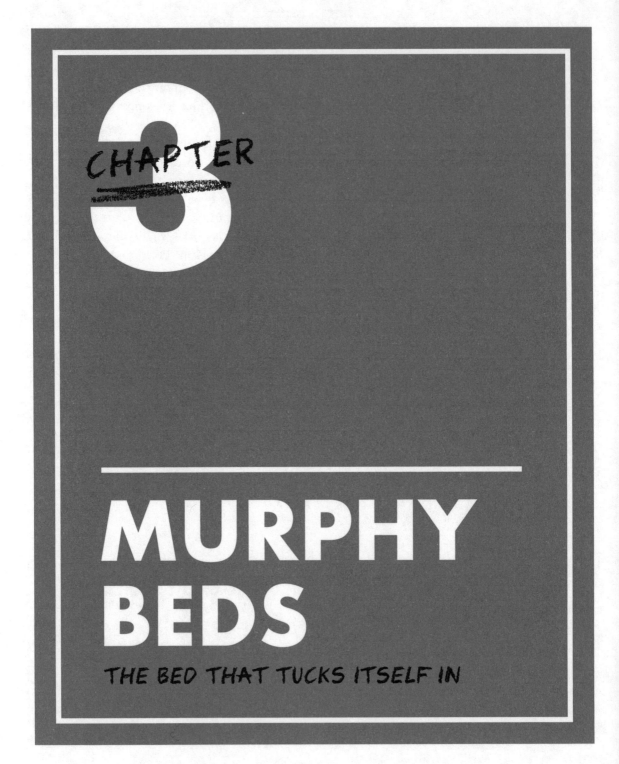

CHAPTER 3

MURPHY BEDS

THE BED THAT TUCKS ITSELF IN

Here's a question: what the heck is a Murphy bed, exactly? It's a bed that folds up into the wall, most people know that, but is that it? Is there more? Not really—and we really looked.

No matter the source, Murphy beds are described pretty much exactly how you'd expect: "a bed that swings up or folds into a closet or cabinet when not in use."[1] But the makers of the original Murphy bed—the aptly named Murphy Bed Company—would beg to differ with that characterization.

According to their website, channeling their inner Benjamin Buford "Bubba" Blue, the Murphy bed has also "become synonymous with wall bed, hide-a-bed, pullman bed, tilt-a-way bed, concealed bed, disappearing bed, folding bed, fold-away-bed, hidden bed, hidden mattress, cabinetry bed, [and] wall unit bed." And you thought there were lots of ways to cook a shrimp.[2]

Still, at first glance, it doesn't seem like there's much more to see or to say about Murphy beds. That's probably because the whole point of the Murphy bed is to go unnoticed. A Murphy bed is at its *murphiest* when it's folded up vertically and it disappears into its resting place behind a door or a wall or inside a cabinet. All that's left behind is empty space, and that's the magic of it.

EARLY HISTORY

And yet, if we take a ride in the Wayback Machine [insert Wayback Machine sound effect here] all the way to the Murphy bed's invention around 1900, what we'll see is far from just nothing. The long history of folding and disappearing beds actually goes even further back in time—*centuries further*. It turns out, a "Murphy bed" is just a patented variation on a

---

[1] That's how the Collins Dictionary described them.

[2] For the young people, and those who hate joy and have never seen it, this is a *Forrest Gump* reference.

whole bunch of earlier folding and disappearing beds. It's such a successful variation, in fact, that the term "Murphy bed" is now used for just about all hideaway beds, even ones not made by the Murphy Bed Company (or MBC, as we in the know call them) which means that Murphy beds have become one of our favorite things: a proprietary eponym.

As far as we can tell, it all started in ancient Egypt. Howard Carter, the British archeologist who discovered King Tutankhamun's tomb, 🎙 found five or six beds inside the burial chamber when he busted the proverbial locks on it in 1922. One of them was a two-fold camping bed that King Tut took with him on expeditions. How they figured that out isn't totally clear, but it seems like a pretty good guess when you consider that it looks surprisingly similar to today's first-class, lay-flat airline seats.

From Egypt, fold up bed innovations seem to have stayed pretty static until Imperial Japan with the first futons, which were more like portable bed rolls than the more familiar dorm room futons that have been compressing the lumbar spines of college students for decades. And while they don't much look like the kind of Murphy beds we would recognize today, it was the ease of storage that baked itself into the DNA of the early folding, disappearing bed.

STUFF YOU SHOULD KNOW . . .
About Language

A proprietary eponym is a brand name or trademark that has gotten so popular that it has become synonymous with the product itself. Think Kleenex for tissue, Coke for soda, Xerox for photocopies, Levi's for jeans, Post-it Notes for . . . whatever those things are called.

Five hundred years later, Renaissance Europe had its moment between the sheets with these beds, first in the form of fancy traveling "field beds," which were giant all-wooden beds that servants had to break down, move, and set up again. Later on, this type of bed became accommodations for servants once they lost their cache with the European elite, becoming a kind of cultural hand-me-down. Eventually, folding and disappearing beds arrived in Great Britain and then in America, where they evolved into furniture that was more about raw functionality[3] than signaling wealth and privilege. You can see this in a pair of seminal patents—one for a cabinet bed that doubles as a desk, the other for a simple folding bed. They were issued to two pioneering African-American inventor-entrepreneurs in the late nineteenth century named Sarah Goode and Leonard Bailey, who sold their wares to working-class customers in Chicago and to the government in Washington, D.C., respectively. Their inventions immediately preceded patents issued to William Murphy—of the Murphy bed Murphys—in the early 1910s for his hinged, pivoting, vertically oriented design.

SO WHO IS THIS WILLIAM MURPHY?

William Lawrence Murphy was born in 1876 to one of the more than 300,000 prospectors who came to the Sierra Nevada foothills in the second half of the nineteenth century hoping to strike it rich as part of the great California Gold Rush. It's lost to history whether his 49er father was successful or not. What we do know is that his son, good ol' Bill the Bed Hider, spent his late teens and early twenties breaking horses and driving stagecoaches before moving down to San Francisco. There he rented a tiny one-room apartment just off Union Square, in a building at 625 Bush Street. That little apartment is important for two reasons. First, interestingly enough, it is the building where Sam Spade's partner, Miles Archer, is murdered in *The Maltese Falcon*.[4] The second, more important reason, is that it directly caused William Murphy to invent his eponymous bed.

....

[3] You only need to look at the photography of Jacob Riis around the turn of the twentieth century to see how crowded things were in American cities. Or, if you like your pictures to move, just watch *Gangs of New York*. So, so cramped.

[4] The 1941 Humphrey Bogart movie is an adaptation of the 1930 detective novel written by Dashiell Hammett, who lived just down the street from this Bush Street apartment building. Today there is a plaque on the alley-side of the building that commemorates the famous fictional death.

It was here, in what we would call a studio apartment today, right around the turn of the twentieth century, that Murphy came up with a way to mount his full-size bed to the doorjamb of a closet using the door's hinges and a special bracket that he designed so the bed could be easily flipped up vertically, then pivoted and conveniently hidden away inside the closet, freeing up nearly thirty square feet of precious floor space.

Now, it may seem weird that a clever, mechanical innovation like this came from the mind of a young guy whose prior job history seems to have begun and ended with making horses behave. But there are two things you need to know about William Murphy: 1) he was an inveterate tinkerer, and 2) he was in love with an opera singer whom he was desperate to court. This invention didn't just create more living space in his tiny apartment—it also allowed him to invite his new love over and entertain her. And we have Queen Victoria to thank in a roundabout way for making William Murphy become the MacGyver of home improvement just to ask a girl out.

THE VICTORIAN AGE:
ALL HOLDS BARRED

The last half of the nineteenth century is generally referred to, in the English-speaking world, as the Victorian era, named for England's Queen Victoria, who reigned from 1837 to 1901. The Victorian era was a remarkable period of both great technological and political progress. It saw the beginning of the Industrial Revolution and the end of the slave trade. That same period also included a return to concerns about morality, of the stifling-propriety variety. This focus on morals called for great personal restraint within every social class, creating an environment that might best be described in modern terms as "a real buzzkill." Somehow, as our understanding of science and technology became more expansive, our mores became more suffocating and our behavior more restrictive. Who would've thought?

This was the stifling, suffocating world William Murphy was born into. A world where a true lady did not eat cheese, or become a doctor,[5] or turn around in the street to look back at someone; where a gentleman could talk briefly to a lady if they bumped into each other on the street, but could only have a full-blown conversation with her if they were on a stroll through someone's garden.[6] And though the Victorian era was drawing to a close when ol' Will found himself in San Francisco and many of these unwritten rules were beginning to relax—people were by this time allowed to make eye contact with their spouses after the twelfth year of marriage—the millions of English and Irish immigrants who'd come over to America during Victoria's reign had brought enough of their crazy rules of etiquette with them that at least a few stuck in one form or another.

....

[5]   Hats off, Elizabeth Blackwell!

[6]   You know what they say: every man wants a lady in the streets and a freak in the shrubs.

VICTORIAN ERA INVENTIONS AND INNOVATIONS
Postage stamp
Typewriter
Sewing machine
Photography
Paddle steamship
Reinforced concrete
Telephone
Pasteurization
Asphalt
Electric light bulb
ICE CREAM!!!!!!
Automobile
Radio
Comic book
Escalator
Coca Cola

VICTORIAN ERA COURTSHIP RULES AND ETIQUETTE

A SINGLE WOMAN COULD NEVER . . .
- go out without her mother's permission.
- go out at night with a single man.
- let a single man into her house if she was alone.
- say hi to a single man, or dance with him at a ball, without an introduction by a mutual acquaintance.[7]
- let a single man touch her . . .
  . . . *unless* the road was uneven, then he could offer his hand for support.[8]

A SINGLE MAN COULD NEVER . . .
- have an "impure conversation" in front of a woman.
- invite an unescorted single woman into his home.
- even think about physical contact with a woman until after they were engaged. Forget about sex until after marriage.

The one big rule Murphy was running up against, at least according to family lore, was the prohibition against inviting a single woman into your bedroom. Which doesn't seem all that unreasonable, if we're being honest. Even today, that would be considered a little forward—Netflix and chill usually starts on the living room sofa (or the parlor sofa, back in 1900) after

---

[7] This sounds ridiculous, but this is pretty much exactly how certain dating apps works.

[8] Maybe that's why there was so little political will in cities like London and Boston and New York to convert their streets from cobblestones to asphalt after its invention in 1870—the uneven road surface was a ready-made excuse to hold hands in public!

all. The problem was that Murphy's studio apartment was effectively just a bedroom with a stove and a sink in one corner. Thus, inviting his beloved opera singer over to his apartment meant inviting her into his bedroom, and that was a no-no. But by flipping up his bed and tucking it into the closet, his room immediately became a parlor. Presto! No codes of conduct violated, either written or unwritten, and courtship could commence forthwith and posthaste.

Which it did . . . successfully! The couple married a year later—the same year Murphy filed his first patent application. Mr. Murphy went on to turn the whole suite of folding, disappearing bed-related patents he would accrue over the next fifteen years into what would become the wildly successful Murphy Door Bed Company.[9]

In doing so, Murphy also created a cultural icon that was fertile soil for comedy . . . *and murder*! Okay, maybe not murder, but definitely quite a few of the world's most comfortable accidental deaths ⏺—including a 72-year-old English grandma from Liverpool who had her bed fold up on her in the middle of the night while she slept. She fit so snugly in the bed, which fit so snugly in its cabinet, that no one found her for five years. Her family thought she'd run away after they'd had a fight about putting her in a nursing home. It was only when they gave up looking and decided to sell Granny's house that they discovered her, mummified in the Murphy bed in her favorite pink and purple nightgown.

The bedroom wasn't the only place the Murphy bed murdered its occupants. It killed on the small screen and the silver screen too. Legends of film and TV, from Charlie Chaplin to Laverne and Shirley to Eugene Tackleberry of *Police Academy* fame, spent time on—and frequently ran into misfortune with—Murphy beds. Chaplin's battle with a Murphy bed in the 1916 silent film *One A.M.* is still one of his most famous routines. Besides being legit hilarious, it also offers a look at what the early versions of the bed looked like. If you want to see another, all you have to do is go to the Smithsonian. They have one. You just have to look closely; it's probably hidden.

....

[9] One of Murphy's first investors was his new father-in-law. Imagine the chutzpah that takes. "Hey Opera Singer's Dad, you know that thing I invented to help me get into your daughter's petticoats? I'm turning it into a business. Can you spare a couple of bucks?"

CHAPTER **4**

HOW TO GET LOST

AND SEVEN WAYS TO STAY LIKE THAT

Do you want to hear an astounding number? 65,439. Sure, it's not so astounding on its own, so you have to know the context: that's the number of search and rescue (SAR)[1] missions launched for people who went missing inside America's national parks between 1992 and 2007.

65,439! That's basically the entire population of Jupiter, Florida.[2]

Over a fifteen-year period, that's nearly twelve lost people per day. One every two hours who just went *poof* and disappeared into the wilderness somewhere across America. Like we said, astounding. Fortunately, the period of time people are typically lost for is rarely ever very long. The average search and rescue mission for a lost hiker or hunter—who make up nearly 50 percent of those national parks cases—lasts about ten hours, which usually isn't a life threatening amount of time, although it's probably several hours longer than it takes to scare the bejeezus out of them.

Interestingly, 2007 marks the beginning of a significant downward trend in missing persons reports that continues today. What happened? It wasn't a country-wide rise in Eagle Scouts or the long-term impact of those Stranger Danger campaigns finally kicking in. It was smartphones. It just so happens that 2007 was the year the iPhone 1 came out, and it had onboard SMS and map software and Internet. The next year, Apple added GPS to the phone, which made tracking people easier and getting lost much harder. With a computer in your pocket that doubles as a satellite beacon and telephone, you almost have to *try* to get lost.

Which, of course, people still did.

Thousands of people around the world continue to get lost every day, and for all sorts of reasons: they get caught in difficult terrain or the weather suddenly turns sour on them; they don't pay enough attention to where they're going (or where they've been), they get separated from their

---

[1] We have done not one, but two episodes on SAR, one of them just on SAR dogs. 🎙

[2] As of 2020, with a population of 65,791 that includes Michael Jordan and Tiger Woods, Jupiter is precisely the 570th largest city in the United States. Even more interesting than that is the fact that there are 569 cities in America with more than a football stadium's-worth of people living in them.

group, or they lose their maps. Sometimes darkness falls and obscures the path, which must be awfully spooky; other times they simply get turned around in a giant mall, or make too many wrong turns in a big city where they don't speak the language.[3] And then there is the age-old problem of getting lost while you're running away from a serial killer at an overly wooded summer camp with no idea what direction leads to town.

There are a million different ways to get lost, but what's interesting is that when people get lost (particularly out in nature), they all act in the exact same ways. This is the discovery of psychology professor Kenneth Hill, who studies the psychology of being lost at Saint Mary's University way up in Nova Scotia, Canada.[4] Independent of race or gender or nationality or outdoor experience or even age, when people get lost, they kind of lose their minds—but in predictable ways. They forget their training (if they had any).

....

[3]   That was pretty jarring, huh? In your mind's eye you'd been imagining yourself lost in the woods, in the rain, in the dark, without a map, then suddenly—BAM!—you're in a big city where you don't speak the language like Jakarta or Casablanca, lost as ever. What a ride.

[4]   Or, if you live in Nova Scotia, "Here."

They forget what they were taught by parents and teachers—some forget themselves entirely and just kind of go berserk. And they engage in some combination of the same eight behaviors, kind of like robots that have been programmed with outdated guidance software that's chock full of bugs:[5]

RANDOM TRAVELING	ROUTE TRAVELING
DIRECTION TRAVELING	ROUTE SAMPLING
DIRECTION SAMPLING	VIEW ENHANCING
BACKTRACKING	STAYING PUT

The thing is: when you take a closer look at each of these "lost person behaviors," as they're called in the search-and-rescue field, it's easy to see how each one of us could fall prey to them. Including you—yes, you!—and everyone you know and love. All of you: lost, lost, lost!

RANDOM TRAVELING

Lost person behavior seems to start here, and it works just the way it sounds: You move around in all sorts of random directions, hoping to find your way out. The irony is that it's usually unconscious random traveling that gets you lost in the first place, which then triggers even more random traveling that gets you even more lost. As Dr. Hill explains it, this is because most people experience "high emotional arousal" once they realize they don't know where they are, and so they start following "the path of least resistance, with no apparent purpose other than to find something or some place that looks familiar." (This is a very calm, Canadian way of saying that when people realize they're lost they "totally freak out and run around like a chicken on mushrooms with its head cut off."[6])

Eventually, though, the adrenaline dump subsides, and the poor lost person starts to behave with a little more purpose and deliberation. They focus on traveling specific routes and directions, instead of letting the panic of having no idea where they are guide them like the world's worst divining rod.

---

[5] It's not a bug, it's a feature.

[6] Shout out to Mike the Headless Chicken from Fruita, CO!

ROUTE TRAVELING

This is one of the first strategies people employ after freaking out. They spot an animal trail, or a dry stream bed,[7] or a ridge line, or what they think is a path, maybe, somewhere in the distance, and they follow it regardless of whether or not they know what direction it's going in. The hope is that eventually they'll stumble across something they recognize. The *theory*, we guess, is that if all roads lead to Rome, and there are 1,000 roads to Mecca, at least one of these routes should lead to the trailhead where their car is parked. Except usually that's not the case. To make matters worse, once the route dead ends, they almost never try to backtrack. Instead they either revert to random traveling (especially if they're younger) or they pick a direction and go.

DIRECTION TRAVELING

According to Dr. Hill, picking a cardinal direction and heading that way is a really bad strategy. That's unfortunate, because this is the one that often gets employed by overconfident outdoor enthusiasts and takes them from really lost to *totally* lost in very short order, because travel is no longer about hooking up to a trail or identifying landmarks, but simply going in whatever direction the lost person has chosen. Under normal circumstances that doesn't make sense. It doesn't make sense under lost circumstances either. There are even stories of hunters and hikers ignoring trails and roads, "cross[ing] power lines, highways and even backyards" because they're convinced those landmarks (which generally point in the direction of civilization) are going the wrong way, while they themselves are headed in the "right" direction. *Backyards.* There does not seem to be an instinct to backtrack on the part of direction travelers either—which is really something for a seasoned nature lover, because if there's one strategy you'd think they would be best suited to for getting *un*-lost, it's backtracking. Mais non.

....

[7] Also known as an "arroyo" or a "wash"—is it weird that there are so many words for "a place where there used to be running water?"

BACKTRACKING

As you might expect, going back the way you came can be a pretty successful strategy once you realize you've lost your way. This is true whether you're lost in the woods or a city or a mall or a park. (It's not so good at sea. You can't really say "well, then we turned left at that one wave. Remember?) The problem with backtracking is that it takes patience and constant awareness of your surroundings—and those are often the first two things that fly right out the window when someone realizes that they're lost. It also doesn't help that many lost people seem disinclined to backtrack, as we've seen. Either they think they don't need to, because their destination is just around the corner (spoiler alert: it isn't), or they don't *want* to, because going back would be an admission of failure or would be like walking right back to square one of being lost.

If a lot of these tendencies sound like traditionally male behavior, you're not mistaken. The two groups most likely to be the subject of a search-and-rescue operation are men ages 20 to 25 and 50 to 60, in that order. All you have to do is spend some time drilling down into the National Park Service's Annual Search and Rescue Dashboard to experience the truth of those numbers. In 2017, for example, there were 319 search-and-rescue operations just in the state of Utah's national parks. Of those 319, the majority were men, and the majority were in their 20s. Way to go, fellas!

To be fair, though, it can be really hard to find your way out of places like Utah's national parks, what with their changes in elevation and topography and all the intersecting animal and human trails that crisscross their many hundreds of thousands of acres. Even experienced hikers who do everything right can get themselves lost when they come to a juncture where different paths converge and then diverge again. Rabbit path? Donkey path? Human path?

That's what happened to a Tasmanian hiker named Andrew Gaskell in 2016 when he decided to climb Mount Mulu in Malaysia's Gunung Mulu National Park. Gaskell summited the 7,795-foot mountain on the morning of his second day in the park. At the top, he took some pictures, then turned around and headed back. Only a few kilometers from home base, in an area where multiple streams crossed the path that led out of the park, Gaskell says he "took a wrong turn, and despite my efforts to backtrack I couldn't find my way."

Despite his vast experience hiking throughout Tasmania—or perhaps *because* of it—Gaskell proceeded to "wander through the jungle, looking for a way out." He started random traveling. *For. Days.* And rather than finding his way home he later said that all he did was lose his bearings even more.

While random traveling is not uncommon after backtracking has failed, what is unusual, at least according to Dr. Hill's research, is the extent to which Andrew Gaskell wandered. "Only a few lost persons—such as some school-age children by themselves—will continue to move randomly during their ordeal,"[8] Hill wrote in the introduction to his book, *Lost Person Behaviour*. "Most lost people show somewhat more purposeful behavior in their attempts to get out of the woods."

....

8   This is a sick Canadian burn if we've ever heard one.

VIEW ENHANCING

The process of ascending to high ground to get a better look at the surrounding area definitely qualifies as one of Dr. Hill's so-called and presumably patented purposeful behaviors. It's a method for getting your bearings that is favored both by experienced outdoorspeople and fictional systems analysts marooned on deserted islands after the Federal Express plane they're flying in crashes into the South Pacific. As a matter of fact, on Tom Hanks' very first day on the island in *Castaway*, he climbs up to the island's highest point to get a better look around.[9] Eventually Andrew Gaskell did the same thing. Unfortunately, what both guys discovered was just how lost and alone they were.

When view enhancing didn't work for Gaskell, he did a little direction traveling, moving west with the sun until he ran into the river that marked the western border of the park, at which point he followed it south to the park's entrance. That was the plan, anyway. Unfortunately, he couldn't hold his direction because "the forest canopy made it hard to keep track of the sun [and] the landscape was a frustrating matrix of mountains and rocky streams." So Gaskell continued to wander about for several more days, where others might have used particular points on that matrix of mountains and streams as a base from which to employ two other lost person behaviors: route sampling and direction sampling.

ROUTE SAMPLING

At the convergence of multiple trails or paths or streams, the lost person picks one of the branches and travels down it as far as they can without worrying that they won't be able to find their way back to the place where the trails intersected. If the lost person is carrying a bucket of DayGlo paint or some other brand of daytime fluorescing paint and a brush suitable for

---

[9] Of course, the behavior of Tom Hanks' character was being controlled by a writer/god and lives in a universe generated and stored on a hard drive, but it was a writer/god who did their research and we can respect that. And, truth be told, maybe the story's the same for Andrew Gaskell, who knows?

painting on rough surfaces like tree bark, they may consider painting a marker on a tree located near the intersection so they can easily find their way back.[10, 11] This may not be an option for most lost people, however.

If that first path doesn't pan out or run into anything familiar, the lost person returns to their base of operations, perhaps demarcated by a painted tree, and tries another route. They repeat this process until they've exhausted all the paths, or they've found their way out.

DIRECTION SAMPLING

This is the same as route sampling, in that the lost person is traveling out from the same point of origin every time, except it isn't converging paths or waterways they are following: just cardinal directions. Typically, someone engaged in direction sampling tries never to go so far that they lose sight of whatever landmark they chose to start out from.[12] That's very limiting when trying to navigate through a forest or a Bornean jungle, and also very difficult to maintain. That's why people who try direction sampling often get re-lost and end up random traveling again for a while, until they finally pick a new landmark and try direction sampling again. Persistence is the key to staying lost.

If you're anything like us, this list of lost person behaviors probably makes a lot of sense, while at the same time inspiring zero confidence that if someone in your life gets lost, no matter how well you teach them, they will never be able to find their way home on their own. That's why the eighth and final survival strategy for when you're lost is the one recommended most strongly by safety programs and park rangers and search-and-rescue personnel: for the love of God, just stay where you are.

....

[10] When painting a mark on a tree to serve as a marker for base camp, paint a one-foot square patch on the tree, using two coats to ensure maximum coverage. Allow the first coat to fully dry before applying the second coat. If the mark is not quite square or is out of plumb, scrape the bark off the tree where the mark has been painted and move to another tree to try again. Continue this process until a well-formed square has been painted or there are no more trees in the area. In the latter case, the lost person may consider random traveling once more until they come to another intersection with plenty of trees.

[11] Josh is the only person who thought this was funny and he stands by it.

[12] A tree, for instance.

STAYING PUT

If you haven't deliberately slipped off the grid, like Christopher McCandless when he walked into the Alaskan wilderness in the spring of 1992, there should be a decent expectation that a search party will be organized once your friends and family and the relevant authorities agree that you have officially been gone way too long. If that is true, by far the best thing you can do once you realize you're lost is to stay right where you are and sit tight, because if there is anything more difficult than finding a needle in a haystack, it's finding a needle that keeps moving around.

And yet, staying put is almost always the last thing people do. It goes against nearly every instinct we have. *Not* doing something is not something we humans can easily do. We have to move. We have to act—unless you're super lazy, which could benefit you here. Even experienced outdoorspeople, who know that hunkering down is the best strategy when they're disoriented, admit that they probably wouldn't stay put as a strategy. Andrew Gaskell certainly didn't. He spent his entire thirteen-day ordeal lost in Mulu National Park wandering, climbing, probing. Not once did Gaskell really consider simply sitting down and waiting for the Malaysian SAR team to arrive. In the event a person is found sitting in one place, it's rarely because they were being cautious and humble, or because they actually thought it was a good idea. It's usually because they are exhausted or injured or asleep or pouting.

As part of the research for his book, Dr. Hill studied more than 800 missing person reports from the Nova Scotia area where he teaches. In those 800 reports, he found only two instances where the lost person purposely stayed put in order to be found. One was an 80-year-old woman who got lost almost immediately upon entering the woods; the other was an 11-year-old boy who had received Hug-a-Tree training[13] at school.

Wanna guess how old Andrew Gaskell was when he got lost in Malaysia in 2016? He was 25. Typical male.

Okay, that's all. Now go get lost in another chapter!

....

[13] Hug-A-Tree was a program created in the early '80s by an empathetic US border agent and search and rescue expert from Texas named Ab Taylor. He came up with the program after the 1981 death of 9-year-old Jimmy Beveridge, who got lost in the woods during a camping trip with his family and died of hypothermia. The program teaches kids to stay put (hug a tree) when they get lost in the woods, and reassures them they can survive by teaching them some basic survival skills and showing them how long they can go without food and water. Since its inception, it has directly saved the lives of a number of kids who received the program training at school and later became lost in the woods but were found by following the program's guidelines.

CHAPTER **5**

MEZCAL

NOT TEQUILA, EXCEPT WHEN IT IS

If you have ever eaten a worm, and you weren't four years old when you did it, there's a good chance mezcal was involved. Mezcal is that distilled spirit made from the agave plant that has been produced in villages and small towns across central Mexico since the early seventeenth century.

It has become a ubiquitous and officially recognized feature of Mexican culture to the point that only nine states within Mexico are allowed to produce the drink and legally sell it as "mezcal."[1] It's the champagne of Mexico, if you will. And yet, despite the fact that Mexico shares nearly 2,000 miles of border with the United States, it wasn't until the mid-1990s that mezcal started to make it into American bars and stores in meaningful enough numbers that casual consumers and fern bar patrons started to notice it. Thanks, in large part, to the efforts of one man.

THE LEGEND OF RON COOPER

Ron Cooper was a popular artist from Los Angeles whose work was part of the Southern California Light and Space movement in the late 1960s and early 1970s. His pieces were very minimalist, and they played with the viewer's sense of perception through the manipulation of, you guessed it, light and space. It was the kind of art that didn't necessarily end up in the most prestigious galleries, but definitely in the coolest ones—which is all you really needed back then to make enough money to do the kinds of neat and interesting things that artists in the '60s and '70s did.

Things like taking impromptu surf trips ⊚ to Ensenada with a big group of art school friends, which is the very thing Ron Cooper was doing in

------

[1] The nine official "Denomination of Origin (DO)" regions are Oaxaca, Guerrero, Michoacán, Puebla, Durango, San Luís Potosí, Zacatecas, Guanajuato, and Tamaulipas. Plan your next trip to Mexico accordingly.

1963 when he first encountered mezcal. Or jumping in a VW bus covered in surfboards and setting out for Panama, like a hippie Jack Kerouac, to see if the fabled Pan-American Highway actually existed.[2] That's what Cooper did with a couple friends in the summer of 1970, having just made a little bit of money from a recent art opening. Like we said, neat and interesting.

For four months, Cooper and his pals drove down the Mexican coast, then through Central America on the patchwork of roads that make up the Pan-American Highway. Along the way, they passed through the city and state of Oaxaca,[3] which sits at the heart of mezcal country and is, today, the culinary epicenter of Mexico.[4] It was here that Cooper rediscovered the

....

[2] It does. If you think the US-Mexico border is long, the Pan-American Highway goes nearly uninterrupted for 19,000 miles. On current roads, it's 3,500 miles and 72 hours of driving time just to reach the Panamanian border from Los Angeles. It's so long, when you put L.A. and Panama into the Directions function of Google maps, it won't even give you directions at first. The map just zooms out to show you how far it is, as if Google is asking: "Are you sure about this?"

[3] In case you've never heard "Oaxaca" pronounced out loud or, conversely, never seen it in print, the "x" in the middle is not like your average "X" in English. The word is pronounced "wha-HA-kah.'"

[4] Oaxaca is like San Francisco, Napa Valley, and Santa Fe smushed into one.

smoky spirit. Though he would say—as he has many times over the years—"you don't find mezcal, mezcal finds you."

Mezcal found Ron Cooper at a traditional days-long wedding that he and his friends had somehow scored invitations to. At various points each day, mezcal was passed around and used ceremonially in ways he hadn't seen before. And this was not just any mezcal. It was *really, really good* mezcal. That's when Cooper learned that the best stuff wasn't the drink you'd get at a bar in the city center: it was an artisanal creation made by *palenqueros* who live in little towns out in the countryside. This sent him scrambling to the villages in the hills around Oaxaca city looking for the best mezcal he could get his hands on. And he got his hands on a lot. Cooper ended up bringing twenty-eight different mezcals back with him to the United States,[5] and over the next few years he injected them into the art scene, first in L.A. and then in New York, where famous artists like Richard Rauschenberg, Jasper Johns, William Burroughs, and Richard Serra helped to make mezcal an underground in-the-know hit.

Slowly mezcal began to find its way into America, though most Americans' exposure to the spirit would continue to be the poor-quality mezcal that bartenders in popular Mexican beach towns served up to unknowing tourists. You know, the kind with the worm at the bottom, that made people do things like Craig T. Nelson did in *Poltergeist II* after he polished off a bottle of the rot gut stuff.[6] It wouldn't be for another twenty years that the good stuff started to come across the border in appreciable quantities, and once again, Ron Cooper was in the middle of it.

In 1990, Ron made a bunch of money on commissions from the city of Los Angeles for two large bronze sculptures. He used that money as an excuse to move down to Oaxaca to focus on his art and to study weaving—another cultural staple for which Oaxaca is well known, and another neat and interesting thing for an artist to do. Mezcal became an important, transformational part of his creative process; so much so that he turned more and more of his focus to it until, in 1995, he founded a company called Del Maguey and began exporting high-quality "single village" mezcal varietals in earnest.[7] And that, really, is when the mezcal boom in America began.

....

[5] At this point "smuggling" might be the more technically accurate term.

[6] Fun fact: the worm isn't actually a worm. It's a moth larva, which totally makes it better.

[7] Note from Josh here: it is really, really good.

YOU'RE MORE FAMILIAR THAN YOU REALIZE

Still, if you asked an average group of adults today if they've ever had mezcal, the vast majority would say, "No." And yet, if any of them had a typical college experience, especially in North America, the chances are actually very good that they've consumed their fair share of it without even knowing. That's because much like scotch is a kind of whisky, tequila is a kind of mezcal. And tequila is often the drink of choice for young revelers who are looking to blow off steam and kill some brain cells. So much so that, of all the spirits, tequila is the only one that produces stories with headlines like these:

"19 People Who Fought Tequila and Lost"

"36 People Share Their Craziest Tequila Stories"

"19 People Share The Reason They'll Never Drink Tequila Again"

"Everyone Shared Their Best 'Tequila Stories' And It's True, Tequila Makes People Do Some Strange Things"

The kind of unwitting, escalating drunkenness in these stories is so consistent that it feels like a universal physical principle that you could chart using the equation for momentum. If momentum equals mass times velocity ($p = mv$), then blackout tequila drunk equals number of shots times frequency of shots ($tD = nf$). The arc of these stories is all some version of this post from a 2017 Reddit thread of tequila stories that amassed more than 300 comments in a day—which is a lot for a subreddit that doesn't involve conspiracies or kitten pics:

"This one time, after a lot of tequila, I swapped clothes with some guy on the street. Another time I almost started crying because I loved Gary Oldman so much. One time I just ran all the way home, after leaving my shoes at a friend's house. I left them there because we were working together the next day and she told me she'd bring them in to work with her."

There's an irony to these stories, though. Of all the spirits to guzzle as quickly and thoughtlessly as we tend to when we're younger, any variety of mezcal (including tequila) should be last on the list. Because compared to all other spirits, compared to beer ⓘ—compared to wine, even—mezcal takes the most time by far to produce, from seedling to sipping.

HOPE YOU'RE NOT IN A RUSH

Now, it's true that many wines are aged for a number of years, and many of the best whiskies can be aged anywhere from six to twenty years before they're released. But when it comes to the time it takes from when the primary ingredient is planted—whether it's corn or wheat or grape or magic deer in the case of Jägermeister—to when it gets harvested, processed, fermented, distilled, aged, and bottled, you're looking at no more than three to five years. And that's for wine; beer and spirits take much less time.

With mezcal, however, it can take anywhere from seven to *thirty* years for an agave plant to mature for harvesting. Thirty years is nuts, of course, but seven years on the low end is still a very long time. The plant species used in 90% of the mezcal that gets exported, called *espadín*, can take up to nine years to mature. If nine years doesn't impress you, please get your pipe out and stuff it with this tidbit: nine years is how long it took the New Horizons spacecraft to travel from Earth to Pluto, a full three *billion* miles from here. How's that taste?

And this is just the beginning of the mezcal production process. The farmers who raise agave, called *jimadors*, then wait for the sign a plant has matured, which is hard to miss since the agave sends up a huge flowering stalk from the center of the plant that grows upwards of twenty-five feet into the sky. The jimador cuts down the stalk with a huge, rounded machete that looks

---

8 Are your eyes crossed now?

a bit like a pizza peel called a *coa de jima*, or *coa* to those hip to the lingo. This prevents all the sugars the flowering stalk needs to bloom from traveling up the stalk. Instead, it forces them down into the *piña*, or the fruit of the agave, the part of the plant that will eventually be harvested and processed into mezcal. "Eventually" is the operative word here, because once the stalk gets cut down the jimador lets the plant rest, waiting anywhere from a couple months to *two years* for the sugars to fully concentrate before harvesting the piña.[9]

This is when the hard work begins, because the agave is no easy plant. Fitting of the dry, sandy, generally inhospitable land in which it grows, the large succulent looks like Mother Nature painted the Iron Throne a lovely shade of green and then wrapped it around a giant egg that can weigh up to 200 pounds and resembles something Godzilla might be hatched from. It's the jimador's job to slice away the plant's large, fibrous, spiky leaves with his coa, rip the piña out of the ground at the root (sadly, ending the life of that agave plant), and then haul it to the *palenque*, or distillery, for roasting.

Traditionally, roasting occurs in a large, stone-lined pit called a *horno* that has been dug into the earth, sometimes in excess of ten feet in diameter. Larger piñas are cut in half for easier roasting, which is a relative term since once the piña is in place, it's covered with agave fibers, rocks, and dirt, and left to smoke for three to five days.

After roasting is complete, the hard piñas are chopped up, placed in a large basin, and crushed to pulp by a large stone wheel, called a *tahona*, which is turned by a donkey or a mule that does not, to our great dismay, wear a traditional hat while performing this work.[10] Some larger producers use mechanical shredders for this part of the process, but purists and pedants say that it sacrifices quality and takes away from the complexity of flavor. This is to be expected because clearly no part of the mezcal-making process should be easy. The pulverized, smoked agave piña fibers are then mixed with water and allowed to ferment for five to ten days.

The resulting liquid, which at this point is somewhere between eight to ten percent alcohol, is then distilled twice and mixed again with water to stabilize its alcohol concentration.[11] By law, the final product has to be

....

[9] We're now in the neighborhood of a full decade from when the agave was planted.

[10] Some places smash the fibers with wooden bats instead. From watching videos of each process, we choose horsepower.

[11] See our episode "Everything You Ever Wanted to Know About Gin" for a bit of a primer on distilling. 🎙️

between 36% and 55% alcohol by volume (ABV). This is a fine law. At this point, the mezcal is aged in barrels anywhere from a month to a year-plus—depending on whether it's going to be a *blanco*, a *reposado*, or an *añejo*—before it's bottled and shipped.

All of this tireless effort and meticulous care—the years and years of growing the agave plant; months and months of waiting for the sugars to concentrate in the piña; the long, hard hours of chopping and shaving and cutting the plant; the days of roasting and grinding and hanging out with a hatless donkey; the week or more involved in the difficult process of fermentation and distillation; and then the mind-numbing waiting around as it ages—all for a beverage that we historically drink with reckless abandon, until the only reminder we have that we drank it is the fact that we don't remember what happened when we did, or why there is a tiny piece of worm stuck between our front teeth.

Ron Cooper must be so proud.

La Medicina

An Old Mexico take on The Penicillin, a classic cocktail that's usually made with bourbon and scotch.

INGREDIENTS

2 oz. reposado tequila

½ oz. ginger syrup*

½ oz. honey syrup*

¾ oz. lemon juice (freshly squeezed)

¼ oz. mezcal (the smokier the better)

Combine the first four ingredients in a shaker with ice. Shake to chill. Strain into a rocks glass. Float the mezcal on top by pouring over the back of a spoon. Enjoy!

*Ginger syrup and honey syrup aren't hard to make. For ginger syrup, combine 1:1:1 ginger juice, water, and sugar and heat it to dissolve. For honey syrup, combine 3:1 honey to water and heat it to mix. Be sure to let both syrups cool before you add them to the shaker, so it's best to make them ahead.

CHAPTER

6

JOHN FRUM AND THE CARGO CULTS

WHEN PRAYERS ARE ANSWERED
IN PARADISE

Come away with us, won't you, as we climb aboard the Way Back Machine, and travel to the white sand and balmy air of the South Pacific. We find ourselves standing on a beautiful beach in May of 1606 as Pedro Fernandes de Queirós stumbles on Vanuatu's largest island with a crew of Spanish and Portuguese sailors.[1]

No Europeans had ever done this before, so, naturally, they drew a bit of attention from the people who already lived there.

Quickly, their presence became a disturbance. According to Don Diego de Prado, a sailor on the voyage, "the Indians came at once with great shouting and attacked us, and paid for their rashness, for about ten were left dead on that ground."[2] Despite being clearly unwelcome, the sailors planned to set up a colony called Nova Jerusalem and claim the whole area for the Spanish crown. The locals didn't give a hoot about the King of Spain, so they harassed the sailors and wouldn't let them move around the island on foot. After six weeks of arguing amongst themselves, the explorers packed up their ships and sailed away.

It would be more than 150 years before the people of Vanuatu were visited by Europeans again. In 1768, it was the French captain Bougainville. In 1774, it was the English captain Cook, who was attracted by the glow of an active volcano on what we know today as Tanna Island. He received a welcome not unlike the one received by the Spanish back in 1606. Cook and his party ended up killing four of the local people, what seems to have become a European tradition when visiting Vanuatu, as they escaped back to their ships. Cook determined that Tanna was probably not suited for any kind of missionary effort. In fact, the first missionary to Tanna would not arrive

---

[1] He named the island Espiritu Santo, which is its name to this day.

[2] We can't help but wonder if they would have paid so dearly had the Spanish and Portuguese also lacked guns in this conflict.

for another 85 years. He would not last long, though he managed to escape with his life, unlike the pair who came before him, John Williams and James Harris, who met grim ends on the nearby island of Erromango in 1839.

Eventually, though, missionaries managed to find their way into the villages in the interior of nearly every inhabited island in the Vanuatu chain. They began plying their trade, attempting to convert natives to Christianity and institute European customs—missionary stuff. They did so with varying levels of success, and cruelty, for several generations. But the local customs were never forgotten, just pushed underground, where they tend to go in these situations, which is really where the story of John Frum and the concept of cargo cults get their start.

VANU-WHAT?

The nation of Vanuatu is a long, spread-out chain of small volcanic islands that extends off Papua New Guinea and the Solomon Islands into the South Pacific. You may have heard of it on the news, as it has lots of big earthquakes, or from our episode on land diving, 🎙 where we learned the people of South Pentecost Island really value yams. Or maybe you saw it on TV, when it was the location for season nine of *Survivor*. Or maybe you read about it in your history book, when it was called New Hebrides and held immense strategic value in the first years of World War II as the base the Allied Forces used to push back the Japanese army at Guadalcanal. It was during this time, at the dawning of that war, that John Frum made his appearance and cargo cults got their name.

No one knows for sure how it happened, but the story goes that one day at sundown in the late 1930s, a man appeared before a group of village elders on Tanna Island, one of the southernmost in the Vanuatu chain. They were gathered on an empty beach for their nightly all-male ritual of shotgunning coconut shells full of *kava*, a psychoactive drink that has a sedative effect on humans, made by chewing kava root and running water through the mash.[3] They were drinking it in preparation for receiving messages from the spirit world, when a figure in "white man's clothes" appeared on

----

[3] Women are prohibited from this traditional nightly ceremony, which continues to this day on Tanna.

the shore. "People were astonished," a Tanna oral history recounts. "They couldn't see his face, but he spoke to them, and he spoke in our language."

The particulars of what the man said were lost to time—and probably also to the kava—but the Tanna people all generally agree that he told them to go back to their traditional way of life. He said to throw away European money and clothes, to take their children out of the English schools, to stop going to the outsiders' churches, and to return to life as they had known it before the first Christian missionaries made landfall almost exactly 100 years earlier, and before the English and French colonizers arrived more than fifty years before them. The Tanna also agree that the man called himself John Frum, and that if they did as he said, and they prayed to him, he would bring literal boatloads of cargo from America. "Radios, TVs, trucks, boats, watches, iceboxes, medicine, Coca-Cola and many other wonderful things," according to a village elder.

It sounds like an odd bargain this John Frum was offering, does it not? Ignore all the "civilized" colonial English stuff; drink your kava, enjoy your ecstatic dance ceremonies, worship your enchanted stones, and in exchange I'll bring you all the newest, coolest civilized *American* stuff. The Tanna people weren't immediately bought in, so John Frum continued to make appearances along the beach for the next couple years until finally, in early 1941, enough of them decided that "maybe this John Frum fella is onto something." Around then the Ni-Vanuatu[4] summarily abandoned every institution and every piece of infrastructure that had been installed and administered by their colonial overseers for as long as most of them could remember.

They pulled their children out of school. They stopped attending church, and those who didn't found themselves excommunicated anyway for expressing their newfound Frumian beliefs. And in a real stroke of creative genius, they spent every last British pound they had, buying whatever the English were selling—they didn't care what—just so they could get rid of the money they had. It was like a proto-*Brewster's Millions* situation, except once there wasn't anything left to buy, they just threw the rest of their money into the ocean.[5]

To the colonial administration, this felt kind of like a rebellion, and they responded accordingly. They cracked down, arresting the leaders of the movement and jailing them in Port Vila on the island of Efate 150 miles to the north. It was a blow to the cause, for sure, but in early 1942 John Frum answered the people's prayers when the American military converged on the islands to set up their forward operating bases on Efate and Espiritu Santo.[6] Tens of thousands of men and hundreds of thousands of tons of cargo came ashore by plane and by ship virtually overnight. The Americans built runways and radio towers. They landed plane after plane after plane. They built barracks and hospitals and movie theaters and miles of roads.

....

[4] This is the name for the indigenous culture on Vanuatu. It's also the plural for multiple Vanuatuans, because Vanuatuans is apparently not correct.

[5] This would have been a disqualifying action for Brewster.

[6] For a period in late 1942 and early 1943, the base on Espiritu Santo was the largest in the South Pacific [pushes glasses up nose].

And they recruited and paid more than 10,000 locals, including 1,000 from Tanna, as the Vanuatu Labor Corps to help build all of it.

Now if you are from one of the Tanna villages where the elders have been going on and on for the last few years about this mythical figure and his promises of American-made salvation, and you've spent your entire life under the thumb of capricious colonial governors, what are you supposed to think is happening? One day you look up into the clear blue sky and it's filled with large, loud planes—some of them dropping huge bundles of man-ufactured goods from thousands of feet up, some landing quite literally at your feet. Then the next day you look out on the horizon and see a flotilla of ships that "are as big as a village."[7] The day after that, the people who come off those planes and ships are driving trucks and jeeps around your island, unloading machinery and other sophisticated objects you've never seen before by the pallet-load. Then a few weeks later some of those same people ask you to work for them and actually pay you for your labor (however min-imally) and feed you while they're at it.

All this stuff, all this cargo, all in a matter of months. How is this even possible for human beings to accomplish? How is this not a bona fide divine miracle? These were the types of questions the Tanna villagers wrestled with, according to legend. And when they put all the pieces together, it was hard not to see this bounty as the prophecy fulfilled and think, *Jesus Christ, this John Frum is like . . . well . . . Jesus Christ!*

WHO, OR WHAT, IS JOHN FRUM?

The presence of US troops and materiel over the next few years—along with fairer (though nowhere close to equitable) treatment—gave the Tannese people all the reason they needed to continue bucking the colonial govern-ment and give their loyalty to the United States. As one elder put it many years later: "I think if the Americans came now, now that we're independ-ent . . . at least we should honor them and what they did for us during the war. They gave everything they had."

....

[7] That's how a Tanna villager described American warships in a 1991 BBC documentary.

Happy John Frum Day

Every February 15, the men of Tanna Island celebrate John Frum Day. Carrying bamboo poles painted to look like rifles with bayonets, wearing denim jeans and "USA" sometimes painted on their chests, they line up and march in military formation in front of the American flag, which flies in their villages at all times, often higher than the accompanying Vanuatu flags. The day is as much about praying for the return of John Frum as it is about hoping for the return of the Americans to help them like they did back during World War II.

All thanks to John Frum, whose place would forever be cemented in the religious hierarchy of the Tanna people. But who is John Frum? Was there ever actually a man by that name? Or a man at all? Maybe the better question is *what is John Frum?* Because there are those who think he isn't flesh and blood at all, but rather the product of a collective hallucination by the kava-drinking men on the beach that night. Some more steeped in the old-time local religion believe he is the spiritual manifestation of Keraperanum, the god of the tallest mountain on the island. The ones who think he's a real person believe he's either an American soldier or a demigod who lives inside Mount Yasur (the island's active volcano) and travels back and forth between Tanna and America through a tunnel under the sea.

If John Frum really was an actual person, most anthropologists believe he was probably a local figure or a village elder who dressed up in white man's clothes in order to cloak his message—rise up against the colonial oppressors!—in some divine or otherworldly way.[8] It's one thing for a bunch of guys to sit around the campfire and complain about their boss, the thinking goes, and it's something else entirely to have some strange figure show up out of nowhere who *looks* like your boss but is taking your side—confirming that you are in fact being treated unfairly and telling you exactly what you should do about it.

....

[8] One early account from 1952, recorded by the French anthropologist Jean Guiart, says the man's name was Manehevi and that he wore "a costume with sparkling buttons."

What's most likely is that John Frum is a combination of man and myth—minus the underground volcanic lair[9]—that have their roots in long-simmering dissatisfaction with the oppressive colonial rule the British had foisted on the Ni-Vanuatu. In fact, "frum" is the Tannese pronunciation for "broom" and, as one colonial governor put it all the way back in 1949, the whole idea behind the John Frum movement was "to sweep (or broom) the white people off the island of Tanna."

---

[9] Between this and the globe-spanning undersea tunnel, if you add sharks with frickin' lasers to the legend, you could make a pretty good case John Frum went on to become Dr. Evil.

THE REAL CARGO IN
CARGO CULTS

Once you start digging into the John Frum cargo cult history it becomes pretty obvious that cargo, in the Maersk-Sealand, Union Pacific, DHL[10] sense of the term, is not at all what a cargo cult is about. What may be less obvious is that John Frum did not produce the first or the only cargo cult in the South Pacific. The German anthropologist Freidrich Steinbauer counted 185 of them in his 1979 book *Melanesian Cargo Cults: New Salvation Movements in the South Pacific*,[11] each one different from the next. And while the promise of stuff sits at the center of a number of their origin stories— thus why "cargo" got baked into their names after World War II—what a cargo cult was really meant to deliver was freedom from injustice, oppression, and tyranny, along with a return to local custom and traditional ways of life. In a word, as Steinbauer concisely put it: salvation.

This has been the purpose of pretty much every cargo cult, from their earliest incarnation with the Tuka Movement on Fiji in the late nineteenth century, before the term "cargo cult" even existed, until well into the late twentieth century when many of the places where these "cults" sprang up finally achieved national independence from their colonizers—Fiji in 1970, Papua New Guinea in 1975, Solomon Islands in 1978, Vanuatu in 1980.[12]

All of this makes sense so far, except for one thing: none of it explains why all these movements seem to involve a mysterious white guy and the promise of lots of stuff. That part can largely be explained by the mythos bending over time to fit the facts on the ground. John Frum doesn't become an American soldier in certain versions of the origin story, for example, until *after* the army arrives in 1942. And the nature of the goods he will

---

[10] These are companies that engage in different modes of freight—by sea, by rail, by air—in case you are unfamiliar because you aren't admirers of the International Hobo Alliance like we are.

[11] A real page-turner if we don't say so ourselves.

[12] The success these parties have had in the fight for freedom is one of the reasons most anthropologists have taken to calling them "movements" instead of cults—movements have a destination and are centered around ideas, whereas cults are meant primarily to perpetuate themselves and are typically built around individuals. "Movement" also seems most appropriate since few, if any, cargo cults have arisen in nations that had already achieved independence.

bring to the Tannese if they pray to him doesn't get enumerated as clearly until after the Americans have left for good in 1945 and all the stuff has arrived.[13]

Anthropologists and ethnologists have been debating the source of these movements pretty much since their first encounter with them in the 1920s. That was when an anthropologist traveled to Vailaila in Papua to look into reports that the indigenous people there had abandoned many of their traditional ways and begun to mimic tea parties and march in formation in anticipation of their ancestors' arrival aboard a "ghost steamship" loaded with stuff. The anthropologist called the phenomenon "Vailala madness," which later evolved into "cargo cult." A surprising amount has been written about them, and there seems to be very little that everyone agrees on.

Perhaps the oddest characteristic that cargo cults share is the belief that the salvation they seek from colonial oppression will come from the same alien world the colonizers hail from. But if you take a step back and squint your eyes, letting all the lines blur together, you start to get a sense of the bigger picture. Cargo cults offer the best of both worlds to the native populations of the South Pacific islands: all the bells and whistles of modern ingenuity without all the rules and repression of modern society. The figures at the head of these movements promise the salvation of local traditions coupled with the advancements of the world beyond their shores . . . on their own terms. And the only way a promise like that could seem even remotely believable to a people who've spent generations under colonial rule and religious repression is if it comes from someone who looks like their oppressor, but talks like *they do*.

Basically, John Frum.

....

[13] Not that they left much in usable condition. Most notably, the Americans dumped millions of dollars worth of materiel—tanks, jeeps, etc.—into the ocean off the coast of Espiriu Santo just so the English and the French couldn't have it once they left. Today that spot, which has become a popular diving destination, is known as Million Dollar Point.

CHAPTER

7

BACK-MASKING

WHEN RECORDING BACKWARDS IS MOVING FORWARD

Late on October 12, 1969, just after the close of the seminal Summer of Love,[1] a man called into a Detroit radio station and blew the lid off a story that had been making the rounds on American college campuses for more than two years.[2]

Paul McCartney was dead.

He died in a car accident nearly three years earlier. November 9, 1966, to be exact.[3] The Paul McCartney the world had been hearing with his Beatles bandmates on the radio and seeing on magazine covers, on television shows, and in concerts since then was actually a look-alike. The remaining Beatles had brought him in to hide Paul's tragic death—though, conveniently, not without leaving a bunch of clues about the insane cover-up hidden within the artwork of their album covers and the lyrics of their songs, including "Abbey Road," which had come out a month earlier.[4]

This late-night caller had "proof" too. Proof is in quotes on purpose, by the way, for reasons that will make sense by the end of this paragraph. He told the DJ, Russ Gibb of WKNR-FM, that if he put on the *White Album* and played the "Number 9" intro at the beginning of "Revolution 9" backward, he would hear John Lennon saying "turn me on, dead man."

"Proof!"

....

[1] We at SYSK are well aware that the Summer of Love really took place in 1969, not 1967 as some unhinged historians claim.

[2] Know what else was making the rounds on campuses between 1967 and 1969? Drugs. So many drugs.

[3] Interestingly, this was the day that John Lennon met Yoko Ono. Which, if you're one of those miserably unhappy Yoko haters out there who thinks Yoko Ono broke up the Beatles, and not drugs or ego, you'd probably say that *something* died on November 9, 1966.

[4] If you don't know who Paul McCartney is but this story still sounds vaguely familiar, no worries - you're thinking of Avril Lavigne.

1969: Another Crazy Year
for the Beatles and for Mankind

JANUARY	The Beatles perform together for the last time, on the roof of Apple Records.
MARCH	James Earl Ray admits to killing Martin Luther King Jr.
	Sirhan Sirhan admits to killing Robert F. Kennedy.
	John Lennon and Yoko Ono get married.
JULY	Apollo 11 lands on the moon.
	Ted Kennedy lands in the waters off Chappaquiddick Island, tragically killing Mary Jo Kopechne.
AUGUST	The Manson Family commits the Tate-LaBianca murders.
	The Troubles begin in Northern Ireland.
	Woodstock happens.
SEPTEMBER	John Lennon quits the Beatles.
	Abbey Road is released.
OCTOBER	The Zodiac Killer murders his last confirmed victim.
	The Amazin' Mets win the World Series as one of the biggest underdogs in sports history.
NOVEMBER	Paul McCartney gives an interview to Life magazine addressing the "Paul is dead" rumors and mentioning for the first time that the Beatles had broken up.
DECEMBER	The Vietnam War draft lottery begins.
	Final members of the Manson Family are apprehended.

Gibb did as the caller urged, heard what the caller suggested, and fell down the rabbit hole that would come to be known as the "Paul is Dead" conspiracy.[5] The story of Paul's death dominated Beatles-related news for the rest of 1969. It got so crazy that at one point John Lennon called in to WKNR to debunk the story and Paul had to come out of seclusion in Scotland, where he was holed up with his wife Linda and their newborn daughter Mary, to confirm that he was, indeed, still alive.

Since then, looking into the clues of the "Paul is Dead" conspiracy has become a rite of passage for every new generation of Beatles fan. Its enduring nature, we think, is due to the fact that what ultimately propelled the conspiracy into the mainstream were those backward messages. As creepy as they are, though, it's something that actually finds its way into music fairly often. It even has a name: backmasking.

Backmasking is a practice that involves recording any kind of sound—vocals, an instrument, a sound effect—then taking that snippet of audio, flipping it around and placing it wherever the artist wants within a given track. The literal definition is the encoding of materials on a recording in a way that it can only be understood properly when the recording is played backwards.[6] In practice, it's not that it's more easily understood this way; it's that sometimes—*most* of the time—it just sounds cool.

TURN LE BEAT AROUND

The technique of backmasking has its roots in a form of musical composition called *musique concrète*, pioneered in the late 1940s by a composer in the French national radio system named Pierre Schaeffer. The idea, made possible by the increasing availability and versatility of modern magnetic tape recorders after World War II, was that you could record any kind of

----

[5] Gibb was no mere one-trick pony. In addition to launching the "Paul is Dead" phenomenon, he also ran the Grande Palace, *the* psychedelic rock venue in Detroit in the '60s, and helped launch the career of The Stooges and MC5 (among others)—hence indirectly helping to launch punk as well. Well-rounded guy.

[6] We talked a lot about backmasking and the like in our excellent—if we do say so ourselves—episode, "Was the PMRC censorship in disguise?" 🎙

natural sounds[7] that you found interesting—hitting two blocks together, banging a copper pot, flicking one of those springy rubber-tipped stopper thingies behind your bedroom door that makes your cat go bonkers. Then you could manipulate and splice those sounds together by cutting and reassembling the tape until you had an arrangement that sounded good and maybe even sounded like music.[8]

Musique concrète techniques were soon adopted by avant garde musicians in the 1950s and eventually spread to a handful of popular musicians in the 1960s. Would you like to guess who two of those popular musicians were? We'll give you a hint: they're named after apostles and they formed the Beatles. The duo were so intrigued by the pioneers in this space that they put a picture of one of them—a German composer named Karlheinz Stockhausen—on the cover of the *Sgt. Pepper's Lonely Hearts Club Band* album.

See, the guy who called into WKNR that night in October 1969 wasn't totally nuts after all. The Beatles actually did experiment with backmasking, and some of it did make it into their albums. What's funny is that it got there, at least in the beginning, entirely by chance.

It started during the recording sessions for the *Revolver* album in the spring of 1966. First, when they were laying down the track "Rain," John came home late one night, high as a kite, and put the tape of that day's recordings on backwards on his reel-to-reel player. He liked the sound so much that he played it for the band the next morning—and they liked it so much that they backmasked lyrics onto the fadeout of the song.[9] A month later, a similar thing happened while recording "I'm Only Sleeping," when the tape operator mistakenly put a tape into the machine backward. Everyone loved it and George Harrison worked into the night rewriting his guitar part so they could flip it on the track and get the sound they were looking for.

Through a combination of drugs and more happy accidents, *Revolver* became the Beatles's most experimental album. On nearly every song, you can hear some kind of recording or production trick, many of them with their roots in musique concrète.[10]

....

[7] This is sometimes called "found sound," as in sounds found naturally . . . in nature.

[8] Many consider musique concrète to be the Big Bang of electronic music.

[9] The technical term for this part of a song is "coda."

[10] "Rain" and "I'm Only Sleeping" became the first pop tracks ever to have backmasked lyrics and guitar, respectively.

THE ORIGINAL TROLL

This is when backmasking starts to come into its own. Two years after *Revolver*, the Beatles released the *White Album*, which contains the track "Revolution 9," which fans are convinced has the phrase "turn me on dead man" backmasked onto the beginning. Here's the thing about that: "Revolution 9" is full of found sounds composed by Lennon and McCartney in the style of musique concrète, which—if you'll remember from, say, a page or so ago—is where backmasking gets its start. And the song does in fact have backmasking in it. It's all backmasking, really, using all those found sounds, just not any of the kind that the conspiratorially minded among us might be thinking of. Is it any wonder, then, why the "Paul is Dead" rumors never really went away? They were built on something that actually existed and that the Beatles were actually doing at the time.

For the next thirty years, many artists would follow the Beatles's lead and experiment with backmasking. Dozens, however, would be accused of far worse than using backmasking techniques to hide the accidental death of a bandmate. Like inserting satanic lyrics into their songs, for instance.

Artists like Led Zeppelin, Queen, the Eagles, Pink Floyd, Deep Purple, ELO, Cheap Trick, Slayer, Judas Priest, Black Sabbath, Motorhead, and our favorite, Styx, all used backmasking to the delight of teenage boys around the world. A few of these certainly contained some dark messages, while others were much lighter in their tone.

Regardless of the actual message, things got so bad by the mid-1980s, thanks to pressure from religious organizations and parents groups like the Parents Music Resource Center (PMRC), that congressional hearings were held, lawsuits were filed, and the recording artists at the center of it all got *super* P.O.'d.

There is an old saying: never argue with someone who buys ink by the barrel. There should probably be a corollary to that: never get into a shouting match with someone whose job involves a microphone. Because that's what they're going to use to fight back. In this instance, all those bands got even with their accusers by doing exactly the thing they were accused of. Motorhead, Iron Maiden, and Frank Zappa each subsequently planted backmasked lyrics aimed directly at groups like the Parents Music

Resource Center[11] as a show of defiance. The Beatles backmasked the line "Turned out nice again" into their recording of "Free as a Bird" in 1995 on the fifteenth anniversary of John Lennon's murder just to mess with people—or in the language of the Internet, to troll them.

"We even put one of those spoof backwards recordings on the end of the single for a laugh," Paul said, "to give all those Beatles nuts something to do."

The champ of trolling misguided groups like the PMRC was ELO. After being accused of planting messages on their 1974 album *Eldorado*, they dropped two on their next album, including the phrase "The music is reversible, but time . . . is not. Turn back! Turn back! Turn back! Turn back!" into a track called "Fire on High." Following that, in 1983, they released an entire concept album full of backward and hidden messages with the rather overt title *Secret Messages*. You get the sense that a lot of middle fingers were used in the writing and performing of those songs.

I DON'T THINK THAT MEANS WHAT YOU THINK IT MEANS

When you read stories about the "Paul is Dead" controversy and the backmasking claims at the center of it, one of the things you will run into time and again is a description of Beatles fan behavior as an example of a passionate fanbase simply getting carried away in their zeal.[12] There's definitely something to that explanation, but there's also something deeper going on. In psychology, it's called *pareidolia*, or the tendency to see or hear things in totally random objects or sounds.

----

[11] The PMRC drove the Senate hearings in 1985 that delved into obscenity and parental advisory. Seriously, check out our episode, "Was the PMRC censorship in disguise?" You. Will. Love. It.

[12] Also, drugs.

On the visual side of things, this phenomenon is at the heart of the Rorshach inkblot test and is responsible for our tendency to see shapes in clouds. It's why people so frequently see Jesus or the Virgin Mary in all manner of objects.[13] Though, weirdly, it's in food where the Lord pops up most often: since 1977, the list includes a flour tortilla, a grilled cheese sandwich, a Cheeto, and a pierogi.[14]

---

[13] The Shroud of Turin is probably the most famous of these objects.

[14] If you believe Jesus died for your sins, it makes sense that he keeps showing up in carbs.

On the auditory side, pareidolia explains our willingness to believe that a Siberian husky with his own Instagram page can say "I love you." Or why two different commenters on a hearing loss discussion forum described hearing voices in their air conditioning units. And it's why, in 2008, Fisher Price had to pull its talking "Little Mommy Real Baby Cuddle 'n Coo" doll from the shelves when a parent heard it speak the words, "Islam is the light." Of course, each of these people was mistaken, just like Russ Gibb was mistaken when he insisted he heard what his late-night caller told him he would hear on those supposedly backmasked *White Album* tracks.

The question, though, is why did any of them hear anything at all? Most experts believe it's because our brains are geared to try to make sense out of randomness, to find order in the chaos. The unknown is scary: We like to feel that there is intention and meaning to the things we don't understand. It makes us feel safe.

Carl Sagan postulated that our tendency to see faces everywhere— and by extension to hear voices in every sound—is a survival mechanism. You can certainly see the evolutionary logic in that theory. In the wild—or

Florida, same difference—survival very much depends on a person's ability to identify friend or foe as quickly as possible, with as many senses as possible. Pareidolia is recognition of the fact that our brains have this need hardwired as a judgmental bias that affects at least two of the senses we know of—sight and sound. In other words, it makes much more sense to see the face of a potential enemy hiding in the bushes than it does to under-notice such things and let your enemy get the drop on you.[15]

All of which we get. What we don't understand is why, when we *see* something in the randomness, it's always God, but when we *hear* something in the randomness, it's always the Devil. Not sure there is a name for that phenomenon, backwards or forwards, but it's definitely real.

....

[15] We know this sounds pretty paranoid but blame nature, not us.

CHAPTER

8

AGING

DO WE GOTTA?

They say there are only two certainties in life: death and taxes. Judging by the laws and scientific innovations of the twenty-first century, however, there seems to be a third certainty: that people will do everything humanly possible to *defer* those inevitabilities.

Especially the death one, though that's not surprising. We've always known that people will hang on to this mortal coil by the very tips of their fingernails with everything they've got.

It's a basic survival instinct, one that probably emerged somewhere early in the 3.5 billion years of the evolution of life and soaked into every living thing on Earth, humans included. But as G.I. Joe would say, that's only half the battle.[1] What good is living for a long time if you're going to be sick for a whole big chunk of it at the end? Who wants that? Nobody. And that's really what we're talking about when we talk about aging. It's not just about extending lifespan, it's about increasing *health*span—and how expanding healthspan elongates lifespan.[2]

LIFESPAN VERSUS HEALTHSPAN

The first known use of the word "lifespan" appeared in 1831. At the time, the average global life expectancy was a mere 29 years (40 if you were lucky enough to be born in the United Kingdom). In order to raise average life expectancy beyond what we consider young adulthood today, humans waged an extraordinary battle against death in the twentieth century. Through

---

[1] Chuck would like to point out that the 12" G.I. Joe doll remains superior to the 3.75" G.I. Joe action figure. Josh disagrees, yet they remain friends.

[2] It's okay if you need to read this sentence a few times. It took us a few attempts to write it.

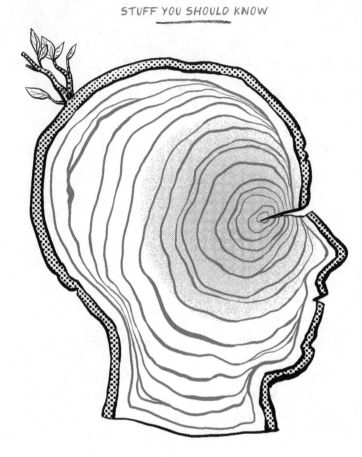

a combination of advancements in medical care,[3] hygiene,[4] food production,[5] and social welfare policy,[6] life expectancy around the globe jumped from 32 to 66 years between 1900 and 2000.[7] In the US, it went from 49 to 76 years. Japan was the true success story, though. Despite the devastation of carpet-bombed cities, capped off by two atomic bombs, the country ended the century with the highest average life expectancy in the known world—81 years. When she passed away in 1997 at age 122, France's Jeanne

....

[3] Thank you, Elizabeth Blackwell. 🎙

[4] Thank you, John Snow. 🎙

[5] Thank you, Upton Sinclair.

[6] Thank you, Frances Perkins. 🎙

[7] This was quite an accomplishment considering the first half of the century featured two of the deadliest wars in human history—both of which were fought principally by men in their twenties, which definitely drove down the average lifespan in those years.

Calment—a smoker who claimed to have met Van Gogh—had held the mantle of the world's oldest person for four years.[8] More than twenty years later, Calment's record remains intact.

For some scientists, as they evaluate all the advances that have been made since her death and the fact that her record still stands, Jeanne Calment's extraordinary age has ostensibly set the outer limits of a human lifespan.[9]

STUFF YOU SHOULD KNOW . . .
About Averages

A common fallacy when it comes to interpreting statistics is that the word "average" means "typical." It doesn't. Average life expectancy refers to the average age of death among the entire population, taking into account the age of every person who died that year. For example, if you have ten people and six of them died at age two and the other four died at age 50, the average age of death of that group would be 21.2 years. To get there you take the number of deaths in an age group and multiply it by that group's age of death (e.g., 6 x 2 = 12 and 4 x 50 = 200). These products are added together (12 + 200 = 212) and divided by the total number of deaths (212 / 10 = 21.2). Usually when you see a low average life expectancy from the past, it means that era had a high rate of childhood mortality. Because so many children died at birth or in childhood, the oversized proportion their deaths represented greatly outnumbered the proportion of people who lived to an old age, and that pulled the average life span toward the lower end.

---

[8] In 2018, Calment's claim to the title of the longest-living human in history was challenged by a Russian mathematics graduate and glass blower named Nikolay Zak. He claimed that Calment was a fraud and was in fact Jeanne's daughter, Yvonne, who had supposedly died in 1934 of pleurisy at age 36. Under Zak's theory, it was really Jeanne who had died in 1934, and Yvonne assumed her mother's identity in order to avoid paying an estate tax on her inheritance, carrying on this masquerade among friends and family for 60 years. The French strenuously dispute this claim and Calment continues to hold her record.

[9] Technically, it was set back in 1825 by an actuary from England named Benjamin Gompertz, who noted that the risk of death increased exponentially with age, doubling every eight years and reaching 50% by age 101. If you follow this to its conclusion, there comes a point where statistically it is impossible to survive.

DECADE	MALE LIFE EXPECTANCY	FEMALE LIFE EXPECTANCY
1900s	47.9	51.1
1910s	49.4	53.7
1920s	57.0	59.5
1930s	59.8	63.4
1940s	63.7	67.9
1950s	66.3	72.3
1960s	66.8	73.7
1970s	68.5	76.2
1980s	71.0	78.1
1990s	72.8	79.1
2000s	75.0	80.2
2010s	76.3	81.2

Not everyone has bought into that idea, though, which brings us to healthspan.

The first-known sighting of the term "healthspan"—defined as the length of time that a person is healthy—is on the previous page of this chapter. Not really, it was in 1931. This was two years deep into the Great Depression when few people were thinking about healthy living and most people were just focused on surviving. Not surprisingly, the term didn't get much use for most of the twentieth century because after the Great Depression came the second great war, and after that came a period of insane abundance marked by the emergence of things like microwave dinners,[10] fast food,[11] remote controls,[12] and smoking on airplanes—all meant to remind us that we'd beaten fascism and to trick us into thinking we were invincible. People weren't thinking about health, and they certainly weren't thinking about healthspans. They were just happy to be alive, let alone living longer.

It wasn't until the end of the century that "healthspan" started making cameo appearances alongside its more famous companion. Still, it had to wait around until the first Baby Boomers started hitting 65 in 2011 before anyone really took notice of it. Boomers, the first generation to hang out at health clubs[13] and visit cosmetic surgeons for facelifts, started asking why they should stick around longer if all it meant was a slow death by disease? They didn't just want to see their grandkids twice a year and putz about until the reaper knocked, maybe winning a few bingo games along the way if they were lucky; they wanted to keep their party going.[14] So they made 70 the new 50 (maybe even 40) and waged war against aging.

By the time "healthspan" finally made its Webster's debut in 2018, 10,000 Americans were turning 65 each day, the global antiaging supplement market was approaching $200 billion, and a Harvard geneticist named David Sinclair had figured out how to reverse aging in mice (more on that later, we promise). The quest to live both longer and healthier had become *the* preeminent First-World preoccupation. Fortunately for those preoccupied with it, it was also becoming a legitimate scientific endeavor that was showing real possibilities.

....

[10] Thank you, Percy Spencer.

[11] Thank you, Walter Anderson and Billy Ingram.

[12] Thank you, Nikola Tesla.

[13] We are purposely not including the wealthy folks behind turn of the century sanitariums like the Kelloggs (see our live episode, "The Kellogg Brothers' Wacky World of Health"), because they were just making up what constituted health and wellness as they went along.

[14] Keeping the party going was pretty much par for the course with Baby Boomers, as they were the generation that started out as hippies, moved onto disco, and ended up as coked-up stockbrokers.

Two Steps Forward, Four Years Back

One of the great advances in the twentieth century was a pretty much continuous upward climb in life expectancy, which is why it was particularly alarming when, from 2014 to 2017, life expectancy actually went down for three straight years. The last time that had happened in America was the four years around World War I. What made this grim statistic more alarming was that the US wasn't involved in any major ground wars to speak of during this period—certainly nothing like WWI. And, don't forget, 2014 to 2017 was also in the middle of an era where healthspan was exploding across the Western world. Researchers found this decline in American life expectancy came from a depressing mix: there was an increase in eight of the top ten causes of death—things like heart disease, stroke, diabetes, and the flu—along with the rise of the opioid crisis and an increase in suicide. The number of deaths by opioid overdose had more than quadrupled by this point since 1999, and all deaths attributed to opioids were up by a factor of six (!). Saddest of all, suicides were up by a third.

THE AGING EQUATION

But let's back up for a second. To understand how to extend a healthy lifespan, you first have to understand its natural rival, aging. What exactly is aging? What makes us become all the things we can't imagine becoming when we're young: old, wrinkled, weak, relentlessly committed to getting up at the buttcrack of dawn?[15] And why the heck do we have to age anyway? For many of us, it's aging's longstanding association with time, which

---

[15] It turns out there is an answer to why our grandparents get up before the garbage man. Aging people produce less melatonin, a hormone that helps us go to sleep and stay asleep. A decrease in melatonin, along with an increase in pain, weird side effects from meds, nocturia (having to get up in the night to pee), and all sorts of other unpleasant accoutrements of aging conspire to rob the aged of their sleep. All of which reinforces why research into how to expand healthspan is a legit public good.

is itself inexorable, that gives us the impression that aging is inevitable. Except, there's more to it than just the simple passage of time.

Even though it has the word "age" in it, aging isn't really about the number of trips we've taken around the sun. On our birthday, people don't say we aged a year—they say we're a year older. Similarly, when we see someone for the first time in years and they look great, we say "you haven't aged a bit." That's because aging is really about the change to our physical condition—on the outside and on the inside—over time.[16]

A review of several dozen mostly incomprehensible National Center for Biotechnology Information articles reveals a fairly consistent definition of aging in that regard: aging is a time-dependent and progressive decline in function that ultimately ends in death—a real bummer from start to finish. The NCBI considers aging to be a cause for a whole assortment of chronic diseases such as cancer, diabetes, and heart disease. The thing is, the NCBI *does not* consider aging itself a disease. That little nuance, it turns out, is the frontline of a very robust and ongoing debate about the nature of aging—whether we can stop it or even possibly reverse it,[17] and whether we have to do it at all.

Whatever their position in this debate, pretty much everyone in the scientific community refers to a 2013 article from the journal *Cell* that identified three categories that characterize aging.

There are *primary hallmarks*—the things that cause damage at the genetic and cellular level. Things such as telomere attrition,[18] which is when the caps on the end of your chromosomes—the ones that make sure your DNA gets copied properly whenever your cells divide—start to degrade and shorten. Telomeres are like those plastic tips on the end your shoelaces,[19] but for chromosomes. Just like your shoelaces are pretty much toast when those plastic tips wear out, the same goes for cells and telomeres—because

---

[16] Remember our *mezcalero* friends from chapter 5? They don't age mezcal just so it will be older; they do it because that process transforms the physical properties of the spirit, and with that transformation comes greater flavor.

[17] Is it worth it? Let science work it.

[18] Great band name. So-so, at least.

[19] These plastic tips are called "aglets" and they date back to Roman times, though an English inventor from the 1790s named Harvey Kennedy often gets the credit for them.

as telomeres wear down, your cells stop dividing and your tissue stops regenerating.[20]

There are *antagonistic hallmarks*—the ways our bodies respond when damaged. One peppy example is deregulated nutrient sensing, the less-than-artful way of describing what happens when the body forgets to be good at taking in nutrients. This is usually because the cellular system for storing excess energy goes on the fritz. Say your hypothalamus sends out signals that make you crave food when your body doesn't need it. It keeps sending the signal until it gets what it thinks you need—but then obesity sets in, and diabetes follows shortly thereafter. Antagonistic!

And then there are *integrative hallmarks*—what happens when all that damage from the primary hallmarks and all those terrible physiological responses from the antagonistic hallmarks start combining and become too much for the body to manage. That's when things like stem cell exhaustion start to happen, and the cells responsible for healing injuries just kind of run out of gas.

When you add all of these hallmarks up, you get aging; pretty much everyone agrees on that. What they disagree on is what we can do about it.

HELLO DOLLY

Some researchers—let's call them Team Cumulative DNA Damage (CDD)—argue that aging is genetically programmed.[21] Their view is that the accumulation of damaged DNA that happens as telomeres shorten and cells get less good at dividing results in aging, which results in death. Team CDD's ultimate proposition is that aging is essentially irreversible because our genome has suffered permanent wear and tear. The best we can do is slow down the aging process (and elongate healthspan) through exercise and

----

[20] The maximum number of times a cell can divide before its telomeres run out is called the Hayflick limit—something we've talked about in the episodes "How HeLa Cells Work" (about Henrietta Lacks) and "Does the body replace itself?" 🎙

[21] That whole Hayflick limit thing.

diet. Team CDD dominated the second half of the twentieth century. Then, in 1996, Dolly the Sheep was born—well, cloned.

Dolly[22] was supposed to be the harbinger of a dystopian era of human cloning and body part harvesting. Real *Blade Runner* stuff. Instead, her big contribution was debunking the long-held belief that only cells from an embryo could yield another animal.[23] Since she was grown from a regular old cell, Dolly's birth and life proved that just about any given adult cell had all the DNA necessary to give rise to another animal. Which meant that you could reprogram an adult cell nucleus back to an embryonic stage. Which meant the idea that DNA damage was irreversible was bunk. Which meant Team CDD's theory was—oh, okay, you get it.

....

[22] Dolly's original name was 6LL3. She earned the nickname "Dolly" after some (male) project members suggested she be named after Dolly Parton, since Dolly the Sheep was cloned from a mammary cell. (As a joke it held up in the '90s).

[23] This is not to say that Dolly conducted any studies or wrote any papers herself; rather, she contributed simply by existing.

Although Dolly didn't bring about the dark world many predicted,[24] she did set the stage for a second set of researchers—let's call them Team Information Loss (IL)—that would become a formidable opponent to Team CDD. Team IL scientists argue that even if Dolly hadn't managed to fully discredit the DNA Damage theory of aging, Team CDD's theory still misses the mark—because the epigenome, not the genome, is the central player in aging. Epigenes[25] regulate gene expression like overbearing helicopter parents, telling DNA exactly what they will become. When genes lose that guidance, which happens when we age, the genes that are supposed to be turned off turn on and vice versa. Chaos ensues. Chronic diseases appear. Dogs and cats living together. Death comes ripping.[26]

Team IL argues that we humans can defeat aging once and for all if we can learn to reset and reprogram our epigenes. It makes sense: problems with epigenes create a whole cascade of issues that trigger all of those hallmarks of aging that the *Cell* study identified. So if we can stop those problems with epigenes from ever beginning, we can forestall the cascade and, hence, the hallmarks of aging.

When news of Dolly the Sheep's birth made headlines, Japanese biologist Shinya Yamanaka got to work developing a biological cocktail that could reprogram a cell's epigenome back to its original form. Yamanaka first used the technique on mice. Astoundingly, a year later, he was able to successfully reset human skin cells to infancy.

....

[24] . . . yet . . .

[25] Epigenetics is the basis for one of our better (and better titled) early episodes, "Can your grandfather's diet shorten your life?" 🎙

[26] If you didn't recognize this as a reference to a Misfits song, it's time for you to listen to more Misfits.

BIOLOGICAL AGING AND CHRONOLOGICAL AGING

Thanks to discoveries like Yamanaka's cocktail, we now have two ages, believe it or not. One is the age our birth certificate says we are—the number of trips around the sun we've taken. The other is the age that an epigenetic clock says we are, based on our health. In 2011, a UCLA geneticist and biostatistician named Steve Horvath stumbled on a way to measure aging. Essentially, he was able to take a DNA sample, measure its methylation (kind of like a genetic rust accumulating over time) and run the results through a machine learning algorithm, maybe go get a cup of coffee while the AI did its thing, and then—presto!—arrive at an estimated biological age. For the first time we were able to see the true impact of epigenes on the aging process. If your biological clock said you were older than your chronological clock, you were aging faster than you should and probably needed to make some lifestyle changes. If it said you were younger, you could stop feeling guilty for lying about your age.

Once Horvath's Clock, as it came to be known, was able to show our biological age, the stage was almost set to begin testing whether that clock could be stopped or reset. Almost.

Yamanaka Factors and Horvath's Clock are both now and forever named after their originators[27]—and both figured heavily in the antiaging breakthrough that Harvard geneticist David Sinclair later made (it took a while, but we told you we'd come back to him). Sinclair compares an aging cell to a scratched CD.[28] The CD still has the information; it's simply unreadable. And just as scratched CDs can be repaired with a little toothpaste, so too can aging cells (not with toothpaste, though; it's a metaphor).

---

[27] Unlike Horvath, Yamanaka won the 2012 Nobel Prize for his achievement. Poor Horvath.

[28] CD is an abbreviation for "compact disc," a form of media storage—typically for music—that was popular between 1982 and 2003.

To test his theory, Sinclair got his hands on a pair of young mice and "scratched" the epigenome of just one of them. In a matter of a month, the mouse with the scratched epigenome began to show all the aging signs of a middle-aged mouse. Within two or three months, the mouse looked downright sick. By the end of a year, its hair had greyed, it developed wrinkly skin, diabetes, dementia, osteoporosis, and it probably even started waking up at 4:45 a.m. too, the poor thing. When Sinclair checked the wrinkly mouse's age using Horvath's Clock, he found it was 50 percent older than its unaltered partner, roughly 80 years old in human years.

Okay, so Sinclair managed to artificially age a poor mouse—not bad, pretty impressive. But the big question was whether he could prevent aging in the first place. Apparently he had the same thought, because he rummaged through his molecular toolbox looking for something that would repair the epigenome. He came up with nicotinamide mononucleotide (NMN), a molecule that gives a shot in the arm to important stuff like metabolism and cell maintenance. Sinclair thought it could be like toothpaste for scratches on the epigenome.

He thought right. After two months of treatment, the aged mouse experienced a 56 to 80 percent bump in endurance for things like running.[29] After being treated with NMN, wrinkly mouse could run as fast and significantly longer than its untreated pair. When Sinclair and his team ran the DNA through the Horvath Clock, it had effectively de-aged.

The next step was to reverse aging back beyond chronological age. As scientists working along the edge between madness and genius are wont to do, Sinclair crushed the optic nerves of a mouse. He shook up a nice batch of Yamanaka's biological cocktail and injected it into the mouse's damaged eye. The results were, as Danny Zuko might say, electrifying. The nerves didn't just wake up—they reset themselves. The mouse could see as well as it could when it was young. In fact, it *was* young. The clock confirmed as much.[30]

....

[29] Mice haven't been the only beneficiaries of NMN. Despite being in clinical trials, Sinclair has been using it on himself for years, and while we don't yet have the results, the man is 50, looks 40, and is a tender 31 according to the epigenetic clock.

[30] Sinclair has since replicated the de-aging process on practically every part of a mouse's body. You should see the ear!

So where does this leave us? Can we stop aging, and even reverse it? Will we ever be able to reset our entire cellular system? Between NMN and Yamanaka's cocktail, it certainly feels like we're heading in that direction. As Sinclair put it: "Ultimately there is no upward biological limit, no law that says we must die at a certain age." Which can mean only one thing: 123 years old, here we come. Watch out, Jeanne Calment![31]

....

[31] If that is your REAL name!

CHAPTER

9

THE
HISTORY
OF INCOME
TAX

HONEST ABE'S OTHER LEGACY

The Inuit have more than fifty words for "snow" and seventy words for "ice." The Sami people of Scandinavia have 1,000 words for "reindeer." And the government, a.k.a. The Man, has thirteen words for taxes—as many as Americans have for "submarine sandwich."[1]

Experts say that cultures often do this with language for things that are a major part of their daily lives—which explains why the British have 3,000 ways to say "drunk." But it can also be a byproduct of complexity. Taxes, like drunkenness, take many nuanced forms. It's hard to *keep it simple, stupid* with things that are not so simple to understand. And few things are more complicated, no matter where you're from or how drunk you may be, than taxes.

TAX	TARIFF	ASSESSMENT
EXCISE	EXACTION	DUTY
LEVY	TITHE	CUSTOM
IMPOST	DUES	TOLL
TRIBUTE		

"THE TARIFF"   "THE TRIBUTE"   "THE EXACTION"

----

[1] Americans love their subs. And also their grinders, hoagies, poboys, heroes, wedges, spukies, blimpies, bombers, garibaldis, zeppelins, rockets, and torpedos.

The US tax code is somewhere between 2,600 and 6,500 pages long, depending on whose interpretation of the code you use. The fact that there's a roughly 4,000-page disparity between versions, and no one is really all that sure how best to define it, should tell you all you need to know about the complexity of the tax code. And we're just talking about the tax law itself at this point; the supporting materials they publish for the experts to explain what the heck they mean in those 2,600-6,500 pages brings the total up to 70,000 pages. That may sound like a lot, but when you consider that it covers all the ways the government can tax, assess, and levy somebody—on what you bring into the country or send out of the country; on what you manufacture here or sell there; on what you own, what you inherit, what you make from investments—okay, yeah, that's still a lot of pages.

The form of taxation that is probably on the easier side to understand, because it touches the most people, is also the one that has historically created the most controversy in the United States—income tax. People don't seem to like this one very much at all.

A PRACTICE AS OLD AS TIME

Personal income tax is the government's levy on the wages one of its citizens earns from doing work. The government then takes that levied amount and uses it for projects that benefit that person and/or their fellow citizens, like building roads and keeping the drinking water supply clean.[2] In most countries, the tax is a percentage of total income and is assessed on an escalating "ability to pay" basis, meaning that the more money you make, the greater percentage you pay.[3] This is sometimes called a progressive tax system—progressive in the "gradually increasing" sense, not in the "2112" sense or the "single-payer healthcare" sense, though both of those rock equally hard—which is to say, a lot.

[2] In theory.

[3] Again, in theory.

Like so many aspects of our modern world, income tax has been around in some form, and for similar reasons, since the days of the Sumerians and the ancient Egyptians. Back then hard currency was far less common than it is today, and so payment had to be made in other ways. In Mesopotamia, payment was made with livestock throughout the year, similar to how wages are withheld from our paychecks today. That makes sense, because who would want a bunch of goats all at once at the end of the year? You want to spread your goats out over the year to make sure there are always goats. In Egypt, pharaohs taxed their citizens in kind. If you were a regular John Q. Tutankhamun, you paid with a portion of whatever goods you made: farmers paid with a percentage of their annual crop yield, potters paid with pieces of ceramic, brewers paid with casks of beer (very popular), and so on and so forth.

This became known as the tithe. Today that term has a more religious connotation, but in early civilizations it was as much about paying the leader as it was about paying tribute to the gods—though often those figures were one in the same. If you were too poor to pay the tithe—say, if you were a peasant—you were spared the expense. Not so fast there, buster: instead, you'd be required to pay with your labor. This was called the corvée and was probably not nearly as fun as paying your taxes in beer.

These tax payments formed the primary revenue stream that leaders of these ancient civilizations could draw from to keep the state running, to fund infrastructure projects (e.g., big ol' pyramids like the ones at Giza), and to raise armies. Fast forward six or eight thousand years and not much has changed. Income tax in the United States accounts for almost half of national revenue and more than 85% if you include payroll taxes, which are effectively a form of income tax.[4] Like Hammurabi and Amenhotep before them, government leaders use this money to pay for the maintenance of roads and bridges,[5] for public sector workers' salaries, and for military expenditures.

Interestingly, the tax burden in the ancient world doesn't seem to have been insanely high or overly complex, at least not on a regular basis—there was a 10% tithe in Mesopotamia,[6] a 1% tax in early Rome, a 20% crops tax in pre-modern China. But if there was one thing that could change all that in the blink of an eye, bringing new, bigger tax policies into being (and protests along with it), it was war.[7] In fact, it was a war that produced the first true income tax in the United States.

....

[4] Kind of makes you feel a weird mixture of important and powerless at the same time, doesn't it?

[5] Also, in theory.

[6] This is basically a flat tax, which as we've pointed out in the podcast is a regressive form of taxation, since 10% of your beer means substantially more to a self-employed small brewer struggling to make ends meet than it does to a huge, Coors-Ho-Tep type brewer making a large sellable surplus of beer.

[7] Flagrant overtaxing by emperors to fund faroff wars during the late Roman Empire is understood to have played a big part in hastening its collapse.

WAR, WHAT IS IT GOOD FOR? THE FIRST INCOME TAX, THAT'S WHAT

Abraham Lincoln began his presidency on a war footing. Addressing the nation from the steps of the US Capitol for the first time on March 4, 1861, Lincoln found himself president of a country with seven fewer states than the day he was elected in November 1860. It must have been tough not to take this personally. In those intervening five months, South Carolina, Florida, Mississippi, Georgia, Alabama, Louisiana, and Texas seceded from the Union and formed the Confederate States of America.[8] Six weeks later, war would start with the Confederate bombardment of Fort Sumter outside Charleston. By the second week in June four more states—North Carolina, Tennessee, Arkansas, and Virginia—would join the Confederate cause.[9]

It's hard enough, economically speaking, for a country to fight a war against an outside enemy. But if the enemy comes from within, it becomes even more difficult, because when the country divides in two the resources at its disposal are divided as well. By the middle of the summer of 1861, the United States of America was a third smaller with the secession of the eleven Confederate states. When it became clear that the war would not end quickly, Congress entered a special session to draft legislation that would generate enough revenue to run the country and fight the war. How, oh how did they do that? Why, taxes, of course.

Under the leadership of Senator William Pitt Crittenden of Maine, who was chairman of the Senate Finance Committee, Congress spent the month of July drafting and passing the Revenue Act of 1861, which President Lincoln signed into law on August 5. This new tax bill instituted a land tax, increased tariffs on certain imports, and for the first time in American history created an income tax: 3% on personal income over $800.

....

[8] Today these states go by a different name: the Southeastern Conference.

[9] Sadly, this included some members of the Atlantic Coast Conference.

The bill was immediately popular for the only two reasons any new tax is ever popular—it only affected the wealthy, and it was totally ineffective. In 1861, only about 3% of the population made more than $800 per year, so there weren't a lot of people who fell under its scope. Not to mention, Congress apparently forgot to build any enforcement mechanism into the bill, so any chance of collecting meaningful revenue while the country was fighting for its life was slim to none.

Fortunately for the Union, this itty-bitty oversight by Senator Crittenden and his committee was rectified the following year, with the Revenue Act of 1862. The sequel not only included a way to enforce the tax by establishing the Office of the Commissioner of Internal Revenue—fit *that* on your business card—it also introduced a progressive taxation model for the first time. Instead of a flat tax of 3% across the board for everyone who made more than $800, the new rates were 3% for annual income between $600 and $10,000, and 5% beyond that. Two years later, the Internal Revenue Act of 1864 repealed and replaced those rates: 5% on income between $600 and $5,000; 7.5% on income between $5,000 and $10,000; 10% on income beyond that.

See what we meant when we talked about taxes and complexity? Within three different laws over just three years, the income threshold moved down for the lowest marginal tax bracket while the rate moved up, then a middle bracket got added and the rate for the highest bracket moved up. Gracious.

A TAX ATTACKS!

There is a not-small group of people who are, shall we say, *unfriendly* to the concept of taxation, who would disagree with our retelling of this history—not so much on the facts as much as on principle. In America, they go by a variety of names depending on their degree of militancy—small-government conservative, libertarian, tax protestor. Their roots extend all the way back to the birth of the nation, which, as every good American school kid knows, had a lot to do with a conflict over taxation. Namely, that the

British government didn't have a right to tax American colonists directly for the sole purpose of raising revenue, especially since the colonists didn't have anyone representing them in Parliament. This is where that whole "No taxation without representation" thing was born.[10]

The British government happened to disagree with this sentiment, and they expressed their disagreement, in one instance, by keeping the tax on tea in place. Well! We don't have to tell you that the American colonists really liked their tea, being lately Brits themselves, so this was quite a finger in the eye.[11] It was another in a long line of friendly little reminders from King George III to his subjects across the pond that he could do whatever he wanted, whenever he wanted.

This didn't sit well with the spiritual descendants of the Massachusetts Bay colony founders—a scrappy group that had enjoyed a twenty-one-year tax exemption from the British crown as an incentive for setting up shop in 1629. As you can imagine, these early colonists had developed a taste for the Tax-Free Lifestyle, what with its panama hats and bottomless mojitos. In this way, it's not hard to see the American colonies as the original tax shelter and to understand the American Revolution that would come 150 years later as a tax rebellion. Those tax/king-wary principles would be carefully baked into the Constitution once George Washington and the Continental Army red, white, and blew the British troops off the continent, declared victory, and let the cast of *Hamilton* get down to the business of "forming a more perfect union."

At first there were just two ways for Congress to tax: they could tax the stuff that people bought and sold through tariffs, and they could tax people directly. So long as the taxes went "to pay the Debts and provide for the Common Defence and general Welfare of the United States," it was all good so far as the Framers were concerned.

---

[10] Interestingly, Washington D.C., where some of those same early American tax rebels lived and worked, faces that dilemma still today. Because D.C. is a district and not a state, it has no federally elected officials arguing for their benefit in Congress. Its residents are, however, American citizens and so they are taxed like any other American—literally taxation without representation. As a bit of a stick in the eye, the District includes the phrase on their license plates.

[11] The Sons of Liberty didn't throw tea into Boston Harbor because they wanted Tension Tamer and all they got was Sleepytime Vanilla. No, there was more to it than that.

And everyday Americans felt pretty much the same way. Early on in its history, the US was apparently run like a lean, mean machine, because for about the first hundred years of its existence those tariffs on trade managed to cover 80-90% of the expense of running the country. This meant that taxes on individual Americans (needed to cover the other 10-20%) remained fairly low. Low enough for everyone to be cool with it.

The three Revenue Acts that later passed during the Civil War, while generally unpleasant to most people, didn't ruffle too many feathers either, because the income tax that came with them was seen as a temporary wartime provision—you know, that whole "common defence" thing.

Oh, you silly, naïve,[12] old-timey Americans. Don't you know that laws are like Pringles? Once you pop, you can't stop.[13] And once you pass legislation, it's very hard to unwind its various implementations.[14]

In 1873, for example, Congress let the Internal Revenue Act of 1864 expire and still the income tax persisted, along with what would eventually become the IRS. It carried on, undead, like some zombie nightmare sucking the coins from honest Americans' mattresses. It continued sucking for twenty more years before it was actually banned; yes, banned. In a famous 1895 Supreme Court case, called *Pollock v. Farmers' Trust & Loan Co.*, the court found the income tax to be a "direct" tax, and therefore unconstitutional since it wasn't apportioned equally across all the states[15]—and thus the income tax was repealed. Though not for long.

....

[12] When we went to verify which letter in the word "naïve" bears the umlaut, we learned that the two dots over the "i" are not an umlaut—which signals a compound letter (as in coöperate)—but a diaresis, which indicates that a vowel should be pronounced as its own thing, not part of the preceding or following letter. We were also delighted to find from our search that we spelled umlaut correctly on the first try, which is sehr schön.

[13] It's possible they were not aware, as Pringles weren't invented until 1967.

[14] This is the lesser known and clumsier second verse of the Pringles slogan.

[15] Apportioned tax meant that any direct tax had to be divided equally among the residents of the nation per capita. So Maryland and New Jersey were expected to cough up the same amount to federal coffers. But there's a problem with this in that if Maryland has fewer people than New Jersey, each Marylander has to pay a higher percentage of their income to make the state's total apportioned tax. As America expanded, this Constitutional requirement made less sense.

In 1909, Congress passed a constitutional amendment that gave itself the power to tax income without having to apportion it. It was ratified by 42 of 48 states four years later and officially became the Sixteenth Amendment to the Constitution on February 3, 1913. To tax protestors, it quickly became a synonym for theft—along with robbery, stealing, larceny, pilferage, plunder, rapacity . . . there's at least thirteen of them. Can't tell if that's a result of it being common or complex.

CHAPTER 10

THE PET ROCK

THE SAVIOR OF 1975 (OR THE DUMBEST
TOY OF THE BEST DECADE)

Are you a cat person or a dog person? Do you value independence in your pets, or is loyalty more important to you? Do you want a pet that can hunt vermin,[1] or one that will play fetch?

Maybe you don't fit into any of these categories and would prefer a pet that matches your decor (consider a chameleon) or your clothes (how about a leopard); maybe one that spouts catchphrases (get a parrot) or eats your annoying neighbor whole and slowly destroys the evidence (look into very large boa constrictors, or consider moving).

Or maybe you want the kind of pet that requires no care or feeding or exercise whatsoever. A pet that will never need a veterinarian or a pet sitter, that will never mate or reproduce no matter how hard you try, and that won't pass away and force you to explain to your distraught kids what this whole "rainbow bridge" thing is all about.

Well, thanks to one enterprising visionary, you just might be in luck, because there is an option out there just for you.

THE PET ROCK FORMATION

In the spring of 1975, a Bay Area freelance copywriter named Gary Dahl was having drinks at a bar in Los Gatos ("The Cats") with a couple long-time advertising colleagues, and they got to talking about how much of a pain it can be to have pets. All the attention you need to give them so they don't get destructive,[2] all the feeding and cleaning they require—they're like children that you're legally allowed to sell. And Dahl would know, as one

---

[1] Do not let your cats do this. Outdoor cats are responsible for such wholesale slaughter of birds and small mammals every year that biologists consider them an invasive species. Chuck and Josh say: keep your cat indoors!

[2] Positive reinforcement only, please.

version of the story goes.[3] With two dogs, two cats, two goats, and two chickens, he and his wife, Marguerite, had basically turned their cabin in the Santa Cruz mountains into a very smelly ark full of very broken furniture.

Wouldn't it be great if there was a pet with none of those drawbacks? one of the friends pondered aloud while they drank. *Yeah, like with my pet rock, I don't have any of those problems*, Dahl joked, *no vet bills except once in a while to scrape off the moss.*

Dahl's friends thought his joke was pretty hilarious, so they all must have been dads. But he couldn't shake the feeling that the idea of a pet rock, while silly, wasn't entirely stupid (which is the standard for all dad jokes; they must be completely stupid). There was an opportunity here. People were feeling down and were tired of their problems, he explained in countless interviews over the years. It had been a rough ten years to that point—the Vietnam War, assassinations, violent protests, Watergate, Hasbro nearly ruining Mr. Potato Head, as you might recall from chapter 2. Dahl thought that people could use an escape, and maybe a laugh.[4]

He started by writing a training manual for future pet rock owners that was modeled quite literally—and hilariously—on dog training manuals. It included a number of commands and tricks that a pet rock would be a natural at mastering, along with others that would be impossible for it to even attempt.

Sit, stay, play dead—the rock was a prodigy; solid. Fetch, come, shake hands—there was little hope. And "roll over," well, the only way that was going to happen was if you trained your rock on the side of a mountain.[5] But the best were the instructions for attack training, which we're just going to quote in full from the manual because no amount of paraphrasing can match a drunk advertising copywriter hitting their stride:

[3] There are two versions of this origin story—the other one doesn't mention whether Dahl had pets, one way or the other. We have chosen to believe the version with more details, since: 1) it's more fun, and 2) we were trained to choose the more detailed answer on multiple choice tests. It works!

[4] They weren't going to get it from movies, that was for sure. The cinema of the first half of the 1970s—which is arguably its golden age—is defined by malaise, cynicism, paranoia, and general dissatisfaction. Here are just ten of the great films from that five-year period: *Serpico, French Connection, Three Days of the Condor, The Parallax View, Dog Day Afternoon, Chinatown, One Flew Over the Cuckoo's Nest, The Day of the Jackal, Mean Streets,* and *Soylent Green.*

[5] One of the neat things we've learned along the way is that mountains are where rocks originally come from. As they crumble and then tumble down into rivers, rocks are carried along, broken down over time, and eventually deposited into the ocean as pebbles and sand, where the waves lap them up onto shores to mix with bits of shell and become beaches. That little tidbit comes from our "We Are Running Out of Sand and That Actually Matters" episode. 🎙

A rock is a loyal, devoted pet that can easily be trained to protect you and your family. Woe be to the burglar or prowler who ventures into the home guarded by a **PET ROCK**—or the mugger who attempts to accost a **PET ROCK**'s master.

When the adversary approaches within arm's length and demands all your money, credit cards, and other valuables follow these easy steps: Reach into your pocket or purse as though you were going to comply with the mugger's demands. Extract your **PET ROCK**. Shout the command, **ATTACK**. And bash the mugger's head in.

As part of the manual, Dahl extolled the advantages of a pet rock over other pets—longer life span, shorter acclimation period—and played up each rock's lineage, claiming that they hailed from some distinguished rock bloodline like the Pyramids of Egypt or the Great Wall of China. In reality, the pet rocks were sourced from the yard of a sand and gravel company on Rosarito Beach in Baja California, Mexico, where Dahl bought them for a penny a piece.

Being an ad man, Dahl also began dreaming up the packaging. He envisioned a cardboard box with air holes in the sides, like pet stores at the mall used for selling plain old boring *animals*,[6] complete with a nest of excelsior that the rock could rest in for the ride home. With the help of his two colleagues from the bar, both of whom he somehow convinced to invest real money[7]—hello tequila—Dahl managed to get the final product ready for the San Francisco Gift Show in August of that same year.[8]

STUFF YOU SHOULD KNOW . . .
About Packaging

"Excelsior" isn't just Stan Lee's catchphrase: it's also the name for the soft wood shavings, sometimes called "wood wool," that shippers often use as packing material around delicate objects.

Remember in *A Christmas Story*, when The Old Man pries open the crate and digs through a giant nest of shavings to reveal his leg lamp? Those shavings were excelsior, and they were in there to protect the lamp, because not only was it a "major award," it was also very fra-gee-lay.

A METEORIC RISE (AND THEN FALL)

The Pet Rock was an instant hit. Dahl came away from the gift show in San Francisco, then the one in New York, with thousands of sales. The high-end department store chain Neiman Marcus ordered a thousand Pet Rocks

---

[6] Yes, there used to be pet stores at the mall and it was pretty great to go visit the cute puppies and bunnies until about the time you hit puberty and realized how terrible those stores were for animals. Lots of states and cities realized too and began to ban pet stores from selling dogs and cats.

[7] One of them, a man named George Coakley, invested $10,000, which was pretty big money in 1975. According to the good people at Westegg Inflation Calculator, it's nearly $50,000 in today's money.

[8] The box ended up taking a shape that was disturbingly reminiscent of a McDonald's Happy Meal container, and what better recipe is there for wholesome family fun than mixing fast food with your pets.

and stacked them prominently in their storefront windows for the holiday shopping season. Bloomingdale's got in on the act, then smaller retailers followed suit. Even though they were going for a ridiculous $3.95 each, or nearly twenty dollars adjusted for inflation,[9] Dahl could barely keep up with demand.

By October, he was selling thousands a day. By Christmas, sales were up to 10,000 daily and well over one million "pets" sold in total. Dahl was an instant millionaire, and before long a celebrity too. Johnny Carson had him on *The Tonight Show* twice; he was profiled in newspapers and magazines nationwide; there was even a hit song—"I'm in Love with My Pet Rock"[10]—further entrenching the 1970s as the head-scratchingest, most manifestly wonderful decade of the century.

Everyone seemed to be happily in on every joke, pet rock included. *Time* magazine wrote about the success of pet rocks as part of a December cover story about the American shopping surge and "trendy Bloomingdale's," commenting that Dahl's creation was "1% product and 99% marketing genius"—a fact that was 100 percent obvious to anyone paying the least bit of attention. One *Time* reader took the gag further in a letter to the editor three days before Christmas, writing in to say that "it saddens me that there are Americans who would buy a Pet Rock from a prestigious store just for one-upmanship. A true pet lover would take in any rock and give it a good home."

And then, just like that, the clock struck midnight on Gary Dahl's igneous pumpkin and the fun was over. The holiday gift-giving season had come to an end, and by early that next year, the pet rock craze had joined it. Dahl tried to keep it going with a bicentennial edition pet rock (sporting an American flag paint job) and ancillary merchandise like T-shirts and shampoo, but demand dropped off so precipitously after the 1975 holiday season that he was forced to give away thousands of unsold rocks to charity—what today we would call "landscaping."

....

[9] Thanks again, Westegg!

[10] Well, if not a hit, a very popular song at least. The song, by Al Bolt, peaked at #85 on the Billboard Country charts.

The 1970s Were Awesome, and Here's Proof

TOYS	If the sturdy, geological permanence of the Pet Rock didn't do it for you, there was always the Stretch Armstrong action figure, released by Kenner in 1976, that basically allowed children to draw and quarter a blond guy in a Speedo without having to worry about breaking him. And what was inside Mr. Armstrong? The most '70s substance ever: corn syrup.
CARS	You had two choices: land yachts like the Chrysler Imperial LeBaron and the Cadillac Fleetwood Sixty Special—both of which you didn't so much parallel park as dock to the portside—or a small, bubble-shaped compact car like the AMC Pacer or the Ford Pinto, which blew up if you rear-ended it.[11]
MUSIC	Disco.[12] 🎙
COLORS	The "trendy" colors for appliances and home furnishings had names like avocado green, burnt orange, harvest gold, and brown. Just brown. Today, those very same colors are the ones your pediatrician says to look for in your newborn baby's diaper to make sure they're digesting food properly.
FASHION	You really had to work for it on the fashion front, from leisure suits and powder blue tuxedos to bell bottoms, peasant blouses, and big-collar shirts. But nothing said '70s like a pair of corduroy trousers and a shrink-top macramé vest made out of yarn. Would you like to light yourself on fire from the friction of your thighs rubbing together as you walked, or would you rather smell like a wet dog in the rain? There's no correct answer!

[11] We did a live episode called "Back When Ford Pintos Were Flaming Deathtraps" that will tell you everything you could possibly know about a car you couldn't possibly ever want to drive. 🎙

[12] See also: Black Sabbath.

TV	This was the golden age for film, but on the small screen TV was starting to come into its own as well, with a number of iconic series that featured fantastic actors, great action, and socially relevant story lines; though not without a less-than-subtle vein of racism running through it, wrapped in a shiny coating of persistent onscreen sexism. And still, even considering all that, the '70s managed to spit out some great TV: *Wonder Woman; Good Times; What's Happening; M*A*S*H; Welcome Back, Kotter; Sanford and Son; The Six Million Dollar Man.*[13]
HAIR	Long, straight hair. Long, frizzy disco curls. The long-feathered Farrah Fawcett hair. Huge perfectly coifed Jackson 5 afros. The Dorothy Hamill wedge. The David Cassidy heartthrob shag. Then whatever you call what the rest of the guys were doing. Just so much hair. And that doesn't even count all the facial hair action . . .
NEWS	The line between news and entertainment began to blur, such that news started to get reported not by journalists, but by pretty faces and handsome figures with entertaining personalities. This led to the birth of the human-interest story and hoaxes like the Amityville Horror murders being reported as real, true news. 🎙 It is not an accident that *Anchorman* is set in 1975, the same year as the Pet Rock.

[13] He'd be The Thirty-Five Million Dollar Man if the show debuted in 2020. You did it again, Westegg!

STUCK BETWEEN A ROCK AND A HARD PASS

Dahl tried his hands at some other gag gifts, all of them pretty great—a "Sand Breeding Kit" offering male and female sand to "grow your own desert wasteland"; a "Canned Earthquake," which was essentially a can with a windup device in it to make it jump around; and an odd scheme to sell "red dirt" from China as a way to take over China one tablespoon at a time. None of them took off.

Even without another hit product, Dahl had made enough money in 1975 to retire from freelancing and do other things. He launched his own creative agency, he started giving motivational speeches about how to get rich quick, he wrote "Advertising for Dummies," and in 2000 he won the Bulwer-Lytton contest for intentionally bad fiction writing.[14] But it was the purchase and renovation of a saloon in San Jose that was Dahl's dream, and fairly soon thereafter his nightmare.

Years later his wife would say that the whole crazy thing "was great fun when it happened"—the pet rock had unquestionably made him rich and famous—but that he'd developed mixed feelings about the whole thing. See, when people found out he owned that saloon, they would "come to him with weird ideas, expecting him to do for them what he had done for himself. And a lot of times they were really, really stupid ideas." It was a veritable onslaught of stupid—everything from packaged bull feces to derivative pet rock concepts like "pet sticks"[15]—that he could only find escape in retirement to Jacksonville, Oregon, and then in death in 2005.

....

[14] The Bulwer-Lytton contest invites authors to submit the worst opening sentence to a book they can come up with. Dahl won for this sentence: "The heather-encrusted Headlands, veiled in fog as thick as smoke in a crowded pub, hunched precariously over the moors, their rocky elbows slipping off land's end, their bulbous, craggy noses thrust into the thick foam of the North Sea like bearded old men falling asleep in their pints." That's awfully great, don't you think? Or should we say, greatly awful.

[15] Pet rocks we get, but pet sticks? You can't even put googley eyes on them.

Pet Rocks are still available online. The company ThinkGeek even developed a USB Pet Rock, which is just a plain rock with a USB dongle sticking out of it. It'd be nice to think Dahl would approve, but he was definitely frustrated with being known as the guru of zany business ideas. He once said that "If people would just forget I did the Pet Rock, I'd be happy."

It sure is a good thing nobody wrote an entire chapter about him for their book of interesting facts!

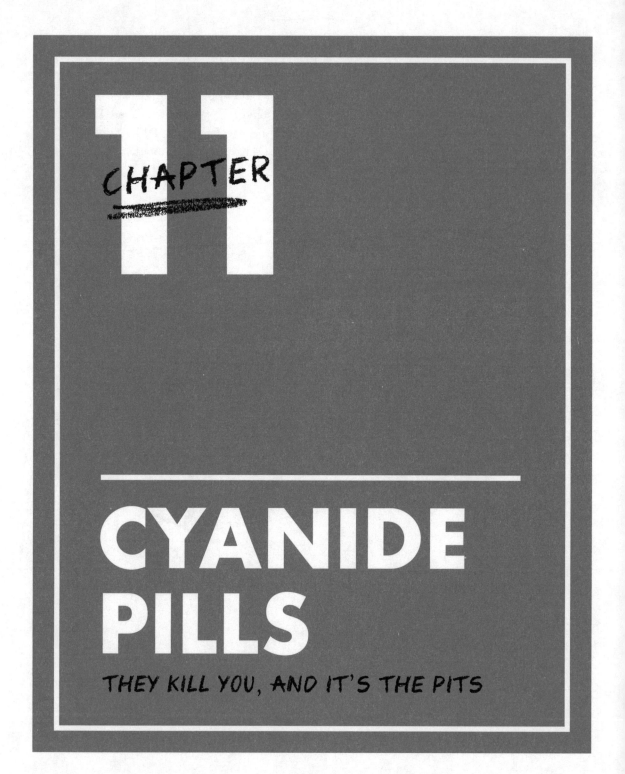

CHAPTER **11**

CYANIDE PILLS

THEY KILL YOU, AND IT'S THE PITS

In Hollywood, cyanide pills are the go-to last resort of captured spies and enemy agents. In *Captain America: The First Avenger*, Captain America chases a dastardly enemy agent and corners him, only for the spy to swallow a cyanide pill and die foaming at the mouth.

In *Skyfall*, James Bond faces off with an agent-turned-villain who bears some profound scarring from a failed suicide attempt by cyanide pill. And in *Wonder Woman*, Diana foils an assassination attempt but can't stop the attacker from taking a cyanide pill to kill himself.

With how often this happens, you'd think by now the world's winningest action heroes would see the cyanide psych-out coming a mile away. You'd think they might ask themselves some key questions before taking their eye off the ball: Did I just thwart an underboss? Maybe catch a henchman or *henchperson*?[1] Do their clothes have pockets? Are we still in the second act? Do they have information that would make defeating the villain *soooo* much easier? Well then don't be fooled, because that's not a Tic-Tac they're reaching for.

It's a pretty effective narrative device, really. The good people over at TV Tropes point out that by taking a suicide pill when their mission has failed, a henchperson shows the audience that their boss—the main villain—is so utterly frightening that taking their life right there on the dirty floor after being soundly beaten up by the hero is preferable to whatever the villain might do to them. That, or the boss has such a hold on them, the henchperson feels they must die for failing them.

Understandable enough. But here's our big question: where did cyanide as the suicide method of choice for spies and villains in the movies come from? The answer can be found not only in the unique properties of the chemical itself, but in its real-world historical usage by a wide range of notorious figures, including lots and lots of Nazis. That's right: as if Hitler didn't have enough to answer for, we can add "inspiring an overused Hollywood cliché" to his long list of crimes.

....

[1] Doing someone's evil bidding is non-binary.

NATURE'S LITTLE SUFFOCATOR

Cyanide is a naturally occurring chemical found, to varying degrees, in all sorts of plants and seeds, including lima beans (not a reason to not eat your lima beans), almonds, and in the pits of all stone fruits: peaches, apricots, cherries, plums, nectarines—basically anything you make a delicious summer pie with. It's not the hard, stony pits themselves that contain the cyanide, however; it's the smaller seeds at their center. Those seeds contain amygdalin, which converts to hydrogen cyanide when ingested, which is when the terrible, terrible party starts.

The first thing cyanide does in the bloodstream is hitch a ride aboard hemoglobin, which is responsible for carrying oxygen to the cells in our body. Once inside a cell, cyanide binds to an enzyme called cytochrome oxidase, whose job is to help mitochondria turn oxygen into energy. Cyanide wreaks its havoc by interfering with the use of that oxygen, thereby halting cellular respiration and preventing the creation of energy (which you need to do things like continuing to live). Cyanide effectively starves the cells in your essential tissues of the energy they need to survive.

And that's when the symptoms begin: nausea, headaches, vomiting, then elevated breathing and a heartrate that quickly progresses to respiratory failure, loss of consciousness, and, oh yeah, death. Cyanide is so lethal that even a half-milligram per kilogram of body weight has been known to kill, and the median lethal dose isn't much higher at 1–1.5 milligrams per kilo range. If the average henchperson clocks in around 180 pounds, it would only take between 80 and 325 milligrams of cyanide in one of its two solid forms—potassium cyanide or sodium cyanide—to virtually guarantee death. That's somewhere around the size of a baby aspirin or a Percocet. Cyanide is the Mike Tyson of poisons: small, compact, with a punch strong enough to put you on your back in an instant, so don't let it anywhere near your face.

Fortunately, it's very difficult to punch yourself in the face by accident—literally or vegetally. Exact toxicity figures vary by fruit and by varietal, but it looks like you would need to eat at least a dozen raw peach pit seeds, twenty

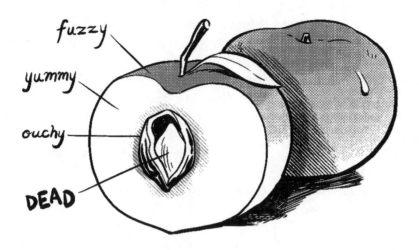

fuzzy

yummy

ouchy

DEAD

or thirty apricot kernels,[2] at least thirty cherry pits, or well over 140 apple seeds to meaningfully flirt with your maker. And simply swallowing them isn't enough. You really have to chew them up to get the amygdalin to release those cyanide compounds that mix with the enzymes in your body to become hydrogen cyanide. That's a whole lot of effort—gathering up all that fruit, cutting away the hard stones, chewing up all those not very chewable seeds. And let's not forget to mention that the seeds emit an unpleasant bitter almond flavor once they're cracked open and chewed. It's Mother Nature's own confirmation dialog box: *Are you sure you want to exit out of this life?*

THE PEOPLE'S POISON

Despite the relative difficulty of extracting an "effective" dose's worth of cyanide from fruits and nuts and seeds, the fact that it's found all over the place in nature is probably why cyanide has been used to kill people for many centuries. Some say its use as a poison goes back as far as 400 BCE,[3] or at least to 50 CE when the Roman Emperor Nero, with the help of his

---

[2] According to C. Claiborne Ray, the long-time writer of the New York Times' "Science Q&A" column, no one has survived eating 38 apricot kernels, so you've got that going for you.

[3] Several historians have made these claims, but there's no conclusive evidence.

personal poisoner Locusta, used cherry laurel water to poison the wells of his enemies and kill off unwanted family members, including his own step-brother Britannicus. Whenever it first came into fashion, we feel bad for the poor sap who originally figured it out, because you can be fairly confident that they found out about the cyanogenic properties of apple seeds and peach pits the hard way.[4]

Despite this potentially ancient legacy, it wasn't until 1782 that cyanide as an actual chemical compound was first isolated, by the Swedish chemist Carl Scheele. Scheele, who died at 43 years old from what many say was cyanide exposure, was also the first individual to notice that cyanide in its gaseous form (hydrogen cyanide) has a distinct bitter almond smell. That discovery was only of so much help since less than 50% of the population is genetically able to smell it. It's like a deadly asparagus pee. Once Scheele let the almond-scented cat out of the bag, though, cyanide quickly found a home in the arsenals of generals and the general population alike.

On January 1, 1845, for example, a Quaker named John Tawell got tired of sowing his oats with a long-time mistress and decided to end things, permanently. He went over to her house in the London suburbs, where she was raising their two illegitimate children, they fought, and he murdered her with potassium cyanide. He tried to flee to the city by train, but was intercepted along the way thanks to another fairly recent discovery—the telegraph, which had been deployed across the British rail system only a couple years prior. Tawell was tried, convicted, and executed a few months later; his cells asphyxiated the old-fashioned way . . . by rope.

Twenty-five years later, during the Franco-Prussian War, Napoleon III had his troops dip their bayonets in potassium cyanide, just in case their rifle-mounted mini-swords weren't stabby enough. That same conflict set the diplomatic stage for World War I, which was eventually precipitated by the assassination of Archduke Franz Ferdinand[5] on a street in Sarajevo in June 1914 by a group of young Bosnian Serbs, all of whom were armed with a vial of cyanide in case they got caught. When one of the assassins, Nedeljko Čabrinović, threw a bomb at the Archduke's car and missed, he took his cyanide and jumped in the nearby river to avoid capture. Unfortunately for Čabrinović, the cyanide was old and only induced vomiting. And this

---

[4] Perhaps it was our dear friend Tuk Tuk the Neanderthal. 🎧

[5] "Take me out" indeed.

being summer, the river was only six inches deep, which together made the would-be assassin very apprehendable, if not also wet and gross.[6]

NO WAY OUT BUT ONE

Čabrinović certainly wasn't the first person to look to cyanide as a way to escape a fate worse than death. In 1904, Whitaker Wright, a conman who was caught and convicted of bilking investors like a turn-of-the-century Bernie Madoff, killed himself with cyanide right there in the courtroom. Shockingly, the cyanide-in-court technique isn't just an old-timey solution to one's legal troubles. As recently as 2012 and 2013, two different men in the US took their lives by ingesting cyanide right there in the courtroom when guilty verdicts were returned in trials for arson and sodomizing a child, respectively.

When World War II rolled around, cyanide pills really took off as the method of choice for offing yourself behind enemy lines. That's when British and American secret services first developed the cyanide pills for their covert agents that have inspired so many Hollywood depictions. The pills were filled with potassium cyanide and hidden inside fake teeth, which if crushed would release the poison and kill the agent, but if accidentally swallowed would just pass harmlessly through the digestive system.[7]

Yet while the Allies may have invented the cyanide pill, it was the Germans who really fell in love with it—not unlike their love for David Hasslhoff's music. Not only did the Nazis infamously use cyanide as a key ingredient in the Zyklon B poison that killed millions of innocent people during the Holocaust, they also used it on themselves. A lot. If you were to judge their taste for the poison based on their frequency of consumption, it appears to have been only slightly less voracious than Tony the Tiger's appetite for Frosted Flakes (*It's Grrrrrrave!*). Cyanide arguably killed more of the Nazi high command than the Allies themselves ever did.

....

[6] So, wait, then how was Archduke Ferdinand assassinated then? Čabrinović's compatriot, Gavrilo Princip, would finish the job later that morning when the Archduke's motorcade foolishly returned to the train station on the same road it came down when it was attacked the first time. He, too, popped his cyanide pill, and it too was expired, producing only vomiting.

[7] There's a (disputed) claim by a CIA chief that Lt. Col. Oliver North was given a cyanide pill to use in case he was found out and tortured when he traveled undercover to Iran to illegally sell missiles. 🎙

The Nazis weren't the last monsters to kill or be killed with cyanide. In 1978, the cult leader Jim Jones ordered his followers to kill a congressman and a number of journalists, then kill themselves en masse with cyanide-laced fruit punch in what became known as the Jonestown massacre.[8] And in 1982, seven people in the Chicago area died from cyanide poisoning after taking Tylenol that had been mysteriously tampered with.[9] The murderer was never found, but the crimes lead to changes in how medicine is packaged and sold.

So the next time you can't get the tamper-proof lid off your bottle of pain reliever and you jam your finger trying to stab through the foil seal, you may not know *who* to thank, but you will definitely know *what* to thank.

....

[8] Though the massacre is the source of the phrase "drink the Kool-Aid," the deadly fruit punch was actually Fla-Vor-Aid.

[9] Interestingly, this appears as a recurring theme in our two-part episode on the very same Tylenol Murders. 📡

Nazi High Command and Their Cyanide Psych-Outs

FIELD MARSHAL ERWIN ROMMEL	Unsuccessfully plotted to kill Hitler in 1944.	Swallowed a cyanide pill before the SS could arrest him.
REICHSTAG PRESIDENT HERMANN GORING	Kicked out of the Nazi party for treason. Arrested by American soldiers and tried at Nuremberg and found guilty of war crimes.	Took a cyanide pill in his prison cell before he could be hanged.
SS CHIEF HEINRICH HIMMLER	Captured by British soldiers after the German surrender and taken to an interrogation camp.	Chomped down on a cyanide pill hidden in one of his teeth before the camp's medical examiner could look inside his mouth.
MINISTER OF PROPAGANDA JOSEPH GOEBBELS	Named Chancellor after Hitler's suicide on April 30, 1945. Spent one day in the role and said *Nein!*	Swallowed cyanide along with his wife, then shot himself. But not before having all of his children injected with cyanide, just in case there was any doubt that he was one of history's most awful human beings.
FÜHRER ADOLPH HITLER	Read the writing on the walls inside the *Fuhrerbunker* as the Soviet Red Army surrounded Berlin.	Bit down on a cyanide pill with his new wife, Eva Braun, then shot himself. Sound familiar? Goebbels copied him to a T.

CHAPTER

12

DO(UGH)NUTS

THE HISTORY OF AMERICA'S
SNACK FOOD

There is a famous deleted scene that didn't make it into *Pulp Fiction* where Mia Wallace (Uma Thurman) interviews Vincent Vega (John Travolta) with a video camera while he waits to take her to dinner at Jack Rabbit Slims.

Mia says that on important topics there are only two ways a person can answer, and how they answer tells you who they are. "For instance, there are only two kinds of people in the world," she says, "Beatles people and Elvis people. Now Beatles people can like Elvis, and Elvis people can like the Beatles, but nobody likes them both equally. Somewhere, you have to make a choice, and that choice tells you who you are."[1]

What Mia is saying—or rather, what Quentin Tarantino is saying through her—is that for all the shades of gray in the world, when it comes right down to it, the important stuff is black and white. You see it in politics—Left vs. Right—you see it in music—Beatles vs. Elvis—you see it in religion—Catholic vs. Protestant, Shiite vs. Sunni—and you see it in . . . *doughnuts?!* Or is it donuts?

See there, it starts right out of the gate with this, what is perhaps the greatest tasty sweet treat. From the spelling, to how they're made, to the variety of flavors, to the best brand, do(ugh)nuts[2] are a study in duality.

----

[1] Exactly what your choice says about you remains as much a mystery as what was in Marsellus Wallace's stolen briefcase.

[2] We haven't trademarked this spelling yet, but we're considering it.

DOUGHNUT VERSUS DONUT

Dough has been fried in oil and sprinkled with sweet, sugary goodness by countless cultures since at least the time of Ancient Greece and Ancient Rome,[3] if not even earlier with prehistoric Native American societies.[4] But the first appearance of the term "doughnut" doesn't occur until the turn of the nineteenth century—and it appears as doughnut, not donut—in the appendix of an 1803 English cookbook that featured American recipes. It then appears in a satirical novel by Washington Irving in 1809, called *A History of New York,* in which his description of early life under Dutch control includes the description of "balls of sweetened dough, fried in hog's fat, called doughnuts or *olykoeks.*"[5]

Most early doughnuts were just strips or balls of dough, but in the mid-nineteenth century a New England ship captain named Hanson Gregory came up with the idea of putting holes in the middle of them. His mother Elizabeth had been in the habit of making doughnuts with lemon rind and warm spices like cinnamon and nutmeg that she would liberate from her son's cargo. She would put hazelnuts and walnuts in the center, where the dough was least likely to cook all the way through—making them very literal "dough nuts"—and give them to her son and his crew for their long stretches at sea. Eventually, Hanson one-upped his mother's culinary inventiveness and started punching holes in the center of the doughnuts with the round top of a tin pepper box, creating their now-traditional ring shape for the first time.

What inspired Hanson to do this? Was he just bored? Some say he was being frugal with ingredients, which honestly doesn't make much sense. Others say getting rid of the undercooked center made them easier to eat and digest. Maybe he didn't like nuts? Then there is the legend that one day he stabbed a doughnut onto the spoked handle of his ship's wheel,

---

[3] Made-Up Fun Fact: Julius Caesar blew out a big mouthful of half-chewed fried dough when he was stabbed in the Senate.

[4] It may be the reason humans exist.

[5] *Olykoeks* is Dutch for "oily cakes." It was they of the tulip and the windmill who brought the food over to New York back when the city was still called New Amsterdam. (Why'd they change it? We can't say. People just liked it better that way.)

either because he needed both hands to control the ship during a storm or he wanted his snack easily accessible while standing at the bridge. Being a sailor, the ability to tell tall tales is as important as reading nautical charts, so it's likely that both versions of that story are apocryphal.[6] Nonetheless! In 1947, on the 100th anniversary of his "discovery," Hanson's hometown of Rockport, Maine, put up a plaque honoring him as the man who "first invented the hole in the donut."

Notice the spelling. "Donut" originally began appearing in the late 1800s as a contraction of the longer, traditional spelling,[7] and became more widespread in the 1920s, especially with bakeries—presumably because three extra letters can take up a lot of space on small storefront windows. "Donut" would pick up real steam only a few years after Captain Gregory's

6   That first ship's wheel story seems particularly suspect, since there's probably never been a human in history who didn't just shove the entire doughnut in their mouth when they suddenly needed the use of both hands. It's like our seventh sense.

7   Haha, "do'nut."

confectionary contribution was memorialized, with the founding of Dunkin' Donuts in 1950[8] by a 34-year-old Boston man named William Rosenberg. Rosenberg had built a sizable mobile catering business after World War II to serve local factory workers and had come to realize that the bulk of his sales came from two items: doughnuts and coffee. 🎙 So he opened a shop, originally called "Open Kettle," that was dedicated to selling those two wonderful things.[9] Rosenberg eventually renamed it and the business became a quick success. Over the next few decades Dunkin' Donuts would expand rapidly across the Eastern Seaboard, and the spelling of "donuts" along with it.

Mostly though, "donut" is a great example of the American preference for simplifying the spelling of commonly used words. It's a longstanding cause that has been taken up throughout American history by luminaries like Benjamin Franklin, Noah Webster (the Daryl Hall of Merriam-Webster),[10] Melvil Dewey (of the Dewey Decimal System), President Teddy Roosevelt (of the Presidents), and the robber baron Andrew Carnegie (of the Mind-Bogglingly Wealthy Strike-Breakers),[11] who went so far as to co-found and fund the Simplified Spelling Board in 1906, which counted among its earliest membership ranks people like Dewey, Mark Twain, and the publisher Henry Holt.[12]

Still, "doughnut" remains the preferred spelling. It's used in print nearly two-to-one, even in American publications. Why that is the case isn't entirely clear, since most dictionaries allow for "donut" as an acceptable alternative spelling. It's possible that many people view "donut" as more of a trademark name, with a capital D, a la Dunkin' Donuts, though your guess is as good as ours. As the great William Safire put it in one of his classic *New York Times* "On Language" columns: "those of us among the elderly . . . spell the circular pastries *doughnuts* because they are made of dough, not *do.*"[13]

....

[8] Dunkin' Donuts is actually a contraction of two words (Dunking and Doughnuts). It would contract again, this time from two words to one, when the company shamefully shed "Donuts" from their name in 2018, to simply become Dunkin'.

[9] Could have ended up as Op'n K'ttl'.

[10] Your kiss is on his list, right between "kismet" and "kist."

[11] See chapter 17.

[12] We need to do an episode on the simplified spelling movement.

[13] Bear in mind that William Safire was arguably the pope of the prescriptivists. *The Onion* once ran a headline that read: "William Safire orders two Whoppers Junior."

The SYSK Vocabulary Test

SIMPLE AND AMERICAN	TRADITIONAL AND FANCY PANTS
donut	doughnut
omelet	omelette
plow	plough
program	programme
check	cheque
draft	draught
yogurt 🔊	yoghurt
airplane	aeroplane
color	colour
flavor	flavour
favorite	favourite
ton	tonne
aluminum	aluminium
ass	arse
oriented	orientated
q	queue

YEAST VERSUS CAKE

Doughnuts are indeed made of dough and not do, though different doughnuts have different doughs that do different things, about that we do not doubt. The main difference is between yeast doughnuts and cake doughnuts. Yeasties, as no one else has ever called them ever, use yeast to make the dough rise, whereas cake doughnuts use chemical leaveners like baking powder and baking soda.

As a result, yeast doughnuts are light and pillowy. They are typically bigger than cake doughnuts and have a smoother, satiny surface,[14] which allows them to take glazing and chocolate coating much better. The honeycomb structure of their insides—created by air bubbles from the proofing yeast—also makes them ideal for filling. If you're eating a jelly- or a cream-filled doughnut, you are eating a yeast doughnut. Of course, the pinnacle of the yeast doughnut variety is the Original Glazed made by Krispy Kreme (more below).

Cake doughnuts, on the other hand, are denser—dare we say, *cakier*—and better for dunking in your coffee. This dunking method was immortalized by Clark Cable's journalist character in the 1934 romantic comedy *It Happened One Night*, when he taught the high society object of his affection, played by Claudette Colbert, how to dunk her doughnut just like working-class folk.[15] The biggest advantages with cake doughnuts are twofold. First, they can come in a variety of flavors, running through the doughnut itself in wondrous veins of precious gems of taste—like cherry and blueberry and oh! apple cider.[16] Second, once the dough is combined and formed, they're ready for the fryer. Yeast doughnuts really only come in one flavor (yeast?) and need time to proof before they get dropped into the oil.

All the earliest doughnuts and doughnut ancestors were yeast doughnuts, for the simple reason that baking with yeast goes back 5,000 years and baking powder wasn't developed until the 1840s—well after the Dutch came over with their oily cakes and unwittingly began the American doughnut revolution. It was baking powder that turned the revolution into an evolution, however, accelerating the doughnut's ascent to the summit of American

---

[14] How badly do you want a do(ugh)nut right now?

[15] In 1941, the famous manners expert Emily Post called dunking your doughnut "as bad an example of table manners as can be found." She and William Safire were probably secretly married.

[16] How about now?

snack food. There is nothing more American, after all, than being able to make a lot of something faster and cheaper, and that's precisely what chemical leaveners like baking powder did with the cake doughnut.

TASTE OF HOME

The ease with which doughnuts could now be made increased their popularity over the course of the nineteenth century, but they grew into a signature American staple during World War I—in France, of all places—when the Salvation Army set up camp wherever American troops were stationed. The camps were staffed with female volunteers who made cake doughnuts by the bushel and often delivered them directly to the front lines, hot out of the frying oil, in an effort to give soldiers a taste of home.[17] The women came to be known as "doughnut lassies" and the campaign they led was such an overwhelming success that other aid organizations like the Red Cross and the Y(!)M(!)C(!)A(!) followed their lead, further imprinting doughnuts on the memories of America's fighting men.[18]

When American troops returned stateside after the war ended, they brought their taste for doughnuts with them. Demand was so high that doughnuts were regularly being served in places like theaters, but things really took off after an entrepreneurially-minded Russian refugee named Adolph Levitt invented the first doughnut machine. He called it the "Wonderful Almost Human Automatic Doughnut Machine" (for real) and put the first one in the window of his Harlem bakery. Lickety split, doughnuts began popping up in bakeries and delis, at festivals and county fairs all over the country. Levitt was even able to wholesale his doughnuts alongside sales of his machine, building a business worth over $25 million in the middle of the Great Depression.[19]

....

[17] This is not where the nickname "doughboy" comes from. We thought of that too. Turns out it's unclear where the name originated—possibly from the clay they rolled along the piping on their uniforms to keep it white—but the doughnuts the soldiers were fed doesn't seem to factor into it.

[18] In World War II, the Doughnut Lassies were replaced by the Doughnut Dollies, though their role was exactly the same. By either name, they were angels on Earth.

[19] The Westegg Inflation Calculator says that's more than $475 million today!

Doughnuts' rise continued through the '30s. In 1934, the same year Clark Gable started dunkin' up a storm on the silver screen, they were named the "Hit Food of the Century of Progress" at the World's Fair in Chicago. Even more monumentally, that year nineteen-year-old Vernon Rudolph opened the very first Krispy Kreme Doughnut Company store in Nashville, Tennessee, with his uncle Ishmael, who'd purchased a yeast doughnut recipe from a New Orleans chef with the whimsical name of Joe LeBeau. A couple years later, Rudolph would move to Winston-Salem, North Carolina, and open his own solo Krispy Kreme shop, establishing it as the official founding headquarters of the doughnut business.[20] By the end of the decade, Rudolph would be wholesaling to grocery stores and bakeries all over North Carolina, and within twenty years Krispy Kreme would be a veritable empire, with twenty-nine factories spread across twelve states, setting up the Doughnut vs Donut battle that Dunkin' Donuts would eventually win.[21]

Today, Krispy Kreme and Dunkin' Donuts have grown to several thousand locations, not just across the United States but around the world—Dunkin' Donuts alone has over 5,000 locations and sells donuts in thirty-seven different countries. In just the United States, over 10 billion donuts are made each year, which comes to about thirty donuts per American citizen—more than that if you leave out babies and the gluten intolerant.[22] With each donut averaging around 300 calories, that's three *trillion* donut calories a year! Or 1.2 billion days' worth of the recommended daily allowance for calories. It's simple math: America loves doughnuts. We rest our case.

To some, what makes doughnuts quintessentially American is the fact that they are deep-fried hunks of dough with little to no nutritional value that get scarfed down by the dozen, which is true. But they're also descended from a long historical lineage that crosses cultural lines and includes not just ancient Romans and Greeks, not just prehistoric Native Americans and colonial Dutch (*olykoek*), but also ancient Chinese (*youtiao*), medieval Arab and twelfth-century Jewish societies (*sufganiyot*), along with German (*cruller*), French (*beignet*), Polish (*paczki*), and Okinawan (*andagi*) cooks from across the centuries.

Whether you're a doughnut lover or a donut lover, a yeastie or a cakey, a Krispy Kremer for life or you ride or die for the Dunk, doughnuts are one of the few things in life where neither side is wrong and both sides win—a kind of duality that is as unique to doughnuts as doughnuts are to America.

....

[20] A year later, in 1938, the Salvation Army started National Doughnut Day, celebrated on the first Friday of June, in part to help those suffering during the Depression, and in part to honor the Doughnut Lassies on the twentieth anniversary of the end of World War I.

[21] When the world has more doughnuts *and* more donuts, does anybody really lose?

[22] A baby eating a do(ugh)nut is a hilarious thought.

CHAPTER

13

THE JERSEY DEVIL

HOO IS THE MONSTER OF THE PINE BARRENS

Boy do we seem to love us some devils. There is the Tasmanian Devil, which is a carnivorous marsupial and aspirational bad boy for a certain subset of T-shirt wearers. There is the Blue Devil, which is a school mascot. There's the Red Devils, the nickname for the Manchester United football[1] club.

There is the Devil Dog, which is the nickname for a US Marine and a snack cake. There is a Dirt Devil, which is a vacuum cleaner brand. There is a *dust* devil, which is a small, fleeting ground-based whirlwind. And then there is the subject of this chapter, the Jersey Devil, which is a famously mysterious, awful-sounding creature that has been haunting south New Jersey for years.

Poor New Jersey. Few states take as much guff and get as bad a rap as the Garden State. The NFL teams the Giants and the Jets both play in New Jersey, but are too ashamed to admit it, insisting that they are New York teams in defiance of basic geography. In movies and TV, it's the home of fictional mobsters like Tony Soprano and non-fictional reality "stars" like the cast of Jersey Shore. As everyone outside New Jersey is well aware, the whole place tends to be treated as a punchline, where the joke is on loud girls with bad spray tans and mama's boys with frosted tips who drop the last vowel on a shocking number of deli items—or so the stereotypes go. Given its largely dubious reputation, it seems fitting that New Jersey is the only state with an official state demon.

....
[1] Soccer 🎙️

121

THIS BABY'S A REAL LOOKER

Sightings of the Jersey Devil go back hundreds of years, to before New Jersey was a state and before "Jersey Devil" was even the creature's given name. Originally it was known as the Leeds Devil, named after a woman called Mother Leeds who lived near the Pine Barrens with her alcoholic husband and twelve children. In 1735, she became pregnant with her thirteenth child. Out of sheer frustration with her circumstances—and who can blame the poor woman—competing accounts say she either shouted to the heavens, "Let this one be a devil!", or she asked the Devil to take the cursed child since this was her thirteenth and thirteen is traditionally an unlucky number.[2]

Why Mother Leeds thought that invoking the devil's name would help anything remains an open question—perhaps she tried the other guy first and got no answer—but a few months later, on a stormy night, she went into labor and gave birth to what seemed like a normal son. Yet within a few minutes, all her cursing came to pass, as the boy transformed into a horrific monster.[3] It grew to a massive size and sprouted horns, claws, and bat-like wings. Its body grew hair and feathers, and its eyes glowed bright red. It turned on its poor mother and killed her, then did the same to the rest of the family and the midwives who attended the birth. Quite a handful, that kid. Fresh out of victims, the monster baby flew up the chimney like some kind of infernal Santa Claus and disappeared into the Pine Barrens, where it has made its home ever since—scaring all manner of people from hunters to cab drivers, military officers to police and firefighters, and park rangers to passersby.[4]

Over time a detailed picture of this heinous beast has emerged from these encounters. Some involved vicious animal attacks, like the one at a pig farm in 1980 where all the pigs had their brains scooped out of the back of their heads as though they'd been attacked by a flying creature with a taste

---

[2] Fear of the number thirteen is called triskaidekaphobia. It's the reason 80% of the tall buildings in the United States go directly from the 12th to the 14th floor.

[3] In another version of this story, in which Mother Leeds is a witch and the real father is the Devil himself, the baby comes out of the womb as a horrific monster—but after all, what else would you expect?

[4] The Jersey Devil has seen a million faces, and it's rocked them all.

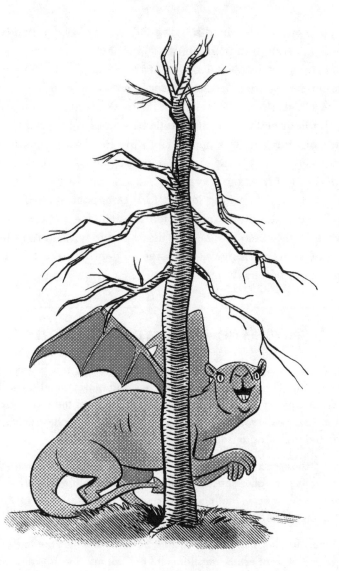

for sweetbreads.[5] Earlier accounts depicted something resembling a flying goat with wings, horns, a forked tail, a strange hiss, and a terrifying scream that sounded neither human nor animal.[6] A more recent sighting near a

[5] Sweetbreads take the prize for best culinary euphemism, as when functioning in the still-alive animal they are known as the thymus gland and the pancreas.

[6] \m/

New Jersey golf course described a flying llama, who a local caddy said was a big hitter—*long*—though not much of a tipper.[7]

Perhaps the most famous account of the Jersey Devil comes from Napoleon Bonaparte's older brother, Joseph, who also happened to be the King of Spain. He settled on a lavish estate in Bordentown, New Jersey, after losing the Peninsular Wars to England and being forced to abdicate in 1813. While out hunting one day in the Pine Barrens, the elder, lesser Bonaparte noticed strange tracks, like a donkey that walked on two legs, and he decided to follow them, we guess because he wanted to get a load of this walking donkey. It wasn't long before Bonaparte heard a "strange hissing noise" and suddenly found himself face to face with a flying creature that had a "long neck, wings, legs like a crane with horse's hooves at the end, stumpy arms with paws, and a face like a horse or a camel," which hissed at him again before flying away.

What Are the Pine Barrens?

The Pine Barrens earned its name from the sandy, acidic soil in which smaller pine species and hundreds of unique grasses and plants could grow, but cultivated crops could not. There are barrens up and down the east coast of the United States as well as some in Kentucky, Wisconsin, West Virginia, parts of Canada, and the Eurasian subcontinent.

All pine barrens lean heavily on fire to clear out undergrowth so that the seedlings of larger, taller species of oak can't take hold and overwhelm the low-growth plant species that need more space and light, both of which get swallowed up by the root system and canopy of large oaks.

Unfortunately for the Atlantic coastal pine barrens—of which the Jersey Devil's habitat is a part—real estate development has cut into the barrens' footprint and urbanization has led to a general policy of fire suppression.

Together, they have made the Pine Barrens nearly endangered. Today it is barely 10% the size it was when Mother Leeds's cursed offspring took up residence there.

---

[7] Though the llama did say that on his deathbed the caddy would receive total consciousness, so you could count that as a pretty good tip.

THE DEVIL'S IN THE DETAILS

What makes this story even more interesting is that Mother Leeds was a real person. Born Deborah Smith, she emigrated from England near the end of the seventeenth century and married a man named Japhet Leeds, who was the son of a controversial figure in New Jersey politics named Daniel Leeds. The elder Leeds was a publisher and devout Quaker who came over to America in 1677. A decade after his arrival, Leeds got himself into trouble by publishing a book called *The American Almanack* that included, among other things, references to astrology. Being an occult divination tool, astrology was considered far too pagan by the local Quaker leadership, who suppressed his book. This got Daniel good and mad. He broke with the group and spent the next thirty years or so taunting and satirizing the Quakers in print, making him not only one of New Jersey's first publishers, but also one of America's first producers of "political attack literature."

These antics earned Daniel a cute little pet name from the Quakers, "Satan's Harbinger," which only made things more difficult for the Leeds family, who were already political pariahs. In addition to publicly demonstrating a fondness for astrology, they'd sided with the widely despised British first royal governor of New Jersey, Lord Cornbury,[8] which was the colonial equivalent of betting the Don't Come line at the craps table or rooting for the rich jocks at Alpha Beta house.

Then in 1716, Daniel retired and turned the family business over to his youngest son, Titan, who redesigned the masthead of the almanac to include the family crest, which depicts three wyverns—a dragon-like creature with clawed feet and batlike wings—on a shield. See where this is going? Fifteen years later, Titan would find himself in a feud with a young Benjamin Franklin, who was trying to get his *Poor Richard's Almanack* off the ground

---

8 Cornbury's full name was Edward Hyde, Third Earl of Clarendon. He was widely loathed as a corrupt, morally bankrupt thief, accused of "squandering public funds and tax revenues for private purposes" and bribing other politicians. There is also a famous portrait of him wearing women's clothing—rather remarkable for the time, but some historians dispute that it is Hyde in the painting and suggest that it may be some unfortunate woman who has been dragged unfairly into a bit of centuries-old mudslinging.

by asserting that a series of astrological calculations were predicting that Titan would die in 1733. When that didn't happen, Titan called Franklin out. Franklin claimed that it must be the ghost of Titan Leeds coming after him, since Titan was obviously already dead. *So* Franklin.

That year, 1733, happened to be a terrible time to get into a public dispute with America's soon-to-be favorite sweetheart bachelor, whose voice was beginning to ring out far beyond the streets of Philadelphia as a leader in the movement for colonial unity.[9] It was also the year the British Parliament passed the Molasses Act, which doubled the tax colonists paid for molasses they imported from the French and the Dutch to make rum. So, not a good time to be open supporters of the Brits in New Jersey, either.

The Leeds were already loathed for their British sympathies; now they had a son back from the dead (according to Ben Franklin), a patriarch labeled the devil's messenger (according to the neighborhood Quakers), and a family crest covered in dragons. *Maybe there is something to the idea that they are associated with the occult*, you could imagine some colonial neighbor thinking upon finding his butter soured in the churn and looking for someone to blame. It's no coincidence, either, that the Leeds Devil's birth aligns pretty closely with Titan Leeds's actual death in 1738. There is, however, no explanation beyond pure misogyny for why Mother Leeds, who was married to neither Daniel *nor* Titan, ended up taking the brunt of the historical blame for the actions of the men of the family she had the great misfortune of marrying into. As if birthing and raising twelve non-devil kids hadn't been hard enough!

By the time the Revolutionary War began in 1775, the "Leeds Devil" had secured its place as a symbol of political ridicule in a fledgling America. But while the political controversy around it died down by the nineteenth century, the story itself persisted. And somewhere along the line, the idea that the whole thing arose from a bunch of townsfolk picking on an unpopular family was lost and only the scary Satan stuff remained. Over the years, magazines like the *Atlantic Monthly* printed versions of the folk tale involving curses, witchcraft, satanism, and monsters.[10] In 1910, the Arch

---

[9] Aside from proposing the turkey as America's national bird and owning two slaves whom he later freed after seeing the light, Franklin's historic track record is remarkably defensible.

[10] So it must be true!

Museum of Philadelphia[11] advertised the appearance of the devil in broad daylight, which the museum manager claimed to have personally captured. In fact, the "Devil" was just a stuffed kangaroo with wings sewn on, and the museum closed for good a few weeks later. Nevertheless, it was around that time that the "Leeds Devil" began to be known as the "Jersey Devil."

IT'S A REAL HOOT

So what is the Jersey Devil, really?

Well, when you put all these descriptions together, as fantastical animals go, the Jersey Devil sits somewhere between the majestic chimera of Greek mythology and the hideous ManBearPig of South Park, Colorado, situated more firmly within the evil quadrant on the graph than the kinder, gentler Bat Boy. Whatever its exact position on this made-up spectrum, the fact remains that *something* is almost certainly out there in those ancient stretches of pine forest. And the likeliest culprit, believe it or not, is the great horned owl, aka *Bubo virginianus*, which is also an awesome name for a band that features a steel guitar and probably a mandolin.

At first blush, you wouldn't think an owl fits with the giant monster that has been described over the centuries by eyewitnesses like Joseph Bonaparte. But when you consider that someone like the French Roger Clinton had probably never encountered this native species of owl, and that most people before the invention of flashlights had never seen this nocturnal animal up close and personal;[12] and then you take those meaty points and throw them in a nice pot and combine them with a good physical and behavioral description of the great horned owl, things start to make a little more sense. More sense than a flying llama, at least.

Here's a description of said owl, cobbled together from various resources to give you a better idea of what we're talking about. The great horned owl is a "savage and powerful nocturnal raptor" that flies virtually

---

[11] The sworn enemy of the Museum of Philadelphia.

[12] Josh saw a bunch of owls up close and personal when he went to an owl cafe once in Tokyo. It was really neat.

noiselessly with a nearly five-foot wingspan. It has big, round yellow eyes that stare out unblinkingly from under a set of feather tufts called "plumi-corns" that function like eyebrows but look like horns. It strikes from above and uses its powerful talons—which are the largest of any owl species as a proportion of body size—to carry away animals several times its size. It's been known to scoop up dogs, cats, rabbits, foxes, even the occasional porcu-pine; and to bend these poor woodland and household creatures to its will, it uses those strong, oversized talons to crush and sever their spines. Oh, and it will also hunt for smaller game by *walking along the ground*.

To the uninitiated and the nyctophobic,[13] the great horned owl was nightmare fuel. To the pious and superstitious, of which there were many when Jersey Devil sightings were at their peak, that nightmare was real, because the owl has been a Christian symbol of death and a manifestation of Satan since medieval times.[14] Is it any wonder, then, when you add in the natural human instinct to exaggerate when frightened or under duress, that a bright-eyed, sharp-beaked bird of prey with oversized talons, feathers that look like horns, and a wingspan wider than a carriage might get mistaken for a satanic monster disgorged from the depths of hell when it descends silently out of the darkness to release a terrifying, ear-piercing screech?

We say it is no wonder at all. But if you're curious (and brave) enough to find out for certain, you could venture into the Pine Barrens to look for yourself.[15] We're sure the National Park Service would be eternally grateful because, like the hit song from another New Jersey icon, it's probably wanted dead or alive.[16]

....

[13] Fear of the dark is called nyctophobia.

[14] The Dutch Renaissance painter Hieronymus Bosch painted depictions of countless religious scenes and stories and was well-known for including owls in most of his work. Honestly, though, what animal hasn't been suspected of being Satan since medieval times? Llamas have probably even been included in that bunch. We would guess especially flying llamas.

[15] Before venturing to the Pine Barrens in search of the Jersey Devil, please sign and return the waiver form printed at the back of this book, releasing *Stuff You Should Know*, its successors, heirs, subsidiaries, and affiliates from any liability should any misfortune befall you during your Jersey Devil hunt (e.g., being attacked by a great horned owl). If your copy of *Stuff You Should Know: An Incomplete Compendium of Mostly Interesting Things* was published without the Jersey Devil Waiver Form, or if you'd just like to get your free catalog, please write to: Consumer Information Catalog, Pueblo, Colorado 81009

[16] It's not. It's really, *really* not.

CHAPTER

14

DEMOLITION DERBIES

WHY WE LOVE TO WATCH THINGS GO BOOM

A demolition derby is bumper cars for grown-ups by way of the Thunderdome—many cars enter, one car leaves. Long before the X-Games or extreme sports or Mountain Dew X-Treme or Mountain Dew MDX,[1] even before Monster Truck rallies came along, demolition derbies were serving up literally explosive spectacles to anyone who enjoyed watching large machines crash into each other at high speeds.

Which, face it, is most of us, since inside every ostensibly mature adult is a small child who just wants to watch things go boom.[2]

It was this particular insight that stock car driver Larry Mendelsohn says he had when he supposedly invented the demolition derby in 1958 at New York's Islip Speedway. Larry noticed that many race fans paid more attention to the crashes than the actual races. So why not, he thought to himself, make up a sport to fill the time between races where the car crashes were the whole point? As Larry later put it when talking about the race cars, "People absolutely love to see them crash. Whenever there's an accident on a corner you have a crowd gather around.[3] You can imagine what the crowd would be like if there were 100 cars, all in one night, deliberately crashing against one another." But Larry is underselling his own genius. It's not just a hundred cars crashing into each other. It's a hundred cars crashing into each other *over and over and over again!*

It's a great story, but there's a good reason to believe Larry wasn't actually the first to come up with the idea of smashing automobiles into each other. That reason is called facts.

....

[1] Mountain Dew X-Treme was an extremely dark purple grape-flavored version first sold in Kuwait in 2010 before spreading to other parts of the Middle East like an extreme wildfire of taste. Its slogan was "Do You Dare?" Mountain Dew MDX was a short-lived energy drink that contained an extreme amount of caffeine.

[2] Search your feelings. You know it to be true.

[3] This reminds us of that famous Weegee photo of the crowd jostling for a better look at a dead body that we talked about in our "Crime Scene Photography" episode. 🎧

WHERE WE'RE GOING
WE DON'T NEED ROADS

No one seems to know who actually staged the first demolition derby. Some say it was a celebrity motor sports promoter named Don Basile, who put on a derby full of famous racers at Gardena's Carrell Speedway in Southern California in 1946. Others believe it was used car dealer (and owner of a magnificent nickname) "Crazy Jim" Groh from Franklin, Wisconsin, back in 1950.[4] Whoever it was, by 1953 the concept was common enough that the term "demolition derby" made it into the Merriam-Webster dictionary—which kind of makes Larry Mendelsohn's claim as shaky as a ten-year-old full of Mountain Dew MDX.

It's easy to see how the idea might have developed when you consider that a very similar kind of proto-demolition derby, called a "crash derby," had been going on at county fairs across America since the thick of the Great Depression in the 1930s—which is not an era where you'd expect to see people wrecking still-usable cars for fun. Still, everybody needs a distraction when times are tough, and crash derbies were a cheap form of entertainment that satisfied a longstanding thirst[5] among American spectators for what one sociologist called, "reenacting technological destruction for public amusement." Or what we called, approximately four paragraphs ago, people's desire to watch things go boom.

These crash derbies did not just suddenly appear whole out of the ether, either. They were expansions of what you might call crash *jousts*—two cars driving head on into each other, or "a terrible idea." Crash jousts had become popular in the early 1920s thanks to a handful of daredevil troupes that performed stunt-driving exhibitions at local racetracks and fairgrounds for slack-jawed locals to enjoy. Groups with killer names like Ward Beam's Daredevils, Lucky Lott's Hell Drivers, and Jimmy Lynch Death Dodgers would jump buses, drive through walls of flame, roll cars on their sides, and then drive into each other at full speed. It was good paying work if you could get it.

---

[4] We're considering adopting our own nicknames, "Crazy Josh" Clark and "Crazy Charles W. 'Chuck'" Bryant. Write in to let us know if you endorse the idea or if you feel it's insensitive.

[5] Just like Mountain Dew can satisfy *your* longstanding thirst.

STUFF YOU SHOULD KNOW . . .
About Depression-Era Job Opportunities

This is the text of an ad placed in a New York-area newspaper in 1931:

WANTED: Single man, not over 25 years, to drive automobile in head-on collision with another car at the Albion Fairgrounds in connection with the Congress of Daredevils on August 19. Must crash with another car at 40 mph and give unconditional release in case of injury or death. Name your lowest price. Write B. Ward Beam, Albion, N.Y.

If you can barely imagine what seeing two old-timey cars crashing head on into one another at 40 mph would be like, prepare for further amazement! Crash jousts too had an antecedent. Between 1896 and 1932, a number of people decided that staging train wrecks—prearranged crashes between locomotives—was a good idea. Organizers would lay track nearly a mile long, then engineers would start locomotives facing each other at either end of the track and jump to safety before they crashed into each other. Spectators would pay to watch the devastation and then scramble to

collect a souvenir from the wreckage after the demolished locomotives came to rest, hopefully not on fire.

At one staged locomotive collision in Ohio, 25,000 people showed up. At another outside Waco, Texas, organized by the brilliantly named William Crush, 40,000 people were lining the track when the locomotives' boilers exploded on impact like massive hand grenades, sending hot metal shrapnel more than a thousand feet through the air at tens of thousands of feet per second, and killing two people. An eyewitness who also happened to be a Civil War veteran was quoted as saying it was "more terrifying than the Battle of Gettysburg," which, as you may know from our episode on the Gettysburg Address, 🎙 was the bloodiest battle of the entire war.

SMASHING SUCCESS

Train collisions crawled, so crash derbies could walk, so demolition derbies could run.[6] And while they clearly existed in one form or another before Larry Mendelohn's event in Islip, it is true that they really took off after he began staging them on a regular basis. By the 1960s, ABC was airing the Demolition Derby World Championships on its popular "Wide World of Sports" program. In the '70s the Los Angeles Coliseum hosted a Demolition Derby on national TV, organized by none other than Don Basile. Much as he had for his 1946 derby, Basile recruited famous racers for this one too. Indy 500 champions like A. J. Foyt, Mario Andretti, Parnelli Jones, and Bobby and Al Unser participated—but unlike his first derby, or any derby really, where drivers competed in cheap, beat-up old cars, the champions in Brasile's derby drove expensive vehicles, including a Rolls Royce donated by the famous daredevil Evel Knievel. 🎙 Even the icon of 1970s cool, Fonzie from *Happy Days*, got in on the trend when he fell in love with professional derby driver Pinky Tuscadero. When the Fonz gives your fake sport two thumbs up and a full-throated *aayyyy*, you know you've hit the big time.[7]

Derbies began to wane in popularity in the 1980s, as commercial real estate development led to the demolition of many of the old tracks where

---

[6] So Mountain Dew X-Treme could fly.

[7] The exception to this rule is stunt waterski shark jumping.

derbies took place. But they made a comeback in the 1990s as a popular event at state and county fairs, returning to their roots, so to speak. They eventually peaked at around 5,000 derbies a year in the US, with between 60,000 and 75,000 demolition drivers competing annually for prize money ranging from a few hundred bucks to tens of thousands of dollars.

ORDERING THE CHAOS

Whenever there are trophies and money to be won, there must also be rules. Lotteries and sweepstakes are highly regulated, for instance. The Laws of the Game for international football (you know, soccer) are more than 220 pages long. Baseball has eleven rules just about the uniforms. Demolition derbies are no different, though fittingly for something so chaotic, the rules tend to vary widely.[8] Still, most derbies share a number of key guidelines, some of which raise serious questions about the kind of person who needs these rules spelled out in the first place:

DRIVERS MUST BE AT LEAST SIXTEEN YEARS OLD

DRIVERS MUST WEAR SEATBELTS

DRIVERS MUST WEAR HELMETS;
FOOTBALL HELMETS DO NOT COUNT

NO HEAD-ON CRASHES

NO INTENTIONAL HITS TO THE DRIVER-SIDE DOOR

**DRIVERS MUST CRASH AT LEAST ONCE
EVERY TWO MINUTES**

ALL GLASS MUST BE REMOVED FROM VEHICLES

ALL CARS MUST HAVE WORKING BRAKES

NO DRIVER CAN PARTICIPATE DRUNK

---

[8] We found the rules sheet for the demolition derby that was held at the 2009 Harrison County Fair in Iowa and it had *thirty-six* different stipulations for car preparation.

Once the drivers and their cars meet those oh-so-rigorous standards, everyone typically lines up around the edges of a dirt arena or track, which has usually been soaked with water to keep the dust from flying, while the crowd chants a countdown. Most drivers will start with their front end facing away from the center of the arena, with the intention of spending as much of the derby as possible in reverse smashing into the other cars with their rear bumper.[9] It is not that this is a better strategy for inflicting more damage; it's a life-extension strategy designed to spare the radiator, carburetor, and engine from repeated collision. Once those go, your day is done.[10]

When the green flag drops, drivers begin crashing into each other at speeds up to thirty miles per hour. That doesn't seem like a lot when you consider the average speed of a NASCAR crash or a highway pile-up, but a collision even at that low speed can produce 8,500 pounds of force, which would be like getting slammed in the chest by a good-sized adult male hippopotamus. That same crash will also simultaneously produce 30 to 40 Gs of pressure in the thirty milliseconds of deceleration after impact.[11] In physics, this is called "no fun." And yet the expectation is that everyone signed up for a demolition derby will crash as often as they need to in order to disable their competition and take the checkered flag. Failure to do so means being disqualified. Avoiding as much contact as possible as a strategy for winning is called "sandbagging" and it is roundly derided by honest demolition derby fans. With rules like these in place, and a stiff dose of social pressure from the fans, a typical derby takes around twenty minutes to complete. In the Thunderdome-iness of it all, the last car still running is declared the winner.

---

[9] Demolition derbies are, as you may have already concluded, no place for a Ford Pinto from any model year, with or without flaming death bolts.

[10] Any usable parts that remain will be harvested from the car, and the driver is likewise harvested for their organs.

[11] To give you an idea of what that might feel like, roller coasters typically produce only 5 Gs on their steepest drops, so this amount is far, far harder on the body and can produce blackouts. There's a cool calculator online that lets you plug in your basic pre-crash stats so you can scare the crap out of your kids (or parents)! https://www.omnicalculator.com/physics/car-crash-force

THE INFAMOUS INDESTRUCTIBLE IMPERIAL

Many derbies, especially the bigger multi-day ones at county and state fairs, will have multiple events that feature different categories of car and racer: there are women's events, RV events, fire department versus police department, compact car and truck events. But the most common derbies involve those full-size cars from the 1960s and 1970s that are sometimes referred to as land yachts. They aren't their own event classification per se, it's just that the most popular cars in the main event tend to be post-1965 American hardtops, station wagons, and sedans with long front and rear ends that offer extra smashability.

But there is one car from this broader genre that is banned, to this day, from nearly every derby held in America: the Chrysler Imperial. Specifically, the 1964 to 1966 models, but also some of the later models from

the 1970s. You may know that we are not car guys, but we can appreciate the Chrysler Imperial. It strikes fear in the hearts of any driver unlucky enough to face off against it—especially when they're not behind the wheel of an Imperial themselves—because it is built like a tank. Its body-on-frame construction[12] makes it heavier, sturdier, and more resilient on uneven terrain. Its V8 engine delivers 500 lb/ft of torque and sends it at the competition like one of those locomotives from the turn of the century.[13] The Imperial's body also sits up a little higher because it's mounted onto the frame instead of having the frame incorporated into it, so when it's hit from behind the impact drives its bumper upward, which pushes its wheels down into the ground, giving it more traction. The Imperial is like a Voltron of invincibility, power, mass, and that time-honored ability to make things go boom. It's almost like it was designed for demolition derbies.

The interesting thing about the ban on Imperials in demolition derbies is that it has nothing to do with increasing the risk of injury to the other drivers. No, it's strictly about their unstoppability. In fact, derby officials say that serious injuries and deaths are rare—a 2004 study found that drivers sustain fewer neck injuries than you might expect (though you might expect that *all of them* have neck injuries,[14] so anything less than that feels like a win). A lower-than-expected incidence of neck injuries doesn't change the fact that cars can flip over and burst into flames, however, putting drivers at risk of other injuries and serious burns.

....

[12] This means (we looked it up) that the body of the car that contains the passengers is built separately and then mounted to the frame of the vehicle that contains the axles, steering column, etc., rather than built as one whole piece. Thus the body can move independently of the frame.

[13] Torque (we looked this up too) is the same type of force you apply to a wrench to turn it. That type of force is handy not just for tightening nuts and bolts, but also for cars because of the way they produce power. Car engines turn a crankshaft, which spins the same way it would as if a wrench was turning it. That then turns the axles, which make the wheels on the bus go round and round, which make the car go vroom. Lots of torque is useful in making a car accelerate quickly and is the power that gets heavy cars like the Imperial to move at all.

[14] Their parents and spouses all probably think they need their heads examined at the very least.

If you're not deterred by this slight possibility of accidentally dying in a car that you crash on purpose, well then, there are plenty of derbies still being staged all across the United States and around the world for you to enter.[15] It's far safer than taking part in an organized train collision, that's for sure. Assuming you can even find one nowadays, what with parents being so overprotective and the government not letting you own your own train.[16]

....

[15] Before entering any demolition derby, we must insist that you fill out our Demolition Derby Indemnity Waiver at the back of the book, which frees us from any legal liability that may arise should any misfortune befall you from entering a demolition derby after reading this chapter. If your copy of *Stuff You Should Know: An Incomplete Compendium of Mostly Interesting Things* does not include the Demolition Derby Indemnity Waiver, please send in for a replacement form. Write to Consumer Information Catalog, Pueblo, Colorado 81009

[16] Fewer than 100 people in the US own their own private rail car, and none of them own a locomotive.

15

CHAPTER

KAMIKAZE

THE LAST GASP OF THE DIVINE WIND

In the late thirteenth century, Kublai Khan was arguably the most powerful man on Earth. Grandson of Genghis Khan,[1] the Mongol ruler had recently upheld the family legacy of brutality by subjugating most of China to form what would become known as the Yuan Dynasty.

Having toppled the Middle Kingdom, he turned his eyes to a task that likely seemed easy in comparison—conquering the much smaller island nation of Japan. In 1274, the Khan's fleet of over 30,000 men set sail aboard hundreds of ships. But just as they were arriving at their destination, a massive typhoon struck, sinking a huge number of ships, plunging 13,000 men to a watery grave, and sending the Khan's forces slinking home with their tails between their legs.

Given the circumstances, the Khan can perhaps be forgiven for thinking the defeat was a fluke. It's not like his men had lost a battle; technically, they just got *rained on*. Would Grandpappy Genghis have given up after some bad weather? Hell no!

So the Khan doubled down. Actually, he quadrupled down. Seven years later, he launched another fleet that made the first seem dinky by comparison. Thousands of ships carrying as many as 140,000 of the Khan's soldiers set sail for Japan in 1281. Yet, unbelievably, just as they were arriving to storm the beaches and steamroll the much smaller Japanese army, *another* typhoon hit. 🎧 The Mongolian fleet was completely wrecked, most of the soldiers plunged to a watery grave again. The survivors who made it ashore were hunted down and killed by Samurai.[2] It was one of the most disastrous attempted naval invasions in human history.

Having twice been saved by incredibly lucky and well-timed storms, the Japanese attributed their salvation to divine intervention. And, really,

---

[1] Even after doing a full episode on the legendary man, called "Genghis Khan: Madman or Genius?," we're still not sure if it's pronounced *gehn-giss* or *jehn-giss*. 🎧

[2] *Samurai* is both plural and singular, as those of you who love linguistic oddities and have heard our episode, "How Samurai Work," may remember. 🎧

can you blame them? They even coined a specific term for it: "divine wind." Or as it's pronounced in Japanese: *kamikaze*. It wouldn't be the last time that word would take on special significance in Japanese history, though it would be the last time the outcome was positive.

THE FIRST **OF THEIR KIND**

On October 25, 1944, in the middle of the Battle of Leyte Gulf, four squadrons of Japanese aircraft from the 201st Navy Air Group took off from Clark Air Base outside Manila. The Japanese had controlled this base since they'd captured it from the American forces during the invasion of the Philippines in the opening days of World War II. Comprising twenty-four young volunteer pilots, flying several different types of aircraft, this was no ordinary unit. These were *tokkotai,* members of a Japanese Special Attack Unit, and this was no ordinary mission. Theirs was going to be a one-way trip. They had no intention of returning to Clark Air Base when the job was done, because their mission was to fly their planes directly into a group of American escort carrier ships from the 7th Fleet that was invading the Philippines. The goal of the tokkotai was to inflict as much damage to these ships as possible, incapacitating them hopefully, sinking them ideally. Success or failure, bailing out was not an option.

This was the first official suicide attack of the first official kamikaze pilots. They took their name from those fortuitous thirteenth-century typhoons, not only because they would be delivering destructive force from the skies, but also because they were hoping to deliver a miraculous victory against a dominant enemy that was poised to destroy them—just like the typhoons did for their medieval countrymen against the Mongols more than 650 years earlier.

Many believe that the idea for kamikaze attacks was first presented as a possible military strategy in June 1944, by a captain named Motoharu Okamura, just as the last of Japan's biggest ships and most of its planes were torn to shreds at the Battle of Philippine Sea.[3] "In our present situation, I firmly believe that the only way to swing the war in our favor is to resort to crash-dive attacks with our planes," he told his commanding officers. "There is no other way. . . . Provide me with 300 planes and I will turn the tide of war." At which point 300 pilots looked nervously around the room as they put two and two together.

Okamura spent the rest of the summer of 1944 exploring how kamikaze attacks could work, and in September his commanding officers put his ideas into practice. Specifically, they commissioned the production of a rocket-powered glider called an *Ohka,* or "Cherry Blossom," that could attach to the belly of a bomber. Once in range, the Okha's pilot would climb into the cockpit, release the glider, and steer it directly into its target. In other words, the Okha was a human-steered one-way missile.[4]

---

[3] The air campaign during the Battle of Philippine Sea was called the Great Marianas Turkey Shoot by American pilots.

[4] Americans called them *Baka,* which is Japanese for "foolish."

One of the reasons something like the Okha rocket glider made sense was that Japan had run out of experienced pilots and modern aircraft. After the Battle of the Philippine Sea, they were being forced to fly older beat-up planes with young, inexperienced pilots. In fact, many of the pilots in those first waves of kamikaze attacks in the Battle of Leyte Gulf had less than fifty hours in the cockpit.[5] That's because the Japanese navy had no choice. They were staring down a true threat to their hold over the Pacific: the United States Navy. The Philippines sat directly between Japan's home islands and the areas of Southeast Asia where it was getting its oil and

....

[5] That is to say, not much. Pilots looking to fly for today's commercial airlines, for example, need a minimum of 1,500 hours before they qualify for a license. Of course, landing a 747 full of passengers requires a bit more skill than flying a rocket glider into the deck of a battleship.

rubber. Once the American military controlled the Philippines, they would have effectively severed the Japanese supply lines and breached their last line of defense. This made Leyte Gulf something of a last stand.

In World War II, if there is one thing you could count on the Japanese military never to do in the face of insurmountable odds, it was surrender. This had been true from the very beginning of the war. When a Japanese pilot ran out of fuel or his plane sustained unsurvivable damage during a bombing run, he would not look for a soft place to land or ditch in the ocean. He would instead aim his plane at the nearest ship and turn himself into a bomb. Now, nearly three years into the war with the fate of the country hanging in the balance, flying their planes into American ships on purpose was no longer a last-second decision when all other options were spent. It was an official strategy where the ending was part of the plan from the very beginning.

BANZAI: THE KAMIKAZE OF THE GROUND

By the end of the war, thousands of young Japanese men would volunteer to join the ranks of the kamikaze. Nearly all of them would die in the cockpit of their planes, in the name of the emperor and in defense of Japan. This particular bent was not unique to Japanese aviators, however, and kamikaze attacks were not the only—or the first—organized suicide missions of the war. Since the early days of the Guadalcanal campaign in the summer of 1942, full-frontal[6] assaults on Allied positions by units of outgunned (and often unarmed and injured) Japanese soldiers had become a frequent part of battle. They were common enough that American soldiers had given them a name: *banzai charges*, after the phrase "Tennōheika Banzai"

---

[6] Meaning head on, not nude.

(meaning, roughly, "Long Live the Emperor") that Japanese attackers would shout as they ran headlong toward the business end of American rifles and machine guns. Apparently, few of the soldiers considered the irony of calling for a long life for their emperor while he asked them to shorten their own, sometimes by their own hands.[7] Much to the relief of the emperor.

In May 1943, for example, Japanese commander Colonel Yamazaki launched a desperate, suicidal counterattack against the American and Canadian troops that had surrounded them on the island of Attu in Alaska. His outnumbered men, some armed just with bayonets lashed to sticks,[8] surprised the Americans' front line positions, killing many and seizing their weapons, until they were finally stopped by a second line of defenders armed with machine guns and howitzer cannons.[9] What was left of Yamazaki's 2,900 men began killing themselves, often by holding grenades against their own bodies, and ultimately taking more than 500 American troops with them. By the end of the battle less than thirty Japanese fighters remained and more than 2,800 had been cut down or died by suicide. Horrific banzai charges like this occurred at large battles and small skirmishes. But it was at Saipan that the notorious maneuver became truly infamous.

The Japanese Invasion of . . . Alaska?!

In June 1942, Japanese forces invaded several islands off the coast of Alaska in an attempt to distract American military planners from the imminent naval showdown in the waters around Midway Atoll, 2,000 miles to the south. The diversion didn't work. Japan took the Aleutian Islands of Attu and Kiska without issue, then badly lost the Battle of Midway, which would be a major turning point in the war. This would be the closest the Japanese would get to occupying American territory in North America, and Attu would be the only patch of American soil upon which a banzai charge was made.

----

[7] Or if they did, they didn't make a big deal about it.

[8] They literally brought knives to a gun fight.

[9] That's a lot of BOOM.

In June of 1944, 8,000 American marines landed on the Japanese-controlled island of Saipan. If that sounds like a lot of Marines, it's because it is. After weeks of pitched battle, in which the Japanese launched numerous devastating ambushes and marines turned flamethrowers[10] against Japanese soldiers and civilians alike, the Japanese forces were driven to the northern tip of the island. The battle was clearly lost, but when word reached Emperor Hirohito he ordered every Japanese citizen on the island to kill themselves rather than surrender. Lieutenant-General Yoshisugu Saitō, the commander on the ground, ordered every one of his soldiers—including the sick, injured, and those armed only with bamboo spears—to commit to an all-out frontal assault. Four thousand Japanese troops rushed forward in a suicidal banzai charge. They killed more than 600 American soldiers and wounded twice as many more. And just like at Attu a year earlier, nearly all of them were killed. When American forces advanced upon the Japanese position, the remaining Japanese civilians began killing themselves en masse, flinging themselves from cliffs or simply walking into the sea. It's estimated that more than 800 Japanese civilians died this way.

THE WEAPONS OF LAST RESORT

To many Westerners, decisions like these—by individual fighters, by civilians, and by military leadership—are hard to comprehend. Purposefully killing yourself is the most quittingest way to quit ever, we often tell ourselves. But Japanese culture offers a different perspective.

In Japan, the concept of a suicidal attack without regard to casualties has its roots in the twelfth century in the Samurai code of *bushido*, otherwise awesomely known as "the way of the warrior," which holds that death is more honorable than surrender. This concept was enshrined in the 1941

....

[10] Flamethrowers are particularly scary implements of death not just because they kill by burning people alive, but because they also suffocate their victims by sucking all the air from around them as fuel for the fire. They are also the subject of one of our great and often overlooked episodes, "How Flamethrowers Work." 🎙

Japanese field service code that guided the behavior of World War II-era Japanese soldiers; the code prohibited surrender and said that "glorious death" was "preferable to ignominious surrender."

In some cases, bushido endorses ritual suicide, known as *seppuku*. Upon the death of their master, or loss in battle, or bringing disgrace to their master or their family name, a samurai would ritualistically plunge a sword or knife into his gut and slice horizontally, disemboweling himself.[11] That tradition made appearances in World War II as well. Colonel Yamazaki would ultimately perform seppuku on the island of Attu after his men's banzai charge failed to breach the second line of American defenses and reach the guns that were positioned in the aptly named Massacre Bay.

You could also argue there is something very ritualistic about marching into the sea the way some of the residents of Saipan did. Keep in mind that unlike the actual kamikaze attacks and banzai charges, the residents weren't employing a military tactic. There was little meaningful advantage to be gained by doing this, but it was a deeply ingrained cultural practice, built on the belief that suicide was an acceptable response to embarrassment, shame, and humiliation—presumably all of which soldiers, leaders, and citizens felt in their defeat by the American military.

Suicide wasn't just acceptable to these citizens—there was honor in it. It showed dedication to the emperor, to the nation, and to the reputation of their families. It showed fearlessness in the face of death. It was also a way of taking responsibility—a perspective, some psychologists and sociologists argue, that persists in present-day Japan, where suicide rates are still higher than virtually every wealthy developed nation in the world.

To most Japanese, going back to the samurai of the twelfth and thirteenth centuries, suicide was also *preferable* to surrender because it was assumed that surrendering meant torture would soon follow. The prospect of brutal torture was very real to the Japanese people during World War II, thanks to the country's propaganda. Japanese propaganda posters depicted Americans as mongrelized demons—literal demons. One poster shows a demonic figure with horns and a bone through its nose and skulls around its neck, pulling off a Franklin Roosevelt mask with its claws. Which is also an awesome, if confusing, Halloween costume idea. Average citizens were

---

[11] An assistant was usually there to behead the samurai shortly thereafter, ending their suffering.

taught in no uncertain terms that if they were captured, they would be tortured, raped, and murdered by the Americans.[12]

Combine the acceptance of suicide, with the threat of unimaginable torture and a cultural focus on honor above all else, and suddenly kamikaze, banzai, seppuku, and mass family suicide (which became epidemic during the final months of World War II) all start to make more sense.

END GAME

The kamikaze attack and the banzai charge have often been depicted as both uniquely terrifying and effective military tactics. There is some truth in that description—one plane could cripple a carrier for a month and one unit of hard-charging Japanese infantry could kill more American G.I.s in an hour than if the unit had maneuvered and fought strategically for a week. But the reality is that they were largely ineffective because by the time Japanese soldiers got around to a banzai charge or a dive bomb, the outcome of the battles—and even the war itself—was already set.

It's hard to think about what it must have felt like during those last months of 1944 and the first months of 1945 to be a young volunteer pilot tasked with delivering the might of the Divine Wind to the enemy. If we were to put it in slightly less cataclysmically apocalyptic terms—considering we've been talking about the deadliest war in the history of the world for the last six pages—imagine the Japanese as a professional baseball team. In late October 1944, the Battle of Leyte Gulf was like the first inning of Game 7 of the World Series against the military equivalent of the 1927 New York Yankees.[13] The Japanese would be, say, the Seattle Mariners from almost any year before 1995, take your pick.[14] Except a week earlier, the Japanese Mariners had lost all their starters in a horrific outbreak of *E. coli*

---

[12] And this proved to be the case to some extent, especially during the Battle of Okinawa and the island prefecture's subsequent occupation, where rape and murder were used as weapons of war by some American troops against the local population.

[13] If you're not super sportsy either, this team had both Babe Ruth and Lou Gehrig, with six future Hall of Fame players in total on its roster. Not too shabby.

[14] We should point out that the best Japanese baseball player in MLB history is Ichiro Suzuki, a longtime Seattle Mariner.

(the Battle of the Philippine Sea), and now they had to figure out a way to quickly get a competitive team together before the big game. What choice did management have other than to look to their minor league farm system and call up all the young guns who threw the hardest and the big bats who hit the farthest, then tell them to swing for the fences?[15]

As came to be expected from the Japanese military, they put up a hell of a fight in those final months. By the end of the war, approximately 3,000 kamikaze pilots[16]—most of them under the age of twenty-four—sank almost three dozen Allied warships and damaged hundreds more, killing nearly 5,000 American and British troops in the process. And yet, despite their lethal impact, most kamikaze attacks were actually failures.[17] It's estimated that only 14 to 19 percent of kamikaze aircraft hit their intended targets. Some of them were shot down in midair, but many more simply missed entirely. As is true in baseball, hitting a moving object is incredibly hard no matter at what speed or from what distance.[18] Just ask Michael Jordan.

Strategically, kamikaze had a minimal impact on the tide of the war, though arguably it may have sped it up and amplified its magnitude. According to the conventional historical narrative, a major part of the calculations that American political leaders used in determining whether to deploy the atomic bomb was how many American lives it would cost to take the home islands through conventional means.[19] Rough estimates from

---

[15] These players would be drawn primarily from the Tacoma (WA) Rainiers farm team, most likely.

[16] The total number of kamikaze pilots varies widely depending on the source, ranging from 1,300 all the way up to 6,000, but the most accurate estimates seem to land somewhere in the 2,800-3,400 range.

[17] To keep the sports metaphor going, they hit their fair share of home runs, but they struck out at a much greater clip.

[18] There's a reason a 30% success rate as a hitter in baseball is enough to get you considered for the Hall of Fame.

[19] Not everyone buys into this conventional expediency narrative. There is a good amount of evidence that by early 1945, the Japanese were resigned to the prospect of a negotiated surrender. There is additional evidence that elements of American leadership felt it was imperative they occupy Japan and establish a permanent foothold there to stave off a Soviet incursion into Asia after the war and as a way to show the world that America was now a dominant player in geopolitics. Dropping the bombs would make that occupation easier to accomplish.

military planners were a half-million. A figure undoubtedly influenced by their experiences with Japan's steadfast refusal to surrender at any cost,[20] the lethality of banzai charges on the ground, and the kamikaze attacks from the air, which were intensifying just as the Allies were beginning to plan the final invasion, codename: Operation Downfall.

If you're looking for us to tell you that this is the silver lining to the radioactive atomic mushroom cloud, you're going to be waiting a long time. The only thing worth taking from the unexecuted plan to lead hundreds of thousands of souls to the slaughter of war the old-fashioned way is the name—because it would be great for a punk band.

....

[20] Prior to the mass surrender of troops to the Chinese and the Soviets at the end of the war, there were only 39,000 Japanese POWs in American custody, compared to a million Germans and 500,000 Italians.

16

TRICHO-TILLOMANIA AND THE BFRBS

THE TICS THAT HAVE PSYCHOLOGISTS SCRATCHING THEIR HEADS

Before we knew enough about psychology and human behavior to speak with appropriate kindness and specificity, we used to call pretty much anything someone did on a repetitive basis a nervous tic. Of course, not all tics are created equal.

Some are innocuous: toe tapping, excessive blinking, hair twirling, nose scrunching. Some, like knuckle cracking, grunting, or sniffing, can be mildly annoying to those within earshot. And yet others, like knee bouncing, are extremely annoying to the entire world, without exception, and must be stopped forthwith and posthaste under every circumstance.

But there is another group of repetitive behaviors that transcends this petty spectrum of annoyance and instead directs their worst onto the very people who engage in them. Collectively they're called body-focused repetitive behaviors, or BFRBs to those who are pressed for time, and they can produce actual physical and emotional damage, not in bystanders and observers, but in the people who suffer from them. Individually they all have names you might hear in the quarterfinal round of a spelling bee: onychophagia (nail biting), onychotillomania (nail picking), dermatophagia (skin biting), dermatillomania (skin picking), rhinotillexomania (nose picking), trichophagia (hair eating), and what appears to be the queen of them all, trichotillomania, or hair pulling.[1]

Trichotillomania,[2] or TTM, or "trich" as it is sometimes called within the community, causes people to pluck their own hair, often one at a time, often in a methodical or ritualistic way. It's a unique disorder with power over its victims that is hard to convey in normal terms. So we'll try to do it in abnormal terms instead.

....

[1] There are a handful of other BFRBs, but these are the most common and get the lion's share of the attention from psychologists and researchers, trichotillomania especially. In fact, one of the most prominent institutions dedicated to the study of BFRBs is called the Trichotillomania Learning Center.

[2] You can say it with us: TRICK-ō-till-ō-mān-ia. It has kind of a sing-song quality to it, strangely.

If you've ever cared for a vegetable garden or a beautiful lawn, you might be familiar with the unique pleasure of pulling weeds. There, sticking out of the dirt or the manicured grass, 🎙 is this long leafy interloper just begging to be yanked out of the ground. Except it's not so simple, because if you don't get the whole thing, root and all, the weed will grow back like it had never been picked. This realization isn't intimidating—it's exciting. You've done it hundreds, possibly thousands, of times before, and you know exactly what you need to do. You know that you've got to separate and clear away any nearby grass or plants so you can isolate the weed you want to remove. You know that you've got to try to get a firm grip on the very top of the tap root, just below the dirt's surface. You know you can't just yank the weed out, but that you have to pull it with confidence. If it's stuck, you know you have to re-establish your grip a little further down in the dirt and start to jiggle it, getting the dirt to release from the secondary filament roots. You know exactly how it sounds and how it feels when you finally get it right and the weed pulls cleanly out. You know what it looks like too, because you turn it over in your hands, marveling at the length and thickness of the taproot in comparison to the size of the rest of it. Maybe you even thrust it into the sky like the decapitated head of a vanquished enemy. 🎙 At that point, it's almost not even about the weed anymore. It's about experiencing the supremely satisfying sensations involved.

Now imagine instead of a garden it's your scalp or eyebrows or eyelashes.[3] And instead of individual weeds, it's individual hairs. And instead of making for a perfect lawn or a lush garden, the pulling makes for unsightly bald spots and skin infections. Everything else though—the ritual, the anticipation, the deliberation, the selection, the satisfaction—is all exactly the same for the hair-puller, with maybe a little dollop of anxiety added on top.

That is trichotillomania. Sound farfetched? Maybe even a little bit romanticized? Then allow us to say it clearly: this affliction is no picnic. It causes real and lasting physical and psychological damage in the people who suffer from it. But it is also complicated by the fact that it involves reward as well. Here is how two psychiatrists described the full sensory experience of TTM in a 2017 paper in the *Indian Journal of Psychiatry*:

....

[3] Chest hair, arm hair, and underarm hair—otherwise known as "axillary hair," as you might recall from chapter 1—will also sometimes be the focus, as will facial hair and pubic hair (though we hope this is not the case for people with trichophagia, for their own sake).

If hair pulling is only the primary goal, the patients should just pull the hair one by one and throw [them away] which hardly happens. They are involved in varied activities seeking pleasure involving all the sense organs . . .

The lead up, they write, is all about touch, combing and twirling and feeling for the "right" hair and then pulling it. The pull can be as much about touch as it is about hearing the snap of the hair releasing from the follicle under the skin. Once it's out, the hair is often then admired by its plucker—the color and length and any other intriguing physical characteristic are examined. They may also tickle their nose with the hairs and smell them, taking in the scent of sweat or shampoo or deodorant or perfume, 🎧 depending on where the hair is being plucked from. Then there are those who engage in chewing, tasting, and sometimes swallowing the hair (i.e., trichophagia).[4]

....

[4] While half of TTM patients engage in some kind of "oral behavior," less than 20% actually eat the hair they pull, and that is on the high end. Some estimates put the instance of trichophagia at ~5%.

Interestingly, what distinguishes trichotillomania from other BFRBs isn't so much these specific, hair-centric behaviors but the outright damage that occurs to the sufferer's body as a result of the pulling. As with other BFRBs, the vast majority of people with trich tend to keep their issues private. But unlike with other BFRBs, trich sufferers can't easily cover up their condition. Think about it like this: it's fairly easy to hide gnawed-down fingernails (it doesn't hurt that biting/picking fingernails is more common, and thus less stigmatized as a result) and there are many explanations for scabs or band-aids on your skin. There are fewer explanations,[5] and fewer ways to hide large bald patches or missing eyebrows or one eyelid with significantly fewer lashes than the other.

Trichotillomania Diagnostic Criteria*

1. Recurrent pulling out of one's hair, resulting in hair loss

2. Repeated attempts to decrease or stop hair pulling

3. The hair pulling causes clinically significant distress or impairment in social, occupational, or other important areas of functioning

4. The hair pulling or hair loss is not attributable to another medical condition (e.g., a dermatological condition)

5. The hair pulling is not better explained by the symptoms of another mental disorder (e.g., attempts to improve a perceived defect or flaw in appearance in body dysmorphic disorder)

*Taken from the Canadian BFRB Support Network

When someone is deep into the disorder, it's not uncommon for them to feel like they can only go out in public if they're wearing a hat or a wig,[6] or fake eyelashes, or painted-on eyebrows. The reason, according to many long-time sufferers, is that if they go out au natural, they may get sympathetic glances from strangers who think they have cancer. When those people find

---

[5] Unless you're in a frat or have roommates in college; for some reason, young guys like to rip each other's hair out as a prank when someone passes out early on the weekend.

[6] Some trich sufferers will even pull individual hairs from their wigs.

out it's not cancer and instead it's an unpronounceable condition they've never heard of, sympathy can quickly morph into awkward confusion, and the stranger may conclude the TTM sufferer has a screw loose or something.

That kind of reaction tends to affect trich patients in a couple of ways: either it roils up the shame and embarrassment that can kick off a new cycle of hair pulling, or it makes them feel even more alien, which sends them retreating further into themselves and farther away from help and support. Or both. This is just one of many reasons that trichotillomania and the other BFRBs have proven so difficult to study and understand.

IMPULSIVE OR COMPULSIVE

It turns out that trichotillomania is one of the more difficult disorders psychology has come up against. It eludes classification and categorization like some shape-shifting imp of the mind and, as a result, being difficult to understand makes it very difficult to treat.

As it stands now, experts believe it probably results from a combination of factors, including genetic predisposition (thanks, Mom and/or Dad!), chemical imbalances in the brain that often produce other concurrent disorders like OCD or ADHD, hormonal changes during puberty (when the onset of TTM is most common), and a variety of environmental factors like stress, anxiety, and trauma.[7] Still, the condition remains so poorly understood that psychologists struggle to even define what kind of basic disorder it is. Back in the go-go '90s, trich was listed as an impulse control disorder in the DSM-IV,[8] which was first published in 1994 and updated in 2000. But

---

[7] This rather expansive collection of explanations is psychology's equivalent of throwing everything you've got at the problem and seeing what sticks. It would not be a surprise if researchers have also looked into lead paint, asbestos, solar flares, and 5G cell phone towers. That's not to say any combination of these factors is incorrect (minus 5G); it's just to say that it's so broad that psychologists clearly feel like they have to say *something* until they really understand what's going on with trich.

[8] The DSM is the Diagnostic and Statistical Manual of Mental Disorders, published by the American Psychiatric Association. The field of psychology is responsible for identifying what behaviors are normal and what are abnormal for society, and the DSM is its reference manual. The numeral on the other side of the hyphen is the version number.

in the DSM-5, the current version that came out in 2013, it's classified as an obsessive-compulsive disorder. (🎙)

This may sound like po-tay-to/po-tah-to, but there's a pretty big difference between a disorder of impulse control and one of obsession or compulsion. Mainly, the difference comes down to whether the behavior is ego-syntonic or ego-dystonic—that is, whether the person feels like the behavior is generally a positive or a destructive force in their life. Initially, as an impulse control disorder, trich was considered to be ego-syntonic, which meant that psychologists generally understood sufferers to be cool with their hair pulling. That weeding-type satisfaction we talked about made it seem alright, in other words. With the switch to an obsessive-compulsive disorder classification, psychologists are now saying that they understand trich to be ego-dystonic, meaning that people with trich are compelled to pull out their hair despite the behavior feeling bad and wrong to them (given that it can lead to bald spots, missing eyebrows, and skin problems, one would imagine).

If this new classification is correct, that's actually good news in a strange way for trich patients, because ego-dystonic disorders are ostensibly easier to treat than ego-syntonic ones. Since ego-syntonic behaviors seem right, good, and normal to the sufferer, even when the behavior is actually destructive—like, say, vomiting to lose weight, as with bulimia (🎙)—the patient doesn't see anything wrong with it. And how can you seek out help if you don't think you have a problem in the first place? With ego-dystonic behaviors, like trich seems to be, the sufferer is truly hurting and is more likely to be a willing participant in their own treatment.

But hold on a minute. It's not like researchers suddenly realized that they forgot to ask trich patients if they felt good about their hair pulling, found out they actually didn't, and then reclassified it as an OCD in the DSM-5. So, what gives with the switch? Psychologists found that trich checks some of the OCD boxes, and it seems they thought it might do better from a treatment perspective by trying that category on for size. The problem is, trich doesn't fit neatly into the OCD category either. Classifying trich (and hence providing a framework for understanding it) turns out to be a lot like nailing Jell-O to the wall.

Trich's multiple personalities, diagnostically speaking, show up in study after study. Regardless of the age groups being evaluated or the geographic locations they are pulled from, researchers found as many (if not more) differences as they did similarities between OCD sufferers and trichotillomania sufferers (or "chronic hair pullers," as they were often called). And the degree of difference even among the similarities was often rather big.

In one study conducted in South Africa in 2005, in the midst of the nosological nerd fight over what trich's entry in the DSM-5 would look like,[9] researchers tried to find what trich might have in common with OCD by comparing two groups of people who suffered from one or the other. Fifty-four trich sufferers and 278 OCD sufferers were compared based on a number of different factors, including how many other disorders they had in common. Of twenty-nine disorders tested for, the two groups only shared five to any notable degree. And two of those five disorders were only common between the groups because no one had them. The other three were kleptomania, 🎙 body dysmorphia, 🎙 and the presence of a "specific phobia." None of this, you might imagine, was super helpful in neatly folding trichotillomania under the umbrella of OCD.

The authors' conclusions say as much. They found that there were "significant differences between OCD and TTM" and that those differences "may reflect differences in underlying psychobiology, and may necessitate contrasting treatment approaches." Basically, what they were saying was that OCD and TTM are probably caused by different factors and require different treatments. Oh, and by the way, they concluded that the "[original] classification of TTM as an impulse control disorder is also problematic." The old saying holds as true as ever: once you let a psychological disorder out of the pen, it might want to come back in, but it can't fit through the gate!

It seems whichever family of disorders psychologists say it belongs to, trichotillomania will always be like Tom Hagen in *The Godfather*—adopted into the family like a brother and a son, but because there is no direct blood relation and he's not a Sicilian, the connection only goes so deep. And also, in this instance, Tom Hagen can't sit on the couch with the rest of the family because he's not shaped for couches, and more to the point his kind doesn't sit, they do something else entirely that no one else in the family does, like crouching high up in a ceiling corner by pressing against the two walls where they meet.

---

[9] Nosology is the science of disease classification.

MEET THE TRICHOTILLOMANICS

Beyond the question of where to house TTM and the other BFRBs within the DSM, TTM makes for a really interesting, if difficult, thing to study because its sufferers are both unique demographically and in terms of what drives them to pull out their hair.

STUFF YOU SHOULD KNOW . . .
About Language

TTM, OCD, BFRB, DSM. These are abbreviations. Some might also call them acronyms, but the correct term for them is initialisms. Here's an easy way to think about and look at these three concepts in relation to each other.

ABBREVIATIONS are contractions of a word or phrase
(St. for street or saint; Mt. for mount; donut for doughnut)

ACRONYMS are abbreviations that you pronounce as words
(NASA, SWAT, 🎙 AWOL, NAFTA)

INITIALISMS are abbreviations that you pronounce one letter at a time
(DMV, DNA, MIA, TTM)

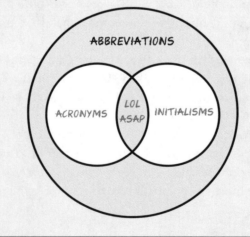

As with all body-focused repetitive behaviors, trichotillomania symptoms tend to start showing up around the time we first begin to focus on our bodies, which is puberty. ⓘ Throughout the teenage years, trich is fairly evenly distributed between the sexes. By the time adulthood rolls around, though, it skews wildly female, to as much as 9:1—about the same wildly skewed ratio as dentists who recommend Dentyne and dentists who do not.[10] In that 2005 South African study, for example, of the fifty-four trich patients interviewed, forty-nine were female and five were male. In a similar study conducted twenty years earlier on childhood trichotillomania— meaning the time when it's still supposed to be evenly distributed among males and females—*all of* the participants were female. Take a guess if psychologists have a good explanation for why this is the case: your options are "no" and "not really."

Beyond the question of *who* pulls out their hair, the question of *why* people pull out their hair is equally complicated, but for the opposite reason. It's not that there is no clear answer; it's that there are many clear answers. For some, it's a release of tension related to stress or anxiety. For others, stress plays no role at all and the moment of plucking doesn't provide release, but pleasure. Some people do it unconsciously when they're preoccupied; others do it consciously when they're bored.

Diagnostically, trich is all over the place, and so clinically we are basically nowhere with it. For years, the primary treatment has been cognitive behavioral therapy and habit reversal training, which together teach people to identify the triggers that lead them to hair pulling in the first place and retrain their brain to think about those triggers differently. Some people with trich are prescribed drugs for treatment, specifically SSRIs (selective serotonin reuptake inhibitors), antidepressants, amino acids that affect neurotransmitters, and an antipsychotic called olanzapine. But the success rate of patients who respond to treatment and stop pulling their hair over the long term is very low. As few as 10 to 20 percent go on to become what the average person might call "cured" by treatment. Even studies showing the high end of positive treatment results have found only about a 50 percent success rate.

....

[10] What *does* that other dentist recommend, by the way? Crest? Tub and tile cleaner? Two-hundred-grit sandpaper?

Rather than continuing to beat their heads against the wall trying to figure out how to include this wide variation into the diagnosis of trich, the psychologists drafting the new DSM-5 had a stroke of genius: why, they could just remove the more difficult criteria altogether! And thus these two formerly important criteria for diagnosing trich didn't survive the move from the DSM-IV to the DSM-5:

- **An increasing sense of tension immediately before pulling out the hair or when attempting to resist the behavior.**

- **Pleasure, gratification, or relief when pulling out the hair.**

Problem solved—for the DSM-5 writers at least. For the psychologists working with trich, however, developing effective treatment protocols remains as difficult as it has always been since patients who pull their hair out but don't fit the revised DSM-5 criteria still show up on their couches. Maybe the DSM-6 will be trich's lucky edition.

We would say in conclusion that the frustrating nature of trichotillomania, combined with the earnest desire to get to the bottom of this behavioral mystery, is making researchers tear their hair out, but that sort of egregious pun is as annoying as a nervous bouncing knee and we would never do something like that.

CHAPTER

17

TRILLIONAIRES

ARE THEY POSSIBLE,
AND WHO WILL IT BE?

1,000,000,000,000. That is a trillion. A one followed by twelve zeroes. It's so long it looks like a freight train with the 1 as the locomotive. A trillion is one of those figures that's so immense it feels more like an idea than an actual amount.

One trillion feels easier to calculate theoretically than to conceptualize practically—like imagining the length of a light-year or the width of an atomic nucleus. That's the crazy part about a number like a trillion: it only shows up naturally on a scale of the infinitely large or the infinitesimally small.

So hold onto your abaci, because we're about to break your brain.

There are 100 trillion atoms in *a single human cell*, and there are about 70 trillion cells in a single human body. But if you add up the weight of all the human bodies (people) in the world it would come to less than a trillion pounds,[1] though it would still be more than the combined weight of all 1,000 trillion ants that live on Earth. God knows what this is in Big Macs.

Astronomers estimate there are 2 trillion galaxies in the universe, composed of a trillion trillion stars. One light-year is 5.88 trillion miles,[2] and the closest star to Earth beyond the sun is 4.25 light-years away: that's 25 trillion miles if you're counting, which you shouldn't be, because if you're counting at one number per second (which is very generous) it would take you a shade over 790,000 years to finish.[3]

....

[1] This isn't nearly as impressive when converted to kilograms, as one trillion pounds equals 454,545,454,545.4545 kg. That's an interesting number, sure, but I think we can all agree that the Imperial system of measurement wins again here.

[2] That's 9,462,942,720,000 kilometers. This one is a wash, since both numbers are very impressive and interesting-looking.

[3] Even David Sinclair would agree there's not enough NMN on this planet to extend human lifespan *that* far (see chapter 8).

YOU GET A TRILLION.
YOU GET A TRILLION!

A trillion doesn't get any more comprehensible when we're talking about money either. A trillion US dollars is just shy of Mexico's entire GDP,[4] for example. It would take the average American family 16 million years to earn it and 2.73 million years to spend it at $1,000 per day. And if you wanted to stack it all in one place so you could see it, you'd need a stadium and a step ladder, because $1 trillion laid out neatly in $100 bills would produce stacks that cover nearly an entire football field at 10 feet high.[5] Make it $1 bills and you're looking at a mound of money roughly the size of the Empire State Building. And the size in Big Macs? Again, who knows?

So how is it that we could even be talking about the idea of one person in possession of such an unfathomable amount of cash? Is that really possible? The short answer is yes . . .

. . . with about 89.7 sextillion asterisks,[6] because that was the effective inflation rate in Zimbabwe at the end of 2008. At its worst, the hyperinflation in Zimbabwe's currency rendered one US dollar worth 2,621,984,228,675,650,147,435,579,309,984,228 Zimbabwe dollars. At that point pretty much every Zimbabwean became a de facto trillionaire, a fact that the Reserve Bank of Zimbabwe made official in 2009 when they rang in the new year by putting a whole suite of trillion dollar notes (10, 50, and 100) into circulation. Not that you could buy much with them. When the story of the trillion-dollar notes broke that January, a loaf of bread cost Z$300 billion and the price wasn't heading anywhere good.[7]

....

[4] Mexico's GDP in 2018 was USD$1.221 trillion.

[5] 3.048 meters; yawn.

[6] There is no metric conversion for asterisks.

[7] Zimbabwe officially discontinued their trillion-dollar notes and abandoned their own currency for the US dollar in 2015. Locals could get USD$5 for every Z$175 quadrillion (that's 16 zeros) they turned in. You can hear all about this economic cluster in our episode "How Currency Works" (and we're pretty sure it makes an appearance in our "How much money is in the world?" and "What is stagflation?" episodes too).

Obviously when we talk about the possibility of trillionaires, we don't mean by the measure of just *any* currency. In certain countries at certain times, like Zimbabwe in 2009, being a trillionaire can be pretty doable. One trillion Iranian rials isn't even USD $25 million, for example. And the top 21 richest people in the world today would all be trillionaires if their USDs were converted to Mexican pesos. But since the US dollar is considered the world's currency, it is the currency upon which any consistent measure of wealth would have to be based. When you look at it like that, the conversation about trillionairity[8] starts to get much smaller and more specific, though not without first navigating through the ever-growing list of world billionaires.

....

[8] It's technically not a word, but it totally should be.

WHO WANTS TO BE A TRILLIONAIRE?

At one time it was generally believed that John D. Rockefeller was the first billionaire. His net worth has since been disputed by his own son, and even though his inflation-adjusted wealth would still rank him somewhere on Most Reputable[9] All-Time Top Ten Richest Persons lists, Henry Ford has firmly supplanted the Standard Oil titan as the first true-blue billionaire.

Whether you ride with the guy who built the cars or the guy who put the gas in them, the billionaire seal was broken long before most of us were born, which means we all grew up knowing that making Richie Rich money was possible, if highly improbable.[10] This fueled our fascination with extreme wealth. We love shows like *Lifestyles of the Rich and Famous* and we eat up stuff like the Forbes 400 list. There's even one list of the richest people of all time that has Joseph Stalin at number 5.[11] That might seem like cheating—maybe not worth a septillion asterisks, but at least one—because Stalin wasn't *personally* wealthy. He didn't have a fortune invested in stocks. He wasn't an oil man or an industrialist or an entrepreneur, either. What he did have was complete authority over an economy that made up 9.6 percent of the globe's GDP. That is a staggering amount of wealth, no matter who wields it and by the standard of any time period, and we would be remiss not to include him. We wouldn't want to hurt Stalin's feelings.

The reality is, if we're going to imagine a world in which trillionaires are possible, we have to consider *all* of the ways that could happen, from Powerball winners to power-hungry dictators. It may not be as fun to imagine a murderous despot becoming a trillionaire as, say, a pot-smoking, late-night tweeting Elon Musk. But let's not kid ourselves: Andrew Carnegie, who ranked fourth on one of those most reputable lists, once hired a militia that killed nine striking workers. Bill Gates, who ranked ninth on that same list, may be a grandfatherly, world-saving philanthropist now, but in his prime he was a ruthless, gawky monopolist. If we're really going to entertain the

---

[9] "Reputable" being a relative term here.

[10] Chuck's favorite comic was Richie Rich and he stands by that.

[11] Stalin may have only been the fifth wealthiest ever, but he had a Top 3 Walrus mustache.

idea of someone becoming a trillionaire when nearly half the world lives on less than $6 a day, then we also have to accept that it probably won't come pretty. And when we look at history, that's exactly what we find.

Of the top ten all-time richest people, two were conquerors who plowed their way across the globe to amass vast fortunes; two were industrialists who gained monopolies over the production of critical industrial age resources and maintained control with force and cunning; five were dictator-emperors who held absolute authority over a global superpower and all of its resources; and one was a software developer who gained a monopoly over the personal computer industry at its inception and used intellectual property laws to amass a personal fortune.

STUFF YOU SHOULD KNOW . . .
About Rulers

Stalin rubs elbows with other historic rulers whose nations' economies were one and the same as their personal wealth. Augustus Caesar personally owned Egypt for a time; India's Akbar I, who ruled the Moghul empire in the sixteenth century, had an economy comparable to Elizabethan England's; and the thirteenth- and fourteenth-century ruler of the Kingdom of Timbuktu, Mansa Musa, is—due to his nation's gold mines—considered perhaps the wealthiest person to have ever lived. There is a tale that when Musa passed through Egypt during a pilgrimage to Mecca, his incredible spending so flooded the market with gold that he temporarily devalued Egypt's currency. That, friends, is how you make it rain in the desert.

It stands to reason, then, that at some point in the past the functional equivalent of a trillionaire has probably already walked the Earth; there just weren't USDs around to use as a measure of their wealth. And whoever becomes the first technical trillionaire won't look awfully different from those who've come before them. They will probably be something of a dictator or a monopolist—if not literally, then figuratively—and utilize some combination of strategies and tactics that have already proven effective.[12]

....

[12] We've grown depressed enough with this question that we now wonder why we asked it in the first place.

This leaves us with two people who've got a legitimate shot at being the first to ride that twelve-zero freight train to Trillionaire Town: Vladimir Putin and Jeff Bezos.

Rootin' Tootin' Shootin' Putin has maintained total control over Russia's USD$1.6 trillion GDP since 2000. His personal fortune—which he totally earned fair and square, in case the FSB 📶 is reading this—is somewhere between $200 to $300 billion[13] according to American and British intelligence reports. But given the cloak of mortal danger and state secrecy that Putin operates behind, his true wealth will probably never be known.[14]

Not to be outdone is Jeff Bezos, who is the world's richest private citizen by a comfortable margin and the founder of Amazon, which has effectively swallowed up retail and has its sights set on pretty much everything that could find its way inside your house, business, car, and body. Even if you opt

....

13 And that is *not* in Zimbabwe dollars.

14 If someone does put all the pieces together, they better watch out, because a nice, warm slice of polonium pie is headed their way.

to stick it to the man (Bezos) and you don't use Amazon or shop at Whole Foods, you are still a cog in the Bezos Empire if you have an account with Netflix, Twitter, Facebook, Twitch, Reddit, and too many other platforms to name because they all run on Amazon Web Services, far and away the largest and most relied-upon cloud service in the world.[15] This is Jeff Bezos's world and we're just living in it. If you listen closely on a quiet night, you can sometimes hear his "mmmwuhhahahaha" carried thinly on the breeze.

By some calculations, Bezos could be the first member of the Trillionaire's Club by 2026, but a lot would have to go right and stay right for that to happen, and even Bezos doesn't think that's likely, having once pointed out that large companies typically last 30 years, not the hundred-or-more-year timeline you can imagine would ease a billionaire comfortably into trillionairehood. Based on that prediction, Amazon will start to fail somewhere around 2024, its thirtieth birthday—two years before Bezos would hit a trillion, if everything were to continue as it has been going. So sad.

But as much money as Bezos can make from his Amazon apparatus here on Earth, it may likely be space rocks that ultimately tip the scale on his balance sheets. Renowned astrophysicist Neil DeGrasse Tyson once triumphantly declared, "It is likely that the first trillionaire will be the person who exploits the mineral resources on asteroids." Well guess what: Jeff Bezos founded a space exploration company called Blue Origin to eventually do just that.

According to Asterank, a database that tracks asteroid contents and value, there are several hundred asteroids in our solar system, *each* with more than $100 trillion worth of minerals and rare earth metals trapped inside them. That's more than the combined GDP of our entire planet . . . in one flying space rock.[16]

Both Putin and Bezos are conquerors in their own ways. But only one has a shirtless picture of himself riding a horse[17] on vacation in Siberia, which probably gives him the upper hand on the race to twelve zeroes.

---

[15] Not uneasy yet? Check out our episode "How AI Facial Recognition Works," which talks about how Amazon Web Services powers the tracking systems of the world's police and governments. 🎧

[16] Of course if Bezos was able to successfully wrangle, mine, and bring to market the mineral contents of an asteroid, we'd immediately be in a Mansa Musa situation where the value of everything starts to collapse. Still though . . . a hundred trillion dollars!

[17] Not a bear; the bear-riding picture is fake. Come on.

CHAPTER

18

THE SCUM
MANIFESTO

THE WORLD WITHOUT MEN
WOULD BE KILLER

Valerie Jean Solanas was a gifted child born to crappy parents on April 9, 1936, in Ventnor City, New Jersey. Uh oh, this feels like another New Jersey story, buckle up.

Solanas was smart, funny, and creative, but she had a hard life—thanks in large part to men. An alcoholic father who sexually abused her. Two pregnancies by age fifteen, one allegedly by a relative, the other likely by an older sailor; both babies taken and given up for adoption. She was kicked out of her Catholic middle school for attacking a nun.[1] Remarkably, despite a rough start to life, she made her way to college where, unfortunately, she found things weren't much easier. As a student at the University of Maryland in the 1950s, she was ordered to undergo anger management counseling multiple times while working in the psychology department's animal experiment lab. Gee, what in Valerie Solanas's life could have possibly made her so angry? Still, through all that, she managed to get a degree in psychology, to find her sexual identity, and to find her voice as a writer and artist.

SPOILER ALERT: Her voice was angry, and she was angry with men.

Eventually, in the summer of 1962, after banging her head against the glass ceiling for a year in a master's degree program at the University of Minnesota, Solanas took her talents to New York City to find her way into the booming Bohemian art scene in Greenwich Village. For the next few years she bounced between residential hotels in and around the village, managing to cobble together a living from a combination of writing and prostitution.[2] These experiences provided the fertile ground from which her first major written work sprouted, a satire completed in 1965 about her life that was proctologically titled, *Up Your Ass*.[3] It featured a street-smart

---

[1] This sounds bad, but anyone who endured a moment of Catholic school education in those days will tell you that there is no meaner figure in the life of an impressionable child than an old Catholic school nun with a ruler in hand. All of which is to say, it was probably a fair fight.

[2] Some might consider these the same things, but we digress.

[3] The full title of the play is *Up Your Ass, or, From the Cradle to the Boat, or, The Big Suck, or, Up from the Slime*. Sometimes it's just too hard to pick between great title options.

lesbian prostitute named Bongi Perez and a supporting cast of oddball characters she meets on the street during her day. The chances are very slim that it will ever be adapted by Disney.[4]

For the next two years, Solanas dedicated herself to two pursuits: finding someone to produce her play and writing what would become *the* radical feminist treatise on the takedown of the male patriarchy and the complete destruction of the social order. The first pursuit didn't pan out so well: she was turned down by every producer she approached, most of them men, including Andy Warhol, who was one of the most famous artists on the scene at the time. The second pursuit, however, was much more fruitful.

MEN ARE SCUMMY, WOMEN ARE SCUM

Solanas self-published her treatise in 1967 and called it *SCUM Manifesto*. The basic premise was that men are inferior (genetically deficient, to be precise), that they have ruined the world, and that to save it women must rise up, overthrow society, and eliminate men from the species.

Your first question might be, *well what about making babies?* Oh boy does Valerie Solanas have an answer for you:

> Retaining the male has not even the dubious purpose of reproduction. The male is a biological accident: the Y (male) gene is an incomplete X (female) gene, that is, it has an incomplete set of chromosomes. In other words, the male is an incomplete female, a walking abortion, aborted at the gene stage. To be male is to be deficient, emotionally limited; maleness is a deficiency disease and males are emotional cripples.

And that's just the second paragraph!

Your next question might be, *c'mon, not all men are that bad, are they?* Valerie would beg to differ. According to her manifesto, the male is . . .

---

[4] But then there was that one frame in *The Rescuers*, so who knows?

...COMPLETELY EGOCENTRIC

...INCAPABLE OF MENTAL PASSION

...A HALF-DEAD, UNRESPONSIVE LUMP

...INCAPABLE OF GIVING OR RECEIVING PLEASURE
OR HAPPINESS

...AN UTTER BORE

...AN INOFFENSIVE BLOB

...IN A TWILIGHT ZONE HALFWAY BETWEEN
HUMANS AND APES

And that's just the *third* paragraph!

Solanas goes on to outline a long list of societal problems that sit at the feet of men. From war and hatred and violence and death and prejudice—okay, fair—to boredom, conformity, depression, suburban isolation, and being really bad at conversation. *Conversation? C'mo*—okay, also fair.[5]

If only we could print all 10,000+ words of the *SCUM Manifesto* here.[6] Valerie Solanas takes a blowtorch to the patriarchy and melts it down into the shape of a Georgia O'Keefe painting. It's kind of breathtaking in its completeness. There is no place for men to hide and no room for interpretation when it comes to her intent: that men are pigs and must be wiped out.

Where there *is* room, apparently, is in the meaning of the term SCUM itself. On the cover of the first "officially" printed version of the manifesto in 1968, published by Olympia Press, SCUM is printed as an acronym.[7] Underneath it are the words "Society for Cutting Up Men." Nine years later, though, Solanas dropped by the New York Public Library and vandalized a copy of the book, claiming that "S.C.U.M." as an acronym was not her title, and that her editor had published a version "full of sabotaging typos." She even went so far as to scratch out her name on the cover and replace it with her editor's, Maurice Girodias, who'd already made a name for himself when he published a little book called *Lolita,* by the Russian author Vladimir

---

[5] In fact, there's very little that Valerie Solanas says about men that isn't mostly accurate. And this is coming from us, who are men.

[6] You can find it pretty easily on the Internet, so check it out for yourself.

[7] A *true* acronym, as we learned in chapter 16.

Nabokov, more than twenty years earlier. Once again, Valerie Solanas had run into men behaving badly, both in practice and in print.

The problem with her interpretation of events is that she used the phrase "Society for Cutting Up Men" multiple times prior to the Olympia Press version of her manifesto going to print. It's in multiple ads she placed with the *Village Voice* in February 1967 promoting a reading of her play, which had still not found a producer. It's apparently on the cover of the first few hundred copies of the manifesto that she published herself.[8] And while it doesn't appear as if the group ever grew beyond just herself, it seems pretty clear that Solanas did view herself as the head of the Society for Cutting Up Men—the birth mother of a movement to punish men for the damage they have wrought.

Her manifesto is a call to arms to SCUM in the fight against scum. And to be SCUM required a certain mindset:

> . . . dominant, secure, self-confident, nasty, violent, selfish, independent, proud, thrill-seeking, free-wheeling, arrogant females, who consider themselves fit to rule the universe, who have free-wheeled to the limits of this "society" and are ready to wheel on to something far beyond what it has to offer . . .

Badasses, basically.

WHAT'S THE DEAL WITH MANIFESTOS?

Have you ever noticed how anytime you see something in the news or in a history book about someone having written a manifesto, violence and death always seem close behind? There's the *Unabomber Manifesto* (three dead, twenty-three injured). There's the October Manifesto that allowed Tsar Nicholas II to crush the 1905 Revolution in Russia. There's Karl Marx and Friedrich Engels's *Communist Manifesto* that arguably inspired a body

---

[8] Interestingly, we couldn't track one down ourselves, so there's still a bit of conjecture there—which explains our use of the word "apparently."

count of around 100 million. There's the manifesto of Christopher Dorner, who declared war on the LAPD and then killed three people in Los Angeles in 2013. The Virginia Tech killer in 2007 and the guy in Norway who killed almost eighty people in 2011 both had manifestos as well.

At its core, the SCUM Manifesto is not much different than any of these others. It's long, it uses violent language, it identifies a common enemy and advocates for the overthrow of the current world order, and when it really gets going you can't escape the feeling that maybe its writer has some mental health problems. Many have argued that the *SCUM Manifesto* is different, that it's a satire and not meant to be taken literally, but judging by what Valerie Solanas did less than eighteen months after its initial publication, you'd be hard pressed to find a meaningful enough distinction from the others.

On the morning of June 3rd, 1968, a young woman named Margo Feiden was returning to her apartment when she saw Valerie Solanas sitting on the steps in front of her building. Feiden was twenty-three years old at the time, married, and a rising star in the New York art scene. As Feiden approached, Solanas introduced herself and said she had an important idea she wanted to discuss with her. Feiden, being a curious and friendly person, invited Solanas up to her apartment to hear her out. What followed was a rambling four-hour pitch for her play, which she insisted that Feiden produce, combined with a recitation of her SCUM-infused theories about the extermination of men. When Feiden asked her how women could reproduce in this fantasy world, Solanas insisted that men could be kept as cattle, bearing numbers on their backs so that women could "request" them.

Ok, now if you think that's bananas, here comes the Chiquita factory. Quite abruptly during the final minutes of her pitch, Solanas reached into her purse and pulled out a gun.

"Do you know what this is?" she asked Feiden.

"Yeah, that's a gun," Feiden responded.

"If you don't agree that you will produce my play, I am going to shoot Andy Warhol," Solanas said. "Then I will become famous, my play will become famous, and you will produce it."[9]

The appearance of the gun adjourned the meeting. Feiden managed to coerce Solanas out of her apartment and immediately called in the threat to

---

[9] She was right about becoming famous, wrong about the other two claims: the manifesto became famous, not the play, and Feiden never produced it.

police, who ignored her. "How would you know what a real gun looks like?" the desk officer reportedly said to Feiden, in another shining moment for men in this story. What neither Feiden nor the sexist cop who dismissed her knew was that while they were talking, Valerie Solanas was on her way to make good on her promise at Andy Warhol's famous studio, The Factory, at its new location on the sixth floor of the Decker Building off Union Square in Manhattan.

GOING DOWN?

When Solanas arrived at The Factory, Warhol was out, so she did what anyone with murder in their heart would do and she waited outside. Around 4:30 p.m., just hours after she had brandished a firearm in the living room of a perfect stranger, Warhol showed up with a London art critic and curator named Mario Amaya, and she rode up in the elevator 🛗 with them. When they arrived on the sixth floor, Solanas shot both men. Warhol three times, Amaya once. Amaya only suffered superficial wounds, but Warhol was rushed to the hospital with a ruptured stomach, liver, spleen, and lungs.[10]

Jeez lady, what did Andy Warhol ever do to you? Turns out quite a lot, if you ask Valerie Solanas. While she'd been unsuccessful in her initial attempt to connect with Warhol in 1965, she found her way into The Factory by 1967. Unlike her encounter with Margo Feiden on that June day in 1968, Solanas was not approaching Warhol as a stranger; the two knew each other. She'd been introduced to Warhol by one of his many hangers-on, and she'd given him a copy of her play to read, which he'd promised to consider because he liked the title. Then he made the grave mistake of losing the manuscript,[11] which enraged her. When Solanas followed up, Warhol tried to make amends by offering her small parts in a couple of his films that year—*I, A Man*[12] and

---

[10] Solanas also tried to shoot Warhol's manager, Fred Hughes, but the gun jammed.

[11] Somehow the manuscript ended up under some lighting equipment in a trunk that belonged to the photographer Billy Name, who was one of the Warhol Superstars, The Factory archivist, and responsible for "silverizing" the entire space with aluminum foil.

[12] *I, A Man* was originally supposed to star Jim Morrison of The Doors, but he backed out and sent his friend Tom Baker in his place instead.

Bike Boy[13]—which she accepted. As it turns out, that was not enough to make things square, and she eventually took her pound of flesh from Warhol's liver, spleen, and lungs, a little love note from the business end of the .32 Beretta she'd smuggled into The Factory in a paper bag.

With both Warhol and Amaya bleeding on the floor, Solanas quickly made her exit and wandered for a while through Times Square before deciding to confess to the first unsuspecting authority figure she came upon. That turned out to be a rookie NYPD officer named William Shemalix.[14] Andy Warhol had too much control over her life, she told the twenty-two-year-old traffic cop. A little while later, she told reporters at the police station to read her manifesto if they wanted to understand "what I am."

In what may not come as a shock by this point in her story, Valerie Solanas would subsequently be diagnosed with paranoid schizophrenia 🎙 and institutionalized until she was deemed fit to stand trial the following June. She was sentenced to two additional years in prison on top of the year she'd already spent under mandatory psychiatric care. When she got out in 1971, she started stalking Warhol, which got her arrested again and ultimately led her into a life on the streets. She just could not let go of the belief that men like Andy Warhol and Maurice Girodias—men of wealth and status

....

[13] You have to imagine appearing in two films with male leads and maleness right there in the titles would not have been Valerie's first choice, but there must have been some consolation in the fact that at least *Bike Boy* is about a macho biker who gets emasculated over and over again in conversation by the Warhol Superstars. What the Brits would call "taking the piss."

[14] It is of the most delicious variety of irony that Officer William Shemalix's fifteen minutes of fame came directly from his tangential involvement with Andy Warhol.

and privilege—were out to steal her ideas and to ruin the world with their oppressive, boorish maleness and their sense of entitlement. Though if we're being honest here you don't need to be clinically insane to believe that, and it doesn't take a 10,000-word manifesto to see the truth in it either.

STUFF YOU SHOULD KNOW . . .
About Andy Warhol

Valerie Solanas's attempt on Andy Warhol's life began a dark, protracted final chapter in his story. He just barely survived the shooting and was left with physical difficulties for the rest of his life. The medical girdle he wore held in his bowels because an abdominal muscle that would normally provide that needed function was pierced by a bullet and left irreparable. When Warhol died in 1987 at age fifty-eight, it was partly due to complications from a surgery to remove his gallbladder, made difficult because of the shape his abdomen was in, and exacerbated by his unwillingness to seek medical help sooner out of the fear of hospitals he developed during his treatment for the shooting. He said in an interview in 1968 that, "Since I was shot, everything is such a dream to me. I don't know what anything is about. Like I don't even know whether or not I'm really alive or—whether I died. It's sad."

BEYOND THE SCUM

Andy Warhol survived the attack by Valerie Solanas, but he would be forced to wear a medical girdle for the rest of his life. Many credit his death in 1987 as a direct result of long-term medical complications from the shooting (see box above). Solanas, who died just a year later in a residential hotel in San Francisco's Tenderloin district, never achieved the kind of fame Warhol enjoyed, though she definitely found a version of it in death. She became a radical feminist icon. Her *SCUM Manifesto* became part of the radical feminist canon. She was portrayed by Lili Taylor in the 1996 film *I Shot Andy Warhol,* and her prized play, *Up Your Ass*, was rediscovered in

1999, and in 2000, it premiered as *Up Your A$$* at the famous George Coates Performance Works in San Francisco.[15]

Still today, decades after she wrote it, decades after she brought attention to it with the shooting of Andy Warhol, decades after she was diagnosed with schizophrenia, the *SCUM Manifesto* is shaping minds. That's a pretty telling testimony to the idea that Valerie Solanas touched on some inherent and inarguable truth—put most generously and in corporate speak, that men have many areas of opportunity for improvement. Maybe it's the mind-boggling violence and dominance she calls for against men. Maybe it's the unrelenting and unapologetic disdain she holds for every last member of an entire sex, no exceptions. Whatever it is, there's something in there that speaks to readers. One professor of feminist theory says that her students who tend to be turned off by most fringe feminist ideas are still drawn to the *SCUM Manifesto*. Which just goes to show that on the right day, even the least revolutionary-minded of the "complete sex" can happily imagine a world without any pain in the a$$ men in it.

....

[15] Having gotten in a fight with a nun in Catholic school, Solanas probably would have appreciated that the Performance Works where her play premiered was a repurposed former Catholic cathedral.

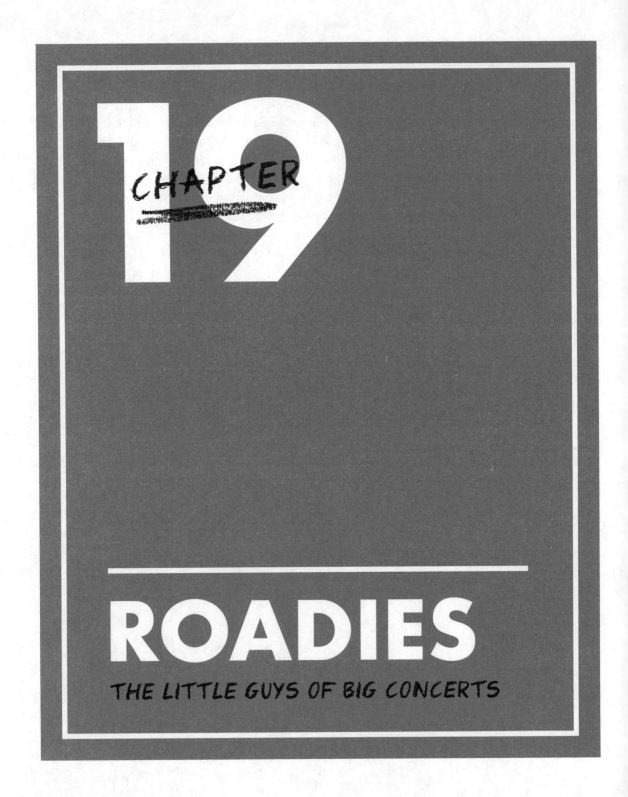

CHAPTER 19

ROADIES

THE LITTLE GUYS OF BIG CONCERTS

Live music lovers will tell you that there are few events as transcendent as a great concert. Ask them about their all-time favorite shows and they will describe the experience of listening to amazing music being performed by brilliant musicians; of being surrounded by hundreds or thousands of like-minded people, moving to a heart-pounding beat being pumped out of massive speaker arrays; of watching lights and lasers and images and sometimes explosions as they flash synchronously with the music and each other.

They'll tell you about the shirt they bought (and still own) from the show and describe how, together, these elements combined to create a kind of communal energy that imprinted the experience onto their minds for a lifetime and brought them to tears in the moment.[1] Thanks, LSD!

When we share these concert memories, it's always the band or the people sitting around us at the show who we end up talking about. But the unsung heroes of those indelible musical moments are really the members of the band's road crew—or "roadies," as they are more popularly known—who make those moments happen, day in and day out, town after town, show after show, for the band's entire concert tour.

---

[1] Watch concert footage of Michael Jackson, Prince, the Beatles, Taylor Swift, or One Direction, to name just a few, and you will see people in the front rows crying like they just finished reading every book and watching every movie where a dog dies at the end. Nonstop waterworks.

OFFICIAL ROADIE ROLES
How to Be the Master of the Professional Resume When You're Just a Slave to the Music

TITLE	TASKS
Tour Manager	• Organize and plan a tour; pay bills • Work with venue managers, ticket agents, and promoters • Travel with band and handle problems as they arise
Production Manager	• Supervise technical crew and coordinate with the local crew • Supervise the assembling, disassembling, and movement of equipment from venue to venue
Stage Manager	• Control performers' movements on stage, as well as crew on and off stage • Give crew cues for the house lights
Advance Person	• Arrive at venue before the band and crew to help the tour manager and make sure arrangements have been handled correctly
Sound Engineer	• Operate the front-of-house console, which controls and mixes the sound the audience hears during a live performance
Monitor Engineer	• Operate the monitor console, controlling the sound the band hears during a concert through on-stage or in-ear monitors
Sound Crew	• Set up, run, and disassemble sound equipment, as directed by the sound and monitor engineers
Lighting Operator	• Operate the control console for the show and supervise the lighting crew
Lighting Crew	• Set up, run, and disassemble lighting equipment • May also handle special effects like smoke machines or hoists
Backline Crew	• Set up instruments and other band gear • Pack up instruments and gear after the show
Drug Guy	• Get drugs for the band

Roadies are responsible for everything onstage and backstage other than the singing and the playing (and sometimes that too, as you will soon learn). They unload trucks, unpack trunks, rig lighting and effects, stack amps and mount backing screens, prep instruments and switch them out between songs, set up mic stands to the exact right height, and lay out those oriental rugs on the stage that literally every rock band seems to have. Then they undo all of that work in reverse order at the end of the night so they can do it again in the next town the next day. As Jackson Browne put it in the first verse of his 1978 ode to roadies, "The Load-Out":

NOW THE SEATS ARE ALL EMPTY

LET THE ROADIES TAKE THE STAGE

PACK IT UP AND TEAR IT DOWN

THEY'RE THE FIRST TO COME AND LAST TO LEAVE

WORKING FOR THAT MINIMUM WAGE

THEY'LL SET IT UP IN ANOTHER TOWN

THE FIRST ROADIE

Considering how long music (40,000 years) and concerts (seventeenth century) have been around, roadies are a fairly recent phenomenon. They began to appear with the arrival of rock and roll in the early 1950s. Before that—during the Big Band era, for instance—most bands were composed of instruments that didn't require much amplification beyond a microphone: horns, strings, woodwinds,[2] percussion, played by musicians who showed up to gigs with their instruments in the trunks of their cars. They were basically mini symphony orchestras with a singer out front. But with the first commercially available electric guitar coming to market in 1946,[3] things started to change, and the kids started to find the rock and/or roll, as their frustrated old-timey parents might say.

----

[2] Those oboes really cooked!

[3] That would be the Fender Esquire.

The first major rock and roll show is generally considered to have been the Moondog Coronation Ball in Cleveland in 1952. Billed as a dance, as was typical of the time, by its radio host promoters, the show took place at the 10,000-seat Cleveland Arena and featured a number of live rock and roll acts. Thanks to a ticket printing snafu and simple enthusiasm, 20,000 people showed up.[4] The following year the world met Elvis Presley. A year or so after that, people got their first big taste of Chuck Berry,[5] and rock-n-roll was on its way.

The sound of rock is, of course, built on electric guitars, which meant that as rock-n-roll got more popular, the fact that those guitars were amplified meant artists could play bigger and bigger venues. This required more and more support. Barely a decade later, the Beatles would show the world what that actually meant, breaking new ground for rock-n-roll artists by playing a show in front of nearly 60,000 people at Shea Stadium in New York on August 15, 1965—the first-ever stadium concert. With Beatlemania in full swing, you can be pretty sure that Ringo wasn't out there a couple hours before the show setting up his own drums.

Even before that whole thirteen-year evolution, a man named Ben Dorcy was already hard at work helping artists tour their act. He'd been at it since 1950,[6] in fact, predating the Moondog Ball by a couple of years, and setting himself up to work with some of the giants of American music: Johnny Cash and June Carter Cash, Patsy Cline, Jerry Jeff Walker, Willie Nelson, Waylon Jennings, Merle Haggard, and a young, good-looking kid out of Memphis named Elvis.

To hear many of these artists talk about Dorcy, who died at the age of ninety-two in 2017, he created the blueprint for the roadie. For one, he was fiercely loyal—a central trait in an exceptional roadie. He knew hundreds of stories that he would take to his grave. He was selfless to a fault. June

---

[4] Ironically, despite double the tickets being printed, there is only one known left to exist. It's housed at the Rock and Roll Hall of Fame in, appropriately, Cleveland.

[5] Whose music is traveling at 38,000 miles per hour across the universe right now on the Golden Records 🏷 aboard the Voyager probes.

[6] Dorcy was a "bandboy" for a big country artist named Hank Thompson. The next time you see a grizzled old biker with a chain wallet breaking down equipment after a show, see what he says when you call him "bandboy."

Carter Cash said that early in his career some artists used him like a slave. He also knew how to get things done, another important quality. "We have seen him pull things out of the air that nobody else could do," the country artist Jessi Coulter said of him during a tour of The Highwaymen.[7] And he knew how to get his people out of trouble. He got Waylon Jennings off the hook for driving the wrong way down a one-way street. He was there when Johnny Cash shot a hole in one of the tires of his brand-new car at a gas station in Encino, California. And even as a ninety-year-old man, still going out on the road, Dorcy was working his magic, getting the Josh Abbott Band out of trouble at the Mexico border in Laredo, Texas when drug sniffing dogs found marijuana in a bag in the luggage compartment of the band's tour bus. When border patrol officers asked who the bag belonged to, Dorcy raised his hand and took responsibility. Agents immediately let the group go. "We're not going to bust a ninety-year-old guy for pot," they said. It was the ultimate roadie move.

ROADIE CULTURE

As romantic as that all sounds, the life of a roadie can be punishingly difficult. In the '60s, '70s, and '80s, some roadies wrote tell-alls about the sex and drug-fueled parties that happened on tour, creating a pop culture stereotype of hard-partying roadies—like the pot-smoking, White Russian-drinking Dude from *The Big Lebowski*, who recalls his stint working as a roadie for Metallica. But the modern reality for most road crew members is significantly less debauched. Roadies often work sixteen- to twenty-hour days, waking up at six in the morning and working until after midnight. Unless they're working for the biggest A-list superstars, they're often sleeping on the floor in packed, cheap hotel rooms and spending hours each day crammed into crowded vans. After a long tour those rooms and vans are often covered in dust, spilled beer, and God knows what else, smelling worse

---

[7] The Highwaymen was an outlaw country music supergroup that included Willie Nelson, Johnny Cash, Kris Kristofferson, and Waylon Jennings, who was Jessi Coulter's husband.

than a Louisiana locker room full of durian fruit, which is generally understood to be the foulest-smelling produce on Earth.

Inevitably, problems will arise on long tours. Buses and vans overheat, get flat tires, and break down. Instruments, amps, and other critical equipment break. Storms and traffic jams can make a mockery of even the most carefully planned tour schedule. Bands can have drama, and so can road crews. With those cramped hotels and vans, there's no real way to take a breather from the coworkers they're squabbling with. Shady or incompetent promoters may try to cheat bands and crews out of what they're owed. If a show is near a military base, the wireless frequencies may even be jammed and unusable.

The harrowing stories from the road are numerous and legend. There was the manager for Ok Go who was fired mid-tour for trying to resolve disputes with his gun and knife collection. Or the lighting designer for a number of major '90s metal and hip-hop acts who watched as one tour bus driver went into full-blown withdrawal and started fighting off imaginary snakes and spiders coming out of the steering wheel—*while driving*. There was the promoter for British bands in the '60s who was shot dead and robbed of the proceeds from one of the concerts he'd promoted—now there's a big hazard right there. And then there was the roadie for Van Halen who had to track down a missing David Lee Roth only to find him passed out and surrounded by naked women, though we're fairly sure David Lee Roth would not have classified that particular situation as the roadie helping out with a "problem."

THE CINDERELLA MOMENT

Experienced tour managers can earn six figures and many roadies average about sixty thousand dollars a year in earnings—enough bread to make the headaches worthwhile most of the time. But this isn't the norm; newer roadies or those working for less successful bands might earn little more than a hot meal and a free spot on a cramped hotel room floor. It is not the kind of gig anyone should expect to get wealthy from. So why do roadies do it?

First and foremost, roadies work for the love of music. Most of them are passionate music fans who put up with all the downsides just to work in the field they love and contribute to putting on great shows for other music lovers. Some do it because they're outgoing types who enjoy travelling, meeting new people, and seeing new places.[8] Others do it because they're friends with the band and like the kind of camaraderie that can develop between people on the road together. Many seasoned roadies talk about the bands they work for and the crewmembers they work with as their second family; sometimes their *only* family. But there's one other perk that a lucky few roadies have received over the years—actually getting to join a band, sometimes temporarily, sometimes permanently, becoming rock stars themselves.

In fact, a surprising number of music stars started out as roadies. In the late '60s, Lemmy Kilmister got a gig fixing Jimi Hendrix's guitar pedals after they were trashed during shows. A few years later he formed

----

8 You know, like flight attendants 🎙 but without the uniforms.

Motorhead, a band that was no stranger to wrecking equipment. Henry Rollins was a roadie[9] for early hardcore band The Teen Idles, who eventually morphed into Minor Threat, while Rollins became the lead singer of Black Flag. Slayer's lighting engineer Gene Hoglan played drums for them on a number of tracks before playing for a bunch of other bands, including Testament and Fear Factory. The Cure's guitar tech Perry Bamonte eventually became a keyboardist and guitarist for the band and coproduced several of their albums. John Marshall was the guitar tech for Metallica's lead guitarist, Kirk Hammett, and got to fill in as rhythm guitarist on two separate occasions for James Hetfield, once because of a skateboarding accident in the '80s,[10] and again because of a pyrotechnics accident in Montreal in 1992 when the band was on tour with Guns N' Roses.

It doesn't stop there: Anthrax bassist Frank Bello started as a guitar tech for the band, but got the full-time bassist job after the band's lead singer fired the guy he replaced.[11] Nirvana bassist Krist Novoselic was a driver for grunge pioneers The Melvins before joining up with Kurt Cobain and Dave Grohl. One of Nirvana's own roadies, Ben Shepherd, later became the bassist for fellow grunge icons Soundgarden. Kliph Scurlock went from Flaming Lips megafan to roadie to full-time drummer for the band. Guitar tech Billy Howerdel was an in-demand roadie for bands like Tool, Nine Inch Nails, and The Smashing Pumpkins before forming A Perfect Circle with Tool's lead singer Maynard James Keenan. Even the legendary rapper Tupac Shakur got his feet wet by working as a roadie and backup dancer for the hip-hop group Digital Underground in the early '90s.[12]

While some roadies make the jump from road crew to band member, most are content to stick to their crew jobs, which they treat with pride and an increasing degree of professionalism as touring has become big business in more recent times. Some even find the term "roadie" a bit dismissive, preferring to be known by their more formal job titles, like "lighting

....

[9] One of the more talkative ones, we would guess.

[10] Metallica once had their own skateboard deck, released in 1988 by the skate company Zorlac.

[11] It probably didn't hurt that the band's drummer was his uncle. Nepotism is so metal!

[12] You can see him doing his thing in the background of the "Humpty Dance" video.

technician" or "production manager" or "guitar tech". A preference most band members fully embrace, because they know how important the road crew is to their success.

We audience members may not know who they are, but they are not unsung heroes to the bands for whom they work. Somebody has to "roll them cases out and lift them amps, haul them trusses down and get 'em up them ramps," as Jackson Browne sang. Somebody's also gotta hide the drugs or take the fall or pay the bail. And then sometimes, somebody just needs to be there at the right place at the right time to save the band members from themselves. Or as Willie Nelson's fourth wife, Annie, put it when talking about Ben Dorcy: "I guess I owe Ben my sanity, because if it wasn't for his timing, we'd have four kids [instead of two]."

CHAPTER

20

THE SCOTLAND YARD CRIME MUSEUM

NOTHING TO SEE HERE

In London, on the first floor of the New Scotland Yard, officially the headquarters for the Metropolitan Police Service, there is a place you can go to learn everything you could ever want to know about the most famous crimes and criminals in Britain and all the cool old-timey ways they did their dirt, got caught, and were punished.

Actually, that's not true. You *can't* go there. Or, we should say, *you* can't go there.[1] The Scotland Yard Crime Museum, or the "Black Museum" as it has been more popularly known over the decades, is closed to the public.[2] Instead, it functions more like a private reference library for British police—a classical training tool for becoming better Sherlock Holmeses and Jane Tennisons.

Video surveillance? DNA analysis? Advanced interrogation techniques? Sure, these modern crime fighting methods are technically responsible for solving most homicide cases these days, and you can learn them *if you want*, but they won't help you as a copper or a detective inspector when you need to know from a distance what an umbrella shotgun looks like (it looks awesome, FYI), or how to tell by weight how many 8-penny common nails are inside a suitcase bomb (a lot), or know by the shape and feel of a murderer's skull whether they were born a criminal or made into one (more on this later).

For that, you gotta go old school. You gotta get your hands on some history. You gotta go to the Black Museum.

....

[1] Got it now?

[2] According to popular lore, the "Black Museum" got its name from an 1877 *Observer* article when a reporter doing a story on the place was denied entry, but it seems more likely that the name was taken from this line in the piece: "The building is, indeed, as it is called, a *Black Museum*, for it is associated with whatever is darkest in human nature."

BLACK MUSEUM: ORIGINS

The Black Museum began with the opening of the Central Prisoners Property Store in April 1874. Soon thereafter it unofficially became a museum thanks to an Inspector Percy Neame, who got the bright idea to train the Metropolitan Police's new recruits in burglary detection by putting together a selection of tools they'd taken off of convicted burglars.[3] Neame's home invasion show-and-tell must have been quite the hit, because within a year his collection of criminal artifacts would expand well beyond burglary, and the place where he displayed them would get the seal of approval as an actual museum. Its doors would soon open to British law enforcement, and for the next 100 years, as if on the lam, the museum would move several times when both the collection and its home, Met HQ, outgrew their previous spaces.

STUFF YOU SHOULD KNOW . . .
About Language

Scotland Yard is home to London's Metropolitan Police and to a crime museum that no one gets to visit, but it's something else too. It's a metonym.

A metonym is a term with its own separate meaning that is also used as a stand-in to describe something to which it is closely related. Hollywood is a section of Los Angeles, for example, but it is also a substitute term for the entertainment industry. K Street is a street in Washington DC, but it is also shorthand for the lobbying industry. Number 10 Downing Street is the address of the UK Prime Minister's official residence, but it is also a term used to describe the whole of the UK government. That makes each of these terms a metonym.

Scotland Yard is the name for the original entrance to the Metropolitan Police headquarters. When it eventually became the substitute name for the London police as a whole, it became a metonym.

---

[3] Victorian society was fascinated by seedy characters who lurked in dark corners, burglars foremost among them. They fill the pages of novels from the Victorian period as both heroes and villains alike.

While the idea for the museum began in 1874, seven years into Neame's tenure with The Met,[4] what made this particular museum possible in the first place was a piece of legislation passed by Parliament a few years earlier, called the Prisoners Property Act of 1869.

The Prisoners Property Act apparently did two things: it required police to hold onto a prisoner's property once they were convicted, then return it to them upon their release;[5] and it subsequently gave police the right to keep a prisoner's property and to use it for instructional purposes in the event that the property was abandoned by recently freed prisoners—or, as was more often the case with the property that has made its way into the Black Museum, the prisoner no longer needed their stuff because they'd been executed.

The Met's collection of crime memorabilia captured the imagination of the British public almost immediately. Too bad for the general public since they would never get a chance to look inside—the museum's contents have not been accessible for public viewing except for one single six-month joint exhibition with the Museum of London from 2015 to 2016.[6] But an odd smattering of famous people was given tours within the first thirty or forty years of the museum's existence. George V and various members of the British royal family, Harry Houdini, Laurel and Hardy, Gilbert and Sullivan, and Sir Arthur Conan Doyle—crime-crazed ghouls, every last one of them.

....

[4] Percy Neame would stay with The Met for another twenty-eight years and retire as the superintendent of the Criminal Investigation Department in 1902. That turned out to be a big year for Superintendent Neame, as he died in 1902 as well.

[5] This is what precipitated the creation of the Central Prisoners Property Store in the first place. It was not a store in the sense that it was a place where things were for sale; rather, it was a place where things were stored. The kind of place where Frank Oz returned Jake Blues's stuff when he got paroled from Joliet.

[6] The fact that this particular six-month period was the only time in history the museum allowed the public to browse a sample of its keepsakes is bad enough, but what makes it worse, at least for us, is that we performed live in London in July 2016, just three months after the exhibition closed. So out of the more than 280 six-month periods that make up the museum's entire history, it's been open for just one of those. And out of the 560 three-month periods in the museum's history, the one we show up to London for is the one that comes immediately after the single six-month period the museum's collection was on display. Cursed!

A LOOK INSIDE THE "MUSEUM"

This inaccessibility brings up an interesting question, though: like the sound of a tree falling in the forest with no one around to hear it, is a collection of stuff really a museum if no one is allowed to look at it? Doesn't the fact that only members of a specific group (British law enforcement) have access mean this place is more like an archive or, worse, some ghastly trophy case?

Maybe we're just being pedantic because we really, really, *really* want to get inside this place, and it sucks that we can't just buy tickets at the entrance and a tote bag as we exit through the gift shop. Museums aren't supposed to be private institutions of instruction (those are called schools)—they're supposed to be houses of inspiration available to *all* crime-crazed ghouls. And that's not just our opinion: it says so right there in the name!

The word *museum* is derived from the ancient Greek *mouseion*, meaning "seat of the muses." As anybody who's ever seen *Xanadu* knows, the muses were the goddesses of arts and science, the source of all knowledge,

in Greek mythology. In modern times they're thought of mostly as sources of creativity and artistic inspiration, occasionally depicted on roller skates. In a way, you could say that the museum as a concept is their physical legacy and—*dammit just let us in so we can see all the death masks!* 🎧

What's that? Death masks, you say? Oh yes, death masks. Masks o' death. Read on for more . . .

DEATH MASKS ARE COOL

Setting aside for a moment whether or not the Scotland Yard Black Museum is, in fact, a museum, what's indisputable is that the place is full of some amazingly cool and interesting things:

- A whole collection of ropes used to execute convicted murderers, complete with noose, just hanging around.

- A pair of bandits' masks, of perhaps the poorest construction of any masks ever (see the sadly accurate illustration on the opposite page), which belonged to Albert and Alfred Stratton, the first British criminals to be convicted of murder on the strength of fingerprint evidence. 🎧

- Three gallstones that were all that remained of Olive Durand-Deacon after she was murdered and dissolved in acid by John Haigh in 1949, and which helped convict Haigh.

- The personal effects of famous apprehended criminals, like an empty bottle of champagne found at the hideout of the gang who pulled off the Great Train Robbery. 🎧

- Tools of various trades, such as counterfeiters, burglars, spies, and detectives (including a forensic kit, called a "murder bag," from 1946).[7] 🎧

- An arsenal of weaponry, from knives and guns to dynamite-filled bombs and a poison-filled syringe belonging to the Kray Brothers,[8] which we guess you could call tools of the murder trade.

....

[7] Once the British got done killing Germans in WWII, they got back to killing each other.

[8] Reggie and Ronnie Kray were immortalized in the Morrissey song "The Last of the Famous International Playboys" and were played by real-life brothers Gary and Martin Kemp from the band Spandau Ballet in a British movie called *The Krays*, and also played simultaneously by Tom Hardy in a movie called *Legend*.

But coolest of all, judging from pictures at least—*since we're not allowed to go inside*—are a series of death masks belonging to some of Britain's most notorious criminals, all of them mounted high up on the walls like hunting trophies.[9]

Death masks are nothing new, to be clear. As a matter of fact, they've been around since the ancient Egyptians.[10] Initially, at least in the case of the Egyptians, they were fashioned to fit over the face of the dead as part of elaborate funeral rituals so that the soul of the deceased could recognize and rejoin its body in the afterlife.

Starting in the Middle Ages, however, death masks evolved into more literal representations of the dead. They were created shortly after death, usually with some kind of wax or plaster material applied directly to the person's face, in order to create the most accurate visage possible. Typically, they were created as molds for sculptors or for use as funeral effigies or on tombs, and over time they became valuable pieces of art in themselves.

Their real heyday, though, was the eighteenth and nineteenth centuries when *everyone* who was *anyone* had a death mask made. Sir Isaac Newton has one. 🎧 Napoleon has one. So many famous composers have death masks—Mozart, Haydn, and Schubert among them—that the Vienna Funeral Museum was able to build an entire exhibition around them in 2020 to celebrate the 250th birthday of Ludwig von Beethoven . . . who has *two* death masks.

It's not immediately clear why death masks became so popular—they were like the Hammer pants of the Romantic Age, except for your dead face instead of your dancin' legs—but their increasing use by scientists in emerging fields of study at that time almost certainly had something to do with it. It is definitely a big part of why the Black Museum's death masks are so interesting.

....

[9] While they were certainly not intended to be viewed as celebratory mementos, it's not hard to imagine British police officers touring the museum, looking up at all the death masks around them, and vigorously shaking their fists at each other (aka The British High-Five) as if to say "Huzzah ol' chap, we got the dastardly buggers!" Or something very British like that.

[10] Perhaps the world's most famous death mask is also one of the great masterpieces of Egyptian art. It is King Tutankhamun's death mask, discovered by our old friend and Egyptologist Howard Carter from chapter 3. Carter found it when he pried open the innermost of three coffins nested within the king's sarcophagus.

PHRENOLOGY:
THE SCIENCE OF THOSE BUMPS ON YOUR HEAD

There are two things (stuffs) you should know about the Black Museum's death mask collection: first, most if not all of them came from London's notorious Newgate Prison upon its closure in 1902,[11] and second, they're not actually masks. Unlike most death masks from earlier periods, which stop behind the ears, these masks are actually full 360-degree casts of the heads of executed criminals dating back to the late 1830s. They were commissioned, ostensibly, for the purpose of studying the size and shape of the skulls—a pseudoscience, though it was not considered quite so pseudo back then, called phrenology.

It's simplest to describe phrenology as the study of the mind from the outside. It involves measuring all the bumps and dents and protrusions you'll find on any given person's skull and using them as a proxy for judging the fitness or quality of various structures that comprise the brain (twenty-seven in all), each of which phrenologists believed was the seat of certain mental traits. In phrenological theory, a large bump or protrusion in one area meant the structure of the brain under that section of skull was bigger, and therefore its associated traits were more pronounced. An indentation, in contrast, usually meant a deficiency in that area of the brain. Nice and tidy and scientific-like.

Prisoners became a valuable resource for phrenologists for two reasons, one practical and one theoretical. Practically, they were an abundant, condemned, renewable population who didn't really have any choice in the matter once they were dead.[12] Theoretically, they were ripe for evaluation

---

[11] According to one of the curators at the Museum of London who organized the 2015–2016 joint exhibition with the Black Museum that we missed by a mere three months, a number of the masks were once displayed by the governor of Newgate Prison at his home. Charles Dickens even saw a couple of them when he visited the prison in 1836.

[12] This will sound eerily familiar when you get to chapter 21, because it's a version of the argument Jack Kevorkian would make 150 years later for experimenting on prisoners on death row.

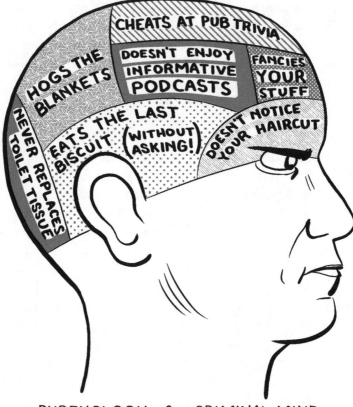

CHEATS AT PUB TRIVIA

DOESN'T ENJOY INFORMATIVE PODCASTS

FANCIES YOUR STUFF

HOGS THE BLANKETS

NEVER REPLACES TOILET TISSUE

EATS THE LAST BISCUIT (WITHOUT ASKING!)

DOESN'T NOTICE YOUR HAIRCUT

PHRENOLOGY of a CRIMINAL MIND

as a kind of control group, because they all had something in common—they were criminals. And if phrenologists (i.e., quacks) could discover some dent or bump common to all of Newgate Prison's late residents' death masks, they might be able to isolate the area of the brain responsible for antisocial, criminal behavior. Not to mention the Criminal Indentation (or the Crooks' Dent, as we've just now decided to call it)[13] might also function as a baseline for measurements related to other behaviors. Why, you could go around feeling schoolchildren's heads and lock up the ones you find with the Crooks' Dent for life—before they could carry out a single crime! Perfectly logical!

....

[13] This is an astounding amount of license we've taken here. Not only did we create a slang term, Crooks' Dent, but we made up the term it's derived from, Criminal Indentation, as well!

Now this idea that the brain has different parts that are responsible for different actions or behaviors—a concept called "localization of function"—isn't so crazy. It would ultimately be proven true in 1861 when pioneering French neurosurgeon Paul Broca[14] proved the existence of the brain's speech center. So it's pretty interesting that the guy who first proposed the very correct localization of function theory back in 1796, a German physician named Franz Joseph Gall, was also the father of the very incorrect field of phrenology—whose twenty-seven structures, their association to specific traits like the Crooks' Dent, and every bit of the skullreadery involved all turned out to be total speculative nonsense.[15]

The Scotland Yard Black Museum and phrenology have a lot in common in this way. There's only so much you can learn about what's on the inside when you can only take a look at it from the outside. No matter how sensitive the contents, if you want to know the truth, eventually you're going to need access. Hint, hint.

....

[14] Broca's area made a number of appearances earlier in SYSK episode history when we talked about things related to language. BA is a great guest star, one of the all-time class acts. Would clean up the green room while waiting, always tipped Jeri, and one time brought us all really nice watches as host gifts. We'd have BA back anytime. 🎙

[15] The product of an overactive imagination which undoubtedly resided within a part of Gall's brain that sat under a section of skull that had a big ol' knot on it.

CHAPTER

21

JACK KEVORKIAN

DR. DEATH AND THE MEANING OF LIFE

In the middle of his Emmy acceptance speech for his portrayal of Dr. Jack Kevorkian in 2010's *You Don't Know Jack*, Al Pacino looked out into the audience and acknowledged his subject. It was a rare and pure Hollywood-meets-real-world moment.[1]

The actor showered the man with kindness in a way he had rarely, if ever, received. Usually, if Kevorkian was being addressed in a public forum about his unpopular ideas, it was with rage, ridicule, and contempt. One can only imagine that for the controversial doctor known best for a theatrical euthanasia crusade that ended in public humiliation, being called "brilliant and interesting and unique" by one of the most celebrated stars of his generation must have been the delight of his twilight.

The irony of that moment and, really, of Kevorkian's fame (or infamy), is that nothing about the first sixty years of his life foreshadowed the late bloom that briefly turned him into a household name.

Not that he didn't try.

THE WONDER (WHAT HE WAS THINKING) YEARS

As a kid, Lil' Jack Kevorkian showed he was different from the other boys: his claim to have taught himself German and Japanese to prepare for World War II service is a good example.[2] Another good example came a little later with Kevorkian's first attempt at making his mark on the medical establishment in a 1956 journal article titled "The Fundus Oculi and

---

[1] The rawness of this Oscar moment is upstaged perhaps only by Dustin Hoffman's acceptance speech at the 1970 ceremony where he brought the real Ratso Rizzo on stage to perform an a capella "MacArthur Park" together.

[2] The war ended before he turned eighteen.

the Determination of Death." It would be interesting just for its potential as a band name, but as a piece of research is utterly fascinating. The paper makes the claim that photographs of the eyes of the dying can help doctors pinpoint the exact moment of death, which would come in handy to determine when to stop costly resuscitation efforts.[3] He admitted later he'd written that first paper because it was interesting and taboo.

Rather than awards and praise, the article earned young Jack, who was still only a resident at the University of Michigan Hospital, the nickname that would follow him for the rest of his days: Dr. Death. It was a fitting name that he would grow into over the years.

Undaunted, Kevorkian pressed on with his end-of-life fixation. In 1958, he presented a paper titled "Capital Punishment or Capital Gain" at a meeting of the American Association for the Advancement of Science (AAAS) in which he proposed that prisoners on death row be given the right to donate their bodies to science beginning *with* the moment of death. Kevorkian suggested that, rather than dying by the chair or the gas chamber, a prisoner would be anesthetized at the moment of their sentenced execution, and some sort of medical or surgical experiment would be performed that would result in the patient/prisoner/subject's death. What kind of experiment? The sky was the limit in Kevorkian's thinking.

Because of the uniqueness of this opportunity, Kevorkian said, the experiments should be "extremely imaginative," they should be done more than one at a time, and they should deal with things that are "uninvestigable" under normal circumstances—hopefully something better than "What Happens When I Squeeze This Spleen?" Kevorkian wrote that human beings are both "the ultimate laboratory" for medical testing and the "most difficult . . . 'guinea pig'" to get your hands on as a researcher, and this population of condemned prisoners represented a pool of subjects they could draw from while not violating any laws. He suggested expanding the effort to all the world's prison systems and routing candidates through a central institution like the United Nations.

....

[3] Unsurprisingly, there is no *House* episode about this little diagnostic trick. And if you've listened to our episode "How Organ Donation Works," you know that dying is an extensive process of turning out the lights and that we still have no sure clue exactly when a person is fully dead. Like dead, dead. 🎙

To anyone whose outlook does not include much preciousness about death, the body, or an afterlife, it is a clear and obvious "win-win." You'd get more scientific breakthroughs at lower costs, using expendable research subjects who were going to die anyway but got to choose how they went.[4] If that sounds a touch too far down the Mengelian side of things for you, you would not be alone. The AAAS rejected Kevorkian's ideas, and for a second time he faced ridicule rather than acceptance. The whole affair led the University of Michigan to ask him to hand in his maize-and-blue lab coat and finish his residency elsewhere.[5]

So began the good doctor's somewhat nomadic medical career. For the next fifteen years, he moved from hospital to hospital, working chiefly in pathology, which was frankly perfect for Kevorkian, since fiddling with dead stuff is part of the pathologist's job description. He continued to publish articles and books on his death row concept, while also introducing a third death-infused idea: blood transfusion from the dead to the living.

Kevorkian pursued this idea while completing his internship at Pontiac General Hospital in his hometown of Pontiac, Michigan, where he landed after the University of Michigan showed him the door. He had read about successful cadaver blood transfusions conducted by Russian scientists as far back as the 1930s and he was determined to recreate them. Astoundingly, he did. In the spirit of other pioneering researchers who used themselves as guinea pigs, 🔊 he did much of the early transfusion experimentation on himself as well as other willing hospital staff, and the work showed promise.

This time, when he wrote up his ideas for publication—they landed in the journal *Military Medicine* in early 1964—he somehow managed not to creep out everyone who read about them, and ultimately found himself at the Pentagon, pitching the idea for transferring blood from soldiers who had just died on the battlefield to their injured comrades.[6] Kevorkian thought the idea would appeal to military planners, what with the Vietnam

---

[4] "Oooh, I'll take the Re-Animator Special, please!"

[5'] In this case, Kevorkian published *and* perished.

[6] We can imagine Kevorkian making his pitch to the Pentagon brass: "You just tilt the dead soldier upside down at a 30-degree angle, y'see, and then you put a needle into his carotid artery, right? And the blood just comes right out, y'see. Just gotta do it within six hours of death or else it gets a bit putrid. And you don't want that! Mmmmwhahahahaha."

War beginning to intensify. The Defense Department rejected the idea, however—one assumes because while they wanted their fighting men and women to be all that they could be, that did not include becoming battlefield ghouls, field stripping the dead of their vital fluids. To make matters worse for Kevorkian, the DoD also rejected his research grant request outright, declining to fund a study. Poor Jack; when it was all said and done, the only thing he had to show for his work was hepatitis C, which he'd contracted as one of the participants in his own study.

FINDING HIS FOOTING

Hep C was just the first of a string of setbacks Jack Kevorkian endured through the 1970s and early 1980s. It was a dark time for a dark guy. He moved to Southern California to take a couple of part-time pathology gigs, but quickly lost them due to fights with chief pathologists (aka his bosses). He managed to get engaged but ended up breaking it off. He quit medicine to dedicate himself to painting macabre portraits,[7] playing Bach on his cello, and spending his life savings on producing a film based on German composer Handel's *Messiah*[8]—which, in the halcyon days of disco, was doomed to be a box office bomb. To support himself, he published articles in fringey European magazines and journals, but eventually he found himself sometimes sleeping in his van, living off of canned goods and social security checks.[9]

Kevorkian finally caught a break in 1984 with a nationwide spike in executions. The California legislature invited him to speak on a bill to give death row prisoners the choice of dying by poison gas or the electric chair, as was standard at the time, or receiving anesthesia and having their organs donated to science.[10] The bill failed, but the media attention energized Kevorkian and he moved back to Michigan the following year to write a history of experiments on executed people (you know, just a little light reading), which was published in 1985 in the obscure *Journal of the National Medical Association*, which sounds made-up but is real. It was also around then that he decided to launch his campaign to euthanize the terminally ill and use their organs to benefit the living. You might not be shocked to learn

---

[7] Including flying llamas, ironically (see chapter 13).

[8] Don't bother; it's not on IMDB and the film seems to be lost to history. In an old interview, *The Los Angeles Times* (go, contemporary journalism!) mentions that it was never shown.

[9] Thanks again, Frances Perkins.

[10] Just to be clear, unlike Jack's earlier focus on experimentation with prisoners, what the state was considering (and Kevorkian endorsed) was execution by organ removal. The sentenced prisoner would go under anesthesia in the operating room, and their organs would be removed and donated to others who needed them. When the procedure was complete, their life would have been ended by a simple lack of the necessary parts needed to live. They'd go under and just wouldn't wake up. Morally speaking it's essentially the same thing (and, you could argue, more moral) as lethal injection, except with lethal injection the prisoner dies of poisoning, not from missing vital organs.

that this wasn't a simple proposition. It turns out that trying to persuade a dying person to sign their body parts over to science just doesn't go over very well; they tend to have other stuff on their minds. Kevorkian was persuaded to abandon this aspect of his efforts accordingly.

STUFF YOU SHOULD KNOW...
About Language

Despite what the phonetically inclined might tell you, *euthanasia* has nothing to do with Chinese children. It is an Ancient Greek word whose etymology is *eu-*, a prefix meaning "goodly" or "well," and *thanatos*, meaning "death." Euthanasia literally means "a good death." That's why it was so hard for Kevorkian's opponents to make headway against him. He wasn't helping his patients die for kicks or as punishment; he was trying to offer them a *good death*. Which stood in stark opposition to the deaths many others with conditions similar to his patients had been forced to endure, in Kevorkian's estimation, through Westernized medicine.

It was around this time that the public debate over *euthanasia,* or "dying with dignity," began to heat up. In 1980, the Hemlock Society formed to advocate for assisted suicide, and Pope John Paul II issued a decree condemning the idea. Elsewhere in the decade, the American Medical Association, the California State Bar, and the Universalist Unitarian Church all came out in some form of support for the right to die. By the early '90s more than half of Americans were generally okay with the idea of physician-assisted suicide. It was a topic that Kevorkian was naturally drawn to and a debate he quickly joined. Conveniently, it also gave him a place to direct his death-related energy that had been continually thwarted over the previous twenty-five years. The world was ready to talk about letting the dying and the doomed control how and when they died; they just weren't as excited as Kevorkian had always been about the prospect of turning them into the human equivalent of a pick-and-pull junkyard for the living.[11] Once Kevorkian realized that, he pivoted his focus to assisting those who were suffering with debilitating illnesses like cancer, multiple sclerosis, Alzheimer's, and ALS, without regard to the value of their remaining organs. He was off to the races.

He began by promoting himself in Detroit papers as a "physician consultant" for "death counseling." The response was nil to zero. Kevorkian found no takers until after he made his first big splash on the national stage by appearing in April 1990 on *Phil Donahue*, the pioneering daytime tabloid talk show of its time. The parts of Jack Kevorkian that drove him to seek the spotlight were on full display: he was outlandish, smitten with his own cleverness, and clearly didn't care what the public thought of him. Kevorkian made for great television. But as *Donahue*-ready as he was, it was the Thanatron, a makeshift suicide contraption he brought with him, that stole the show.

Perhaps even more grim than the machine's purpose was the fact that his new "death machine" was constructed from spare parts that he purchased at flea markets and garage sales for $30. It was despair assembled. The Thanatron held three liquid substances, which were each connected to a needle that would inject the liquids into a person's arm. Upon inserting the needle, the first substance, a harmless saline solution, would begin to enter their body. Only after the patient pressed the switch did the coma-inducing thiopental get released. Sixty seconds later the third liquid, a deadly dose of potassium chloride spiked with a muscle relaxer to prevent those unsightly convulsions, stopped the heart.

"It's really the way executions are carried out by lethal injection," a matter-of-fact Jack explained to a faux-flabbergasted Donahue,[12] "except this is self-execution."

Self-execution? Yeesh. Work on your messaging there a little bit, huh fella? Although he was emerging from a downtrodden chrysalis to

---

[11] His efforts with death row inmate experimentation earned that proposal the name, "Death Row Organ Harvest." While yet another fantastic band name (probably speed metal), it was not the kind of title that gave policymakers the warm fuzzies when they evaluated the program.

[12] There is no one who could do faux-flabbergasted like Phil Donahue; he was the master of the method. Try it sometime—it's really hard to do without cracking yourself up. In fact, try it next time you are served dinner at home or a restaurant and see if you can pull it off.

transform into a media darling, Kevorkian himself hadn't changed much; he clearly still had one foot in that old world of death row inmate experiments that had piqued his fascination with death as a scientist.[13] Nonetheless, at sixty-two years old, Dr. Death had finally found his true calling.

THEY DON'T KNOW JACK

Two months after *Donahue*, Jack oversaw the death of his first patient—a woman named Janet Adkins from Portland, Oregon who suffered from Alzheimer's disease. The procedure, if that is even the right term for it, occurred in one of the sketchiest places possible: at a park in Michigan in the back of Jack's 1968 Volkswagen van. Nothing good has ever happened in the back of a van in the woods. Kevorkian understood this in the moment, as he told a writer for *Vanity Fair* in a huge profile a year later: "I didn't want to do it in a van," he said. "Anything. Anything but the van." Except no one would help him. Funeral homes, hotels and motels, private residences— they all turned him away.

As a result, he tried to talk Janet out of going through with the assisted suicide, because without a third party present there'd be no witnesses,[14] which would more greatly expose him to criminal prosecution. But Janet's suffering was so complete that she insisted, according to Kevorkian, which put him in the position of having to choose between his fate and hers. "She was so distraught," he told *Vanity Fair*, "I decided I had to do it anyway. For the patient. That's what a doctor is for. To hell with the goddanged ethicists."[15]

....

[13] Jack Kevorkian puts us in mind of the old eighteenth and nineteenth-century teaching physicians in the British Isles and America who purchased stolen cadavers from grave robbers. We covered them in our live episode on "The Golden Age of Grave Robbing." Kevorkian totally would have bought stolen bodies to conduct research on had he lived in that era, say we. 🛜

[14] Not enough room in the van for three, apparently.

[15] Language, Dr. Kevorkian, language!

The government responded swiftly but futilely, because the law wasn't totally on their side. And even when it was, Kevorkian didn't care. Prosecutors charged him with the murder of Janet Adkins, but a judge dismissed the charge because Michigan had no law against assisted suicide. Another judge then issued an injunction forbidding Kevorkian from helping patients kill themselves. Citing the legal principle *Nulla poena sine lege* (Latin for "no penalty without a law"), Kevorkian defied the order by assisting another person in their suicide. When the Michigan Board of Medicine suspended his license so he could no longer get his death cocktail, Dr. Death just shrugged. He had already built his second device, the Mercitron, which didn't use those chemicals, and which he first tried out on a forty-three-year-old woman suffering from multiple sclerosis.

Dubbed the "mercy machine," the Mercitron relied on carbon monoxide rather than potassium chloride. Kevorkian kept the CO in cylinders in the back of his van, where most of the early procedures ended up happening (despite his initial trepidation). He would first encourage his patient to take a muscle relaxer to calm the body and numb any pain. Then he would place a mask over the patient's nose and mouth and instruct them to inhale deeply. Finally, he would hand them a clothespin attached to the canister and leave it to them to open the valve. The patient typically joined the departed within ten minutes, give or take.

The press couldn't get enough of Jack Kevorkian. He appeared on the cover of *Time*. Peter Jennings interviewed him on *Nightly News*. Barbara Walters was photographed with him wearing the Mercitron mask. Some people loved him, and other people hated him, but everybody had an opinion about him. For a moment, Jack Kevorkian was one of the most recognizable figures in the country,[16] and at every turn he used his platform to bludgeon the profession that had shunned him for so many years. In his view, the medical field had failed to defend what he considered a person's "last civil right." Denying the terminally ill a dignified death, he said, was no better than Nazi doctors torturing Holocaust victims. (Yep, he went there.)

....

[16] Like, Gorby-level famous. (Look it up, younger readers.)

THE TRIALS OF JACK

NBA legend Shaquille O'Neal often brags that the league changed its rules because of his dominance. It was quite the accomplishment, forcing a fifty-five-year-old league to change its rules just to stop him, but it was nowhere near as impressive as what Kevorkian did. He got Michigan, a 156-year-old state, to create an entire law just to stop *him*. In 1993, the state passed an assisted suicide ban for the sole purpose of stopping (and some hoped, putting behind bars), a small, frail senior citizen who worked out of a van, ate out of a can, and wore mostly secondhand clothes from Goodwill.

At Kevorkian's first trial, his lawyers argued that he had acted to relieve suffering, not aid suicide. It was an artful linguistic dodge of the statutory language. And the jury bought it; Jack was acquitted.[17] His second trial ended in victory as well. He was two for two.

For trial number three, Kevorkian arrived in a colonial costume to protest the 1993 common law statute against assisted suicide under which he was being tried. His attorneys argued that their client couldn't be tried for a law that hadn't been written down. Common law, they pointed out, isn't "law" as much as it is a set of English traditions and legal precedents that form the foundation of modern US law. It's the legal equivalent of using the width of your hand to measure the height of a horse.[18] Under this view, Kevorkian's lawyers said that not only did he not *intend* to kill his patients, he had no way of knowing what he was doing was a crime. *Nulla poena sine lege.*

The jury agreed, and he was three for three. Rather than bring him to justice, the first three trials brightened the spotlight on him and widened the stage Kevorkian craved to trod.

He had worked out a selection process for mercy machine candidates that he was happy to share with the press and prosecutors: a patient may want to end their suffering, but he had to determine whether that wish was medically justified. "The two must coincide: the wish of the patient and the

---

[17] A month later the state's court of appeals struck the ban under which he was charged as unlawful.

[18] Good rule of thumb: don't use body parts to measure important things.

212

medical justification." He could show that he denied the vast majority—97 percent, he once claimed—of the requests he received. He could prove that he never charged anyone a single penny for his services, and he had the crappy clothes as evidence.

Most important, Kevorkian's lawyers could press play on the home videos he shot with his patients and their loved ones in the days before he assisted them in taking their own lives. Jurors could never convict once they saw and heard the clarity and conviction of dear ol' Jack's patients with their own eyes and ears.

BREAKING THE CODE

Al Pacino made his career playing antiheroes who live by a code, a higher truth. Serpico, Michael Corleone, Carlito Brigante, Jack Kevorkian.

And Kevorkian's code protected him—until he broke it. And boy, did he break it.

After the third trial came a fourth that ended in a mistrial and was later dismissed. At that moment—June 1997—Jack Kevorkian had arguably won the battle of attrition. Voters in Oregon, the state his first patient traveled from for her appointment with him, had passed the nation's first Death with Dignity law. Studies were showing that more doctors supported assisted suicide than didn't. The federal appeals court in California ruled that the terminally ill had a constitutional right to aid in dying from doctors. And in Michigan, Kevorkian had hammered out a detente with local prosecutors: they would leave him alone to do his work (kill, kill, kill!) as long as he didn't make a big stink about it. In a little over a year Kevorkian assisted with more deaths (56) than he had in the previous six years combined (52).

But then Michigan passed a new ban that closed the loophole that Kevorkian had exploited: the one that allowed for medical procedures intended to relieve suffering, even if they resulted in death. A pro-euthanasia ballot measure would have superseded it, but the people of Michigan voted against it.

This set the stage for the downfall of Dr. Death.

Hoping to argue, once and for all, the legality of assisted suicide in open court, he sent a now infamous tape to *60 Minutes*. It showed Jack Kevorkian injecting deadly drugs into the arm of Thomas Youk, a patient suffering with ALS. This was a very big deal; to some he may as well have strangled Mr. Youk in the video. Over the previous ten years or so, Jack Kevorkian had come to believe that the line between a patient doing the final deed and him doing it for them was both arbitrary and capricious. The line wasn't based in logic or sound science or even morality. Still, he knew the line existed and that he had definitely crossed it according to the letter of well-established law.

As he expected, Kevorkian was charged with murder and assisted suicide under the new law. What he didn't expect was that the prosecution would toss the assisted suicide charge. This was huge. By charging him only with murder, there was no lesser charge that a jury could go with. It also rendered patient and family consent—his talisman that had protected him all this time—irrelevant. You simply cannot consent to murder.

Undaunted, and convinced that no lawyer could address the jury the way he could, Kevorkian represented himself *pro se*. This move has worked maybe once in the entire twenty-season run of *Law & Order*, which should tell you exactly how bad an idea it was. Jack Kevorkian was convicted of second-degree murder and handed a sentence of ten to twenty-five years in prison, of which he served eight. He was mercifully released on the condition he give up his assisted suicide trade because by then his hep C was terminal.[19] He spent his remaining time giving talks and writing. A little over a year after *You Don't Know Jack* premiered, he died from pulmonary thrombosis. In lay terms, blood clotting killed him.[20]

The exact number of people that Jack Kevorkian helped die is disputed. Depending on where you look, it ranges anywhere from 110 to 130. Given the relatively short period in which he was active and how much of it he spent on trial, that's either impressive or disturbing, or impressively disturbing. Either way, his van was super busy for a while there.

....

[19] Done in by his own experiments on the dead; if there isn't a special word for that sort of irony, someone needs to call the people at the dictionary.

[20] As for his van, it came into the possession of a Detroit pawnbroker who sold it to ghost hunter Zak Bagans for a little over $30,000 in 2015.

Jack Kevorkian remains a polarizing (if not nauseating, for some) figure. His supporters insist that his flaws notwithstanding, he changed society for the better. He forced America to talk about the idea of a good death and the right to die with dignity. His detractors say that at best he was the wrong face of the right cause. Be that as it may, Washington, Montana, Vermont, New Jersey, Hawaii, D.C., California, Colorado, and Oregon have all either passed Death with Dignity laws or made it legal under court ruling—and you can chalk up at least some of the credit for that to Jack Kevorkian.

Michigan, his home state and where all of his deaths took place, still has a ban.

CHAPTER

22

WELL-
WITCHING

THE ANCIENT ART OF
GUESSING WITH A STICK

Every March in Tanzania, 1.5 million wildebeest, along with another half-million zebras and antelopes, begin tracing an invisible 1,800-mile elliptical circuit that moves clockwise from the southern Serengeti, northwesterly through the Upper Grumeti River woodlands, into Kenya's Masai Mara and back again, following the rains in pursuit of fresh grasslands.

At some point in spring a few wildebeest simply get up and start walking. A couple million animals just sort of agree now's as good a time as any and start following the leaders. A few months later, in June and July, at the start of the dry season, the herds of African savannah elephants who share the region with the wildebeests begin their long, ever-shifting treks in search of more reliable sources of water and abundant vegetation.[1]

These annual migrations 📶 have likely been going on for millions of years and the whole thing has a certain mystical quality to it. It's possible the traveling wildebeests begin their trek based on changing levels of phosphorus and nitrogen in the grass that vary with the wet or dry seasons. Or maybe it's just a million years of survival instinct coded into their DNA. Elephant herds, for their part, rely on the remarkable memories of their matriarchs to get moving, as well as an intricate set of senses and behaviors (vibrations, touch, chemical secretions, specific gestures) to pass along information to the rest of the herd about where they're headed.[2] And while

....

[1] While all the wildebeest in East Africa tend to migrate, not all savannah elephants do. A 2018 study revealed that only 25% of elephants reliably migrate. The rest kind of do whatever they want, which we suppose is to be expected from the largest land mammal on Earth.

[2] Elephants don't only know where to go, they know where *not* to go. They can carry mental "Do Not Enter" signs attached to specific locations for generations, only to take those signs down when the coast is clear, even though the elephants who first sensed the danger are long dead. As you may already know from our episode, "Elephants: The Best Animals?," elephants are incredible. 📶

scientists haven't pinpointed exactly how these migrations occur or what triggers them to start, what they do know (or at least suspect) is that there are a number of deeply ingrained evolutionary processes at work, all guiding the animals' fundamental search for water.

Then there's us (humans). We've been around for 200,000 years—50,000 if you're only counting modern humans like you and me—and we have an evolutionary lineage that stretches millions of years farther back than that. And yet, for at least the last 8,000 of those years, when we've gone searching for water during droughts and dry seasons we haven't relied on evolutionary instinct, or heightened olfactory ability, or a finely tuned taste for phosphorus, or sounds or scratching or touch. We've just used a stick.

Locating groundwater with a stick has been given different names over the centuries: water-finding, water-dowsing, water-witching, willow-witching, well-witching.[3] So much witching. But whatever the name, the practice is, at its core, a process of divination whereby the holder of the stick *divines* the location of an underground water source based solely on the movement of the stick in their hands as they walk the land.

H₂OVER THERE!

Here's how the process is traditionally supposed to work. First, an aspiring well-witcher cuts a branch from a tree.[4] Not just any branch, but one that is naturally forked in a "Y" shape, with each of the three segments ideally measuring between twelve and sixteen inches, then trimmed of smaller twigs and leaves so that the stem of the Y is as smooth as possible. Now the limb is no longer a useless branch but a dowsing rod, ready to find water for its maker.

The well-witcher then grabs the forked ends of the dowsing rod with a loose under-handed grip, like they're doing a biceps curl with the handle of a push mower, and holds the rod parallel to the ground as they walk slowly

---

[3] Not quite as many synonyms as there are for taxation or sub sandwiches, like we saw in chapter 9, but more than you might expect for something that, spoiler alert, doesn't actually seem to be real.

[4] It doesn't appear to matter what kind of tree the branch comes from, but willow trees, witch hazel, and fruit trees, particularly peach trees, seem to be the most popular. Willows certainly make sense because their presence indicates an underground water source is nearby and relatively near the surface. Or it could just be that they're popular because they're very pretty.

across the terrain, visualizing the water beneath its surface. According to the *Farmers' Almanac*, maintaining a loose grip is an important part of the dowsing process because as you approach water the rod will begin to bend toward the earth, so you need to give it enough slack to do that. But not too much! When you get really close, the rod will bend sharply, and you want to maintain control of it . . . for reasons that are not at all clear.

If this sounds like a bit of an inexact science, that's because it isn't exactly science. Like phrenology, it is considered a pseudoscience by many. Other, less charitable types prefer the more technical term "total nonsense." For instance, The National Ground Water Association, or the NGWA as it's known by all the cool kids in hydrology class, opposes the use of "water witches" because "controlled experimental evidence clearly indicates that the technique is totally without scientific merit." Well, okay then, when you put it like *that*.

THE DURABILITY OF DOWSING

Except it's not quite that simple. Water-witching, or dowsing, which is the more general term for the practice, has been around for thousands of years, spanning the entire known world. It's depicted in cave paintings in the Sahara Desert that date back to at least 6000 BCE. Prehistoric Peruvian peoples did it. The Egyptians were doing it in 3000 BCE, and Moses and the Hebrews were doing it a thousand years after that as they fled from Egypt. In between, it showed up on the statue of a Chinese emperor and in the writings of Confucius. Over the next 2,000 years it made an appearance in Homer's epic poem *The Odyssey* as "the caduceus"[5]; on the isle of Crete and

---

[5] The caduceus is the familiar symbol of two snakes intertwined around a staff, with wings at the top, which tends to be (incorrectly) associated with doctors. The caduceus isn't the symbol for doctors, it's the symbol of the god Mercury, or Hermes, the messenger, who also happens to be the patron god of thieves and outlaws, not doctors. The correct symbol for doctors is the Rod of Asclepius, who was the Greek god of physicians and whose symbol is a single snake coiled around a rod, no wings (see our fancy modified illustration back in chapter 21 about Jack Kevorkian). The two seem to have gotten mixed up somewhere along the way. So the next time you notice your doctor using the caduceus instead of the Rod of Asclepius, you might want to take it as a sign that you should get a second opinion.

with the Oracle of Delphi; and in Ancient Rome, where Cicero wrote about the use of a dowsing rod, which he called a *virgula divinatorium*. In the sixth century, the Indian mathemetician Varahamihira included all sorts of information about "water divining" in his Sanskrit encyclopedia, *Brihat Samhita*. By the middle of the sixteenth century, dowsing had made its way fully across Europe, drawing the attention of religious figures like Martin Luther, who insisted it was the work of the Devil.

That kind of spiritual castigation did little to slow the practice or popularity of water-witching, however, which should surprise no one who has ever watched *Footloose*. In the twentieth century, dowsing was studied intently by the English and the Germans, and in the Soviet Union, where it was called "biophysical locating," and you could actually get a degree in it.[6] Today, dowsing does not get that kind of official institutional recognition but there are still plenty of dowsing societies all over the world. The biggest of them all, The American Society of Dowsers, has more than seventy-five local chapters. As far as we know, none of them are affiliated with the Devil.

One of the big reasons dowsing seems to have endured throughout history is that it doesn't just apply to water. It's also been used for hundreds, sometimes thousands, of years to find other valuable things buried in the ground: precious metals like gold, minerals and gemstones, oil and natural gas foremost among them.[7] In the first century BCE, for example, legend has it that Cleopatra brought dowsers with her whenever she traveled so they could search for gold wherever she went. The Germans were among the first to dowse for minerals as far back as the 1400s and an illustration of mineral dowsing appears in *De Re Metallica*, the awesome title to Georgius Agricola's seminal text on mining and metallurgy that was published in 1556.[8]

....

[6] The Soviets believed in "bioenergetics," which was the term they used to describe the energy emitted by all living things through normal metabolic processes. This not only explained what dowsing was detecting but also formed part of the foundation of Soviet research into the paranormal during the Cold War.

[7] As we talked about in our episode on Project Stargate, the self-proclaimed clairvoyant and telekinetic Uri Geller has made quite a bit of money as a consultant hired by oil and mineral companies to find deposits by dowsing. Dowsing for oil in particular has its own name—doodlebugging—coined by Americans, because next to Australians only Americans can come up with words and phrases that give you no clue about the things they describe.

[8] This is not, by the by, where the band Metallica gets its name. That came from a guy named Ron Quintana, who drummer Lars Ulrich met at a keg party in San Francisco in 1981. Quintana asked Ulrich which name he thought would be best for a new metal fanzine Quintana was creating—MetalMania or Metallica. Ulrich told Quintanta to go with MetalMania, and then used Metallica himself.

Tools of the Dowsing Trade

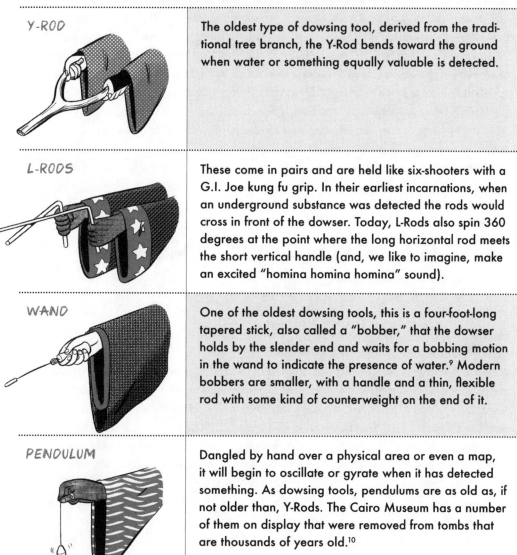

Y-ROD

The oldest type of dowsing tool, derived from the traditional tree branch, the Y-Rod bends toward the ground when water or something equally valuable is detected.

L-RODS

These come in pairs and are held like six-shooters with a G.I. Joe kung fu grip. In their earliest incarnations, when an underground substance was detected the rods would cross in front of the dowser. Today, L-Rods also spin 360 degrees at the point where the long horizontal rod meets the short vertical handle (and, we like to imagine, make an excited "homina homina homina" sound).

WAND

One of the oldest dowsing tools, this is a four-foot-long tapered stick, also called a "bobber," that the dowser holds by the slender end and waits for a bobbing motion in the wand to indicate the presence of water.[9] Modern bobbers are smaller, with a handle and a thin, flexible rod with some kind of counterweight on the end of it.

PENDULUM

Dangled by hand over a physical area or even a map, it will begin to oscillate or gyrate when it has detected something. As dowsing tools, pendulums are as old as, if not older than, Y-Rods. The Cairo Museum has a number of them on display that were removed from tombs that are thousands of years old.[10]

---

[9] Egyptian hieroglyphs describe a magic wand of sorts, called Ur-Heka, that was also used for dowsing and which translated to "great magical power (that) makes water to come forth."

[10] Camping beds, death masks, now dowsing pendulums. These ancient Egyptian tombs can hold almost as much stuff as Mr. Potato Head's butt.

That type and level of interest continues to the present day and has extended beyond what is buried to include what has gone missing—wallets, keys, planes, and ships. There is a big market for custom dowsing rods designed specifically for finding ~~suckers~~ all manner of buried treasure and lost items. In America there's a market for dowsing expertise among miners, prospectors, ranchers, and farmers who can't afford the more accurate (and much more expensive) geological surveys or test drilling that organizations like the NGWA recommend. Which probably helps explain why the NGWA felt the need to come out against dowsing with both water guns blazing: dowsers are their competition. When money's tight, resources are scarce, and time is of the essence, the impulse is to get on the horn and call the guy with the biggest dowsing rod around.

WHAT'S REALLY (NOT) GOING ON?

Something like dowsing doesn't persist across the millennia or spread around the world unless there's something to it. If it were total nonsense, someone would have definitively disproved it by now, we'd have all had a good laugh, and it would become one of those little oddities from history that ends up as a *Jeopardy!* clue.[11] Like how we used to believe the sun revolved around the Earth, or that the speed and movement from riding on trains could cause people to go insane,[12] or that red meat and cigarettes were good for you. You'd think that's the conventional thinking anyway.

Alas, you'd be wrong, because here we are, knee-deep in the twenty-first century, with seventy-five separate dowsing clubs in the United States and an entire international network beyond them, all totally unaffiliated with the Devil and all ready to point us in the right direction toward water, wallets, or any manner of desirable things.

....

[11] Or as a chapter in a book about random stuff you should know about.

[12] The Victorian belief in "railway madness" was helped along by reports of agitated people removing their clothes, fighting with other passengers, and trashing passenger compartments, only to fully regain themselves when the train stopped once again.

The issue is that the persistence of dowsing's existence does not controvert scientific standards, which have definitively disproved the effectiveness of dowsing for a number of decades now, as far back as the 1870s. According to numerous controlled studies since then, in fact, dowsers are no better than chance at detecting anything in the ground no matter what it is. And it's not exactly hard to find water hidden beneath the ground. Something like 90 percent of Earth's surface has groundwater beneath it and the NGWA says that the groundwater hidden out of view beneath the Earth's surface is 60 times more plentiful than surface freshwater deposits. Indeed, the last remaining bit of the mystery of dowsing—why a dowsing rod or a bobber or a pendulum moves in the hands of a dowser—can be explained not by what's in the ground, but rather what's in the dowser's mind.

In psychological terms, this is called the "ideomotor effect." Normal neurological behavior, unconscious mental activity, and subconscious thoughts are all known to be capable of producing subtle but perceptible muscular reactions in a person's body that make it seem like whatever is in their hands at that moment is moving on its own, or in response to something outside their control.[13] The vast majority of dowsers honestly believe they are not moving the dowsing tool in their hands, and consciously they are not wrong. The mind can have a mind of its own sometimes.

Ironically, that is exactly the argument a dowser would make in support of dowsing's legitimacy. It's not actually about the rod or the wand or the pendulum, they will say, but the power of the human body to perceive and respond to the buried or missing material being sought. The rod is just an outward "indicator" that the person holding it has found something . . . with their mind. It's the ideomotor effect in reverse. Or thrown back in your face, depending on your perspective.

Some dowsers believe all humans possess a kind of dowsing sixth sense that can be homed in on and sharpened with practice. Others have described a "dowsing reflex mechanism" that, it seems, has been tracked physiologically through brain waves by at least two researchers using EEGs when it's in action. Here's how research on this phenomenon by an American doctor named Edith Jurka in the 1980s was described in the updated third edition of *The Essential Dowsing Guide,* published in 2013:

[13] Yes, this is the phenomenon behind the "effectiveness" of Ouija boards as well. 🜨

> When in the dowsing mode, the brainwave beta frequency of the
> thinking state lowers in frequency to the alpha state, which is a
> meditative state. When a dowsing target is found, there is a burst of
> the lower frequency theta state of around four to seven cycles per
> second, which corresponds to brainwave activity in dreaming sleep.

According to this idea, dowsing arises from a state of being entranced. Or as Edward Stillman, the scientific advisor to the American Dowsing Society, put it: "Dowsing appears to be a truly unique and creative altered state of human consciousness." One that requires us to abandon logic-dominated left brain thinking and to engage with the intuitive right brain as much as possible so we might achieve that "contemplative alpha state."

What would our right brains be intuiting in this contemplative state? Well, in the case of water, at least, possibly the electromagnetic field and radio waves emitted by underground water running faster than two miles per hour.[14] According to a British researcher named Alf Riggs, as the water passes through rock and sediment, it produces a "positive vertical electrical field," a "DC magnetic field," various radio frequencies, and both high-energy and ultrashort waves. This, the author of *The Essential Dowsing Guide* suggests, might be what some of the best dowsers and well-witchers are perceiving, and thus what their dowsing rods are responding to when they bend toward the earth, bob up and down, gyrate in a circle, or cross in front of them.

WHERE WE GO FROM HERE

Regular listeners of *Stuff You Should Know* may recognize that we seem to have traipsed pretty far into Rupert Sheldrake territory by this point.[15]

---

[14] This is like the Soviet idea of bioenergetics but extended to all matter, not just living things.

[15] After our episode, "How Morphic Fields Work?," 🎙 the classically trained but fringe scientist Rupert Sheldrake has become SYSK shorthand for pseudoscientific stuff that sounds fairly convincing but upon closer inspection does not have any basis in current scientific understanding. This is not to say it's necessarily bunk, just that it *may* be bunk (probably is bunk). It is worth saying that we love minds like Rupert Sheldrake's; they make the world interesting and push science to look into areas outside its comfort zone. And we are critical of blind scientific fundamentalism and dogma too, but we also tend to put stock in peer review and the scientific method. 🎙

The idea that deposits of water can create disturbances within Earth's magnetic field certainly seems plausible.[16] And there are such things as alpha, beta, and theta brain waves. Perhaps most of all, the idea that humans have some innate sense that can pick up on these disturbances, which we can use to find water hidden underground, is an attractive one. It has a certain sensibility; like the wildebeests, we too are products of natural selection, so a sense like that would have contributed greatly to our survival as a species earlier in our evolutionary history. (Using that same sense to locate a lost wallet seems slightly more farfetched.)

But as far as we can tell no one's managed to successfully show in any reliable, repeatable way that humans—or even just *some* humans—have any kind of innate sense that would make us capable of dowsing. And almost all of the studies that have been done have shown the opposite, that it does not seem to be a sense that humans possess.

Still, this one captured our imagination and we don't feel good about poo-pooing it at this point. Perhaps the studies carried out thus far have been flawed in some way we aren't yet aware of. And it's become pretty clear that we have senses far more numerous than the standard five—who's to say we won't discover a sense for groundwater? Not us.

Maybe we should just let Occam and his trusty razor cut through the confusion instead. 🛈 He usually has the simplest explanation, and it's almost always the right one. Or maybe we should look to the wildebeest and the savannah elephant of Africa, take to heart their ancient evolutionary wisdom and, in the words of Atlanta's own TLC, stick to the rivers and lakes that we're used to. The trick is to still keep our minds open to finding hiddens ones we haven't discovered yet.

---

[16] We found a cool paper from 1971 called "The Detection of Magnetic Fields Caused by Groundwater," by Utah State University's Duane G. Chadwick and Larry Jensen, that explains how it might work, but we didn't see much else on it. In no small part, we imagine, because since 1971 there have been significant technological advances in things like detection and electromagnetism.

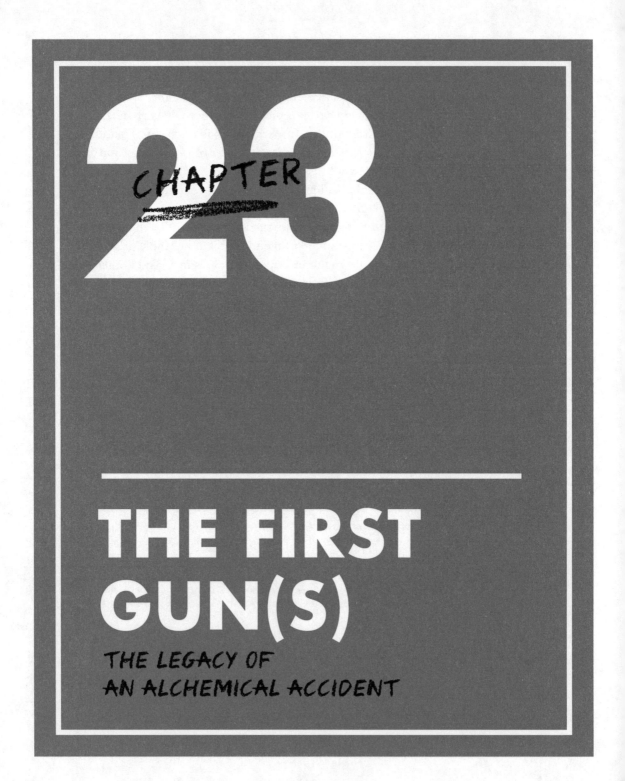

CHAPTER 23

THE FIRST GUN(S)

THE LEGACY OF
AN ALCHEMICAL ACCIDENT

Never bring a knife to a gunfight. That now-familiar American saying, taken from a Sean Connery line in the 1987 movie *The Untouchables*, has come to be useful shorthand for the importance of being adequately prepared in a difficult situation.

The idiom gained popularity fairly quickly after the movie came out because everyone was into Sean Connery at the time, but also because it's universal: everyone can imagine themselves in pursuit of a goal that will require them to battle for it. Perhaps, though, it's so readily accepted because everyone understands that, literally speaking, it has been true pretty much ever since the moment the first gun was invented.

Just think about it. Knives are great for dicing onions or if you're into whittling, and they're even good at poking holes in people, assuming you're close enough to make contact. But if your opponent can poke those same holes from fifty feet away, with little exploding pieces of lead that travel 1,000 to 3,000 feet per second, well then, as Sean Connery might have put it if *The Untouchables* had been set in the late 1940s, it's all over but the crying (and this time you can't blame the onions for your tears).[1]

Imagine not getting the memo and being the first guy to actually bring a knife to a gunfight. Or as he might have referred to it, bringing a knife to a revolutionary new handheld explosive technology fight. There he is, dressed in full armor on the battlefield, unsheathing what is undoubtedly a large and fairly heavy steel sword. Standing across from him is a dude with a large stick in his hands and a big, wide grin on his face, because he knows how things are about to go.

What must that have looked like? Well, it depends on what we mean when we use the term "gun" and therefore when in history this knife-and-gunfight took place.

---

[1] "It's all over but the crying" is a phrase that traces back to a 1947 song of the same name, by The Ink Spots, a vocal jazz quartet that was immensely important to the evolution of R&B and doo-wop, and who were one of the first all-African American groups to cross over with white audiences.

WHAT IS A GUN, REALLY?

Broadly speaking, we could define a "gun" as any weapon that launches a projectile at a target by igniting gunpowder or another explosive material. But that actually includes a lot of weapons that might not (a) best be described as a "gun," or (b) function better than a knife in one-on-one combat. Is a cannon a gun? Sorta. Is a bazooka a gun? Kinda . . . but it's more like a cannon that you rest on your shoulder. They're almost *too much* gun. In a duel between a guy with a machete and a guy trying to load and aim a seven-thousand-pound cannon or a shoulder-mounted missile that could blow up a tank, our money is on Jason Voorhees.[2]

Guns, in the sense that we have come to understand them and that we are talking about them here, are the portable, handheld firearms—pistols and rifles, mostly—that eventually outclassed any other weapons system ever invented for self-defense, hunting, and infantry tactics.[3] They trace back to the tenth century, but were actually developed over several hundred years, and it took even longer to refine them into the efficient and lethal machines we know today.

The origins of gun *technology*, however, begin in ninth-century China with the accidental invention of gunpowder. Alchemists had been combining charcoal, sulfur, and saltpeter in the search, ironically enough, of an "elixir of immortality."[4] To what must have been their great surprise, they discovered that the resulting powder was also extremely explosive when exposed to an open flame. They called their concoction *huo yao*, or "flaming medicine," which is both literally very accurate and figuratively maybe the coolest thing an '80s action movie hero could ever say right before dispatching the villain ("Open wide and take your flaming medicine, you filthy animal!"). As one Buddhist alchemist of the era wrote, "Some have heated together

---

[2] Despite not covering any films from the series (yet) on his Movie Crush podcast, Chuck would like to note that there are a staggering forty-six machete kills across the *Friday the 13th* franchise.

[3] The first lines of the US Marine Corps Rifleman's Creed (which you may remember Pvt. Pyle reciting in *Full Metal Jacket*) are "This is my rifle. There are many like it but this one is mine. My rifle is my best friend. It is my life. I must master it as I must master my life. Without me, my rifle is useless. Without my rifle, I am useless." So you're saying it's important? Roger that.

[4] It ended up being good for skin infections and insect fumigation.

the saltpeter, sulfur, and carbon of charcoal with honey; smoke and flames result, so that their hands and faces have been burnt, and even the whole house burnt down." At which point, one can only assume, the alchemist thought to himself, *well if this stuff can burn down a whole house by accident, what could it destroy ON PURPOSE?* And thus fireworks, mines, bombs, and, in the following century, rudimentary guns called *huo qiang,* or "fire lances," were born.

FIRE LANCES

Despite their objectively badass name, the earliest fire lances looked like giant bottle rockets and were about as lethal. They were basically just spears with single-shot explosive charges strapped to the shaft just below the spearhead, which shot flames out kind of like a flamethrower when ignited. Think Wile E. Coyote, and you're on the right track. Their primary purpose was to repel an advancing opponent by creating distance with the shooting flames, possibly even setting them on fire in the process as a special bonus. But since they were fairly inaccurate and really only effective inside ten feet, the main benefit was psychological, which is to say that they scared the crap out of people.

Not much changed with the fire lance over the next couple hundred years. The way it's depicted in tenth-century books, for instance, is very much the way it is described during its first recorded use by the Song in 1132, one of the early years of the century-long Jin-Song Wars: "The fire lance burns through as a flamethrower from the attached tube of gunpowder, then becomes an ordinary spear." Is it going to win you a war? Probably not. But it's sure as heck going to repel those pesky Jin soldiers climbing up siege ladders trying to breach the walls of your garrison and take control of your land.

Eventually, the fire lance started to evolve as it took on a greater role in the Jin-Song wars and found a place as a cheap weapon for the people—whether they were rebels besieging a city or townsfolk defending it. Armorers got rid of the spear altogether and turned the whole thing into a flamethrower. Instead of a little tube full of gunpowder attached to the shaft of the spear, the spear got hollowed out and became a big tube of gunpowder itself. By the end of the twelfth century, armies started shoving rocks and shards of porcelain and various types of metal shrapnel into the gunpowder tube, giving the fire lance a shotgun-like quality. In some instances, they even coated the shrapnel in toxic substances, turning the pieces into poison darts.[5]

For the most part, these fire lances were still being made out of bamboo and were therefore one-shot weapons. That all changed by the end of the Song Dynasty in 1279, as armorers shifted to the production of metal barrels and introduced an iron "pellet wad" in place of whatever random shrapnel a person could get their hands on as ammunition. This, for all intents and purposes, marked the invention of the bullet[6] and set in motion the next big leap in the evolution of portable firearms: the hand cannon.

HAND CANNONS

By the end of the thirteenth century, as Chinese armies perfected their weaponry, gunpowder made its way to Europe and fire lances found their way to the Middle East, both over the Silk Road (the ancient central Asian trade route, not the sketchy dark web marketplace we talked about in our "How the Deep Web Works" episode where people use bitcoin to buy drugs). 🎧 By 1320, it wasn't fire lances debuting on European battlefields, though, it was cannons. These were huge, stationary, incredibly heavy artillery pieces that shot large, fiery projectiles into an enemy's fighting lines with devastating power and thunderous booms.[7] It took a while because gunpowder

---

[5] As if being shot in the face with a fire lance wasn't enough to ruin your day, the ancient Chinese poisons you might find coating a projectile coming at you from one were no joke. A book called *Instructions to Coroners* written by Song Ci in 1247 during the Song Dynasty includes the passage: "For those who die of poisoning, their orifices open, their face turns greenish black or green, their lips go purplish green, their nails appear dark green, and blood spews out of their mouth, eyes, ears, and nose."

[6] No small thing, for being such a small thing.

[7] Like gunpowder and so many other things, the Europeans didn't invent the cannon—they only advanced it. It was the Chinese who invented artillery cannons, concurrently with fire lances as a matter of fact. Indeed, the Chinese proto-cannons, known as Flying-cloud Thunderclap Eruptors (*feiyun pi li pao*), were basically scaled-up fire lances held in wooden frames that could launch gunpowder bombs. It virtually goes without saying that when combined with Fire Lance as the band name, Flying-cloud Thunderclap Eruptors perhaps takes the prize as the best name for an album in these pages.

was still volatile[8] and forging metal barrels of any size was still a rather inexact science, but eventually military aspirations among rival nations pushed innovation in cannon technology toward miniaturization and portability. What popped out was the hand cannon, which you could describe as a rather handy cannon.

....

[8]   Armorers and alchemists would spend the next couple centuries experimenting with gunpowder, tinkering with the optimal recipe for maximum boomage. Eventually they would find it—75% percent saltpeter, 15% charcoal, 10% sulfur—and it would be one of the keys to stabilizing firearms and ultimately increasing their usefulness and popularity.

Unlike the first cannons, hand cannons could be carried and operated by just two people. Gunners would ram gunpowder and projectiles—which could be early lead bullets, or perhaps just shrapnel or random objects like arrowheads—down the barrel, then one would aim the weapon while the other lit the gunpowder with hot iron or a match through what was known as the "touch hole."[9] These hand cannons had a lot of drawbacks. They were slow to load, unreliable, and inaccurate, not to mention they were extremely dangerous to their operators. Arguably the hand cannon's greatest advantage, like the Chinese fire lance, was the psychological impact of the loud noises they made when firing.[10] But they were also relatively cheap to mass produce, even back then, and required very little training to be effective, especially compared to capably wielding a sword or accurately firing a bow and arrow.

With their mass producibility, durability, and capability for shooting all manner of projectiles from a distance, hand cannons managed to transform warfare and presaged the first generation of true handguns. And in a roundabout way they helped to kick off the Renaissance, because if you didn't want your army to be left behind by the hand cannon trolley or buried on the battlefield by it, as a ruler you were now forced to dedicate a significant portion of the national treasury to equipping a professional standing army as well as to financing advancements in science and technology, each of which was a brand new concept in the fourteenth and fifteenth centuries. The hand cannon and the arms race it triggered gave monarchs and despots no choice but to abandon old medieval strategies, like handing spears to a bottomless well of expendable serfs and wishing them luck,[11] and instead compelled them in the direction of human ingenuity and technological progress, with the end goal of ingeniously killing other humans more effectively and efficiently.

....

[9] Pro tip: don't google "touch hole" at work.

[10] The armies of fourteenth-century Europe should consider themselves lucky vuvuzelas wouldn't be invented for another 500 years.

[11] The Chinese strapped spears to oxen, lit their tails on fire, and sent them charging at the enemy. But unlike the very imaginative, polysyllabic names they gave to their other terrifying weapons, these the Chinese simply called "fire oxen."

Glossary of Awesomely Named Chinese Gunpowder Weapons*

WEAPON	CHINESE NAME	ENGLISH TRANSLATION
Gunpowder	Huo yao	Fire medicine
Flame-throwing spear	Huo ziang	Fire lance
Cannon that fires large bursting rounds	Feiyun pi li pao	Flying-cloud thunderclap eruptor
Sea mine	Shui di long wang pao	Submarine dragon king
Paper-cased bomb filled with shrapnel	Qun feng pao	Bee swarm bomb
Flamethrower that shoots poison and porcelain shards	Man thien phen thung	Filling-the-sky erupting tube
Flamethrower that shoots out sand, chemicals, poison gas, and salammoniac	Tsuan hsueh fei sha shen wu thung	Orifice-penetrating flying sand magic mist tube
Flamethrower that shoots numerous lead pellets	Chong zhen huo hu lu	Phalanx-charging fire gourd
Cannon that fires shells that release poison smoke	Du wu shen yan pao	Poison fog divine smoke eruptor
Poison flame-thrower	Tu lung phen hup shen thung	Poison dragon magically efficient fire-spurting tube
Seven-barreled organ gun	Qi xing chong	Seven-star cannon
Earthenware bomb filled with gunpowder, quicklime, resin, and poison plant extracts	Wan huo fei sha shen pao	Flying-sand divine bomb releasing ten thousand fires

* Taken from the *Huolongjing,* or Fire Dragon Manual, a fourteenth-century encyclopedia of Chinese "fire weapons," and the *Wu Pei Chih,* a seventeenth-century book on Chinese military technology.

LOCKS AND RIFLING AND REPEATERS, OH MY!

Beginning in the fifteenth century, a series of crucial inventions began to address the many flaws and shortcomings in existing gun designs—the first of which was the lock. Not the type you use to keep your bike from getting stolen, but the actual firing mechanism on a gun that ignites the gunpowder without needing a separate person to light it directly. No touch hole involved.

The first gun to include a lock was the arquebus, a short-barreled weapon favored by the French that could be held and operated by one person.[12] It used a matchlock, which is basically a gunpowder-soaked cord that would burn until it touched a pan of flash powder, which would then launch a half-ounce bullet. The arquebus was lighter and more reliable than any gun before it, but was still so slow to load it could only fire once every two minutes.[13] Perhaps for this reason, archers continued to outnumber gunmen for several more centuries, while additional refinements in gun design were developed.

Rifling, which involves carving long parallel spiral grooves into the inside of gun barrels to give them greater accuracy, started in 1498. The mechanical "wheel lock," which unlike the matchlock generated a spark without needing to be lit, was invented in 1509. In 1630 the flintlock was developed, which allowed a user to spark a piece of flint by simply pushing back the lid covering the gunpowder. This became the dominant firing mechanism for more than a hundred years and was still in widespread use during the American Revolution.

Eventually, with all these advancements building and compounding on each other, soldiers with guns began to replace archers, swordsmen, and every other weapon-wielder for a simple reason—guns were easier to use.

....

[12] The arquebus is not to be confused with its cousin the blunderbuss, which is a short rifle with a barrel that spreads out into a funnel. The blunderbuss is the kind of gun you often see cartoon pilgrims carrying when they go on the hunt for animals that will inevitably outsmart them.

[13] In that same amount of time today, an AR-15 can shoot nearly 2,000 bullets, because that is totally necessary.

As gun design began to be refined, the time it took to train a person to use one was reduced from a few months to a few weeks, if not days. In contrast, swordsmen and archers might require years of training to be effective, no matter how their respective technologies evolved. This facilitated the widespread adoption of guns, which, in a way, also helped collapse certain class divisions. A sword-wielding knight has a big advantage over a peasant, but not if the peasant is packing heat, as anyone who's ever seen *Raiders of the Lost Ark* is acutely aware. The advantage offered by firearms was so significant that eventually even the knight-loving aristocrats themselves came around, and by 1750 pistols had replaced swords as the weapon of choice for dueling, 🎙️ though it unfortunately took quite a bit longer for people to realize that "not dueling each other at all" was an even better option.

Guns transformed society by transforming every aspect of warfare, from the distances that armies engaged each other to the wounds most commonly sustained in battle. This trend only accelerated as more modern firearms were invented. In 1835, Samuel Colt created a revolver that became the first mass-produced, multi-shot handgun. Designs for similar weapons had existed for centuries, but the Industrial Revolution made it possible to create them en masse, cheaply, and with the necessary precision to be effective. As America pushed westward, claiming native lands as its own and wiping out entire tribes, it was able to do so because of the firepower that had come to its disposal in the previous few decades. If you've watched any Western, there's a good chance the cowboys are carrying prop versions of one of Colt's weapons. Small wonder the Colt .45 is sometimes called "the gun that won the West."[14]

Fifteen years later the first shotgun was invented as a way for the upper class to hunt birds. The first carbine repeater—which could fire seven shots in fifteen seconds—was invented in 1860, but the US Army opted not to use it at first because they were worried it would make soldiers go through too much ammunition. *Oh, the ever-loving irony of it all!* Three years later, Abraham Lincoln finally put them into widespread use, turning the repeater into the weapon of choice for the Union. Around that same time

----

[14] Colt doesn't have the market cornered on "winning the West"—the Winchester Repeating Arms Company's rifles were also said to have "won the West" and, by the by, went on to produce the fortune that built the Winchester Mystery House in San Jose, California, which we examined in detail in our episode, "What's with the Winchester Mystery House?" 🎙️

the first fully automatic weapon, the Gatling gun, was invented. Within another thirty years, the technology was adapted into fully automatic handguns like the Luger and Mauser, and not long after that the Thompson submachine gun (better known as the Tommy gun) was invented and widely used in World War I, as well as by Prohibition-era gangsters. 🎧

In 1947, Mikhail Kalashnikov invented the AK-47 for the Soviet military (the AK stands for "Automatic by Kalashnikov"), which offered the rapid-fire rates of Tommy guns but were lighter and more reliable. In response, the US military developed their own lightweight automatic weapon known as the AR-15.[15] Both guns are gas-operated, meaning high-pressure gas from their cartridges is used to simultaneously fire a bullet and push the next round into the chamber, allowing for fire rates of over 900 bullets a minute.[16] This is pretty much when all hell started breaking loose.

WORST INVENTION EVER?

Which brings us to the tricky thing about bringing a knife to a gunfight: What do you do if you didn't bring anything anywhere and the gunfight just sort of shows up and breaks out all around you? That is kind of the proposition a lot of us could potentially face out there in modern times. The reliability, stability, usability, rapid-fire capability, and ubiquity of guns—all of which evolved over the last thousand years—have helped to turn the world into a killing field.

That sounds like hyperbole, but consider that the four largest wars of the twentieth century—all of them fought primarily with guns—killed more than 100 million people combined, which would have been almost half of the entire global population when gunpowder and fire lances were invented in

---

[15] The AR stands for ArmaLite Rifle, not "assault rifle" as is often assumed by people who are concerned about the existence of assault rifles and don't own one.

[16] It would take an arquebus thirty hours to fire the same number of shots. Ahh, the good old days.

the ninth and tenth centuries. And those are just four of the innumerable wars, skirmishes, conflicts, and battles that have taken place in the history of guns. Also taking into account the countless millions of people around the world who've died by gun violence outside of war (250,000 a year worldwide, these days)—in everyday disputes, during crimes, in mass shootings, in accidental shootings, by suicide, at the hands of the police—it's hard to ignore the possibility that maybe guns were the worst invention in human history.

Well, either guns or the Pet Rock.[17] Jury's still out on that one.

----

[17] To judge for yourself, see chapter 10.

CHAPTER

24

KEEPING UP WITH THE JONESES

THE UNWINNABLE HUMAN RACE

In 1913, a newspaper sketch artist named Arthur "Pop" Momand returned to New York from a year studying abroad in France with an idea for a comic strip. It would be about a family called the McGinises: Aloysius, the father; Clarice, the mother; Julie, their daughter; and Bella Donna, their housekeeper.

The premise of the daily strip was simple, with a bit of a twist. It would chronicle the funny moments from the small family's normal, everyday life—like, say, *For Better or For Worse* or *Hi and Lois*. But that everyday life the McGinises led was defined by a hilarious obsession with their neighbors, who they were perpetually envious of, and whose opinions they were always concerned with, and who we, the reader, would never actually see.

Momand's comic strip gained a good amount of popularity over time, though it never reached *Peanuts* or *Archie*-level fame and ubiquity. Still, it had a respectable run for twenty-five years in the *New York World*[1] and in as many as 150 other newspapers across the country.

It was called *Keeping Up with the Joneses*.

Who exactly were the Joneses? According to Momand they could just as easily have been the Smiths. Why Smith? Why Jones? Well, since the beginning of the twentieth century, Smith has been the most popular surname in America, and Jones has been right up there with it.[2] In the 2010 census, Smith retained the championship belt, occurring nearly 2.5 million times, while Jones held steady at #5 with 1,425,470 occurrences.

....

[1] The *World* was owned by Joseph Pulitzer—namesake of journalism's Pulitzer Prize—which, by the way, is *not* pronounced PEW-lit-zer, but rather PUH-lit-zer. Or as Pulitzer himself instructed people, 'pull it sir.' The name derives from the village of Pullitz, in southern Moravia, which was part of the Austrian empire when Pulitzer was born in neighboring Hungary just to the south in 1847.

[2] There were apparently some sexually prolific blacksmiths and men named John in England in the near past, since the surname Smith is derived from "blacksmith" and Jones basically meant "John's son" around England and Wales.

STUFF YOU SHOULD KNOW . . .
About Surnames

Arthur Momand was not the first person to play with the Jones and Smith surnames when trying to convey the pervasiveness and commonness of contemporary cultural phenomena like social competition and conformity. In 1901, in his essay "Corn-Pone Opinions," Mark Twain wrote:

> "[O]utside influences are always pouring in upon us, and we are always obeying their orders and accepting their verdicts. The Smiths like the new play; the Joneses go to see it, and they copy the Smith verdict . . . speaking in general terms, a man's self-approval in the large concerns of life has its source in the approval of the peoples about him . . ."

He tinkered with both names for the comic strip's invisible antagonists but ultimately settled on Jones because, in his words, it was more "euphonious,"[3] which is 1910s (Nineteenteens?) talk for "it sounded better." By giving them a famously generic last name and never showing them in the strip, Momand was intimating that there were no Joneses—or, rather, there were Joneses everywhere. So rather than who specifically were the Joneses, a better question might be, *what* were the Joneses?

The simplest way to think about the Joneses is as a symbol of the kind of wealth and high status that many Americans learned to aspire to during the prosperous last decades of the nineteenth century, otherwise known as the Gilded Age.[4] *Keeping up* with the Joneses was about maintaining

---

[3] Momand was onto something. There are more than a few great songs with "Jones" in the title: "Mr. Jones" by Counting Crows; "Casey Jones" by the Grateful Dead; "Me & Mrs. Jones" by Billy Paul; "Crackity Jones" by the Pixies; "Jones Crusher" by Frank Zappa; and of course the deep cut "Keeping Up With the Joneses" by Little Feat. There are no popular songs with "Smith" in the title, though one of the greatest bands of all time is called the Smiths.

[4] Though the Gilded Age deserves its own episode, we talked a lot about it in our "Robber Barons!" episode. 🎙 Mark Twain, who now makes a second appearance in this chapter, coined the term as an unflattering name for an era that seemed to offer prosperity and benefit for society as a whole but masked profound economic inequality and saw the development of vast and amoral wealth concentrated in the hands of a select few people who amassed it by exploiting everyday workers. Steel tycoon Andrew Carnegie—who shows up in chapter 17 on Trillionaires—captured the ethos of the Gilded Age when he said, "It isn't the man who does the work that makes the money. It's the man who gets other men to do it."

that wealth and status (or at least the appearance of it), typically through conspicuous consumption, most often in relation to neighbors or peers. It's a phenomenon Momand was intimately familiar with, actually, because he and his wife fell into its bad habits during their time living in Cedarhurst, New York.[5] They lived "far beyond their means," he said, trying to keep up with "the well-to-do class." It was that experience, he claimed, that inspired the entire idea for his comic strip.

BREAKING WYNDCLYFFE

Except there *was* a prominent wealthy Jones family in Pop Momand's New York. They had a lineage that went back to the earliest days of the American colonies, and their influence kept apace right through to the twentieth century. It is these particular Joneses who many believe are the inspiration for the Joneses of Momand's comics.

This real-life Jones family rose to prominence by multiple generations of property accumulation throughout New York City,[6] Long Island, and the Hudson River Valley. Their wealth derived in part from those holdings and in part from their role in the early growth of Chemical Bank over the forty years that two Jones men served as its president (one of whom married the daughter of the bank's founder, John Mason).[7]

....

[5] A small, quaint village on the southern shore of Long Island whose main street used to be the "Rodeo Drive of Long Island," today Cedarhurst's most famous neighbor is Runway 4R/22L at JFK International Airport, about a mile away as the crow flies (and potentially gets sucked up into a jet engine).

[6] Their Manhattan holdings included a large tract between what is now 66th and 75th Streets, east of Third Avenue, called Jones Wood, that was the subject of a protracted fight that went all the way to the Supreme Court when city leaders and lawmakers effectively tried to confiscate the land for use as a large public park. The family won and eventually planners moved onto a more centrally located area west of Jones Wood called Seneca Village. It was an integrated African American and Irish working-class neighborhood—surprise, surprise—and thus easier to "acquire" and develop. That area would become Central Park. 🎧

[7] Founded in 1823, Chemical Bank was originally a division of an actual chemical maker, the New York Chemical Manufacturing Company. The bank division outlived the chemical division but kept the name until it absorbed Chase Manhattan Bank in a 1996 merger and adopted the more popular Chase name. Today, it is better known as JPMorgan Chase, after their acquisition of JPMorgan in 2000. Chemical Bank is also the bank used by Jerry Seinfeld's nana, who is on a very fixed income, and who briefly goes missing after she learns her account is overdrawn in the sixth season "Pledge Drive" episode of *Seinfeld*.

But it wasn't until 1853 that we really started to feel the fingerprints of the Joneses on American society. That was the year that Elizabeth Schermerhorn Jones completed construction of the largest home ever built in the Hudson River Valley. Situated on eighty acres in Rhinebeck, New York, and intended as a weekend and summer residence for the New York City socialite, she called the twenty-four-room Gothic-style mansion Wyndclyffe.[8] Made of imposing red brick, with tall spires, big arched windows, and access directly to the Hudson River, the place looked like a cross between a castle and a cathedral. And *everyone* was envious of it.[9]

Wyndclyffe kicked off a building boom up and down the Hudson River Valley. Neighbors began upgrading their places. Members of prominent families who traveled in the same circles started looking at plots in the area and planning their own massive estates. For instance, William Astor Jr.,

---

8 The two "y's" and the "e" at the end let you know it's extra fancy, like when an outdoor mall calls itself a "Towne Centre" because they have a Sur La Table and an Armani Exchange. Or it could just be that the Jones family is Welsh.

9 Well, maybe not everyone. The famous novelist Edith Wharton, who was Elizabeth Jones's niece (her father was Elizabeth's brother) called the place a "gloomy monstrosity" in her book *A Backward Glance*.

grandson of John Jacob Astor, bought a large tract of land in Rhinebeck the very same year Wyndclyffe was completed and built a huge mansion on it called Ferncliff Farm, with large castle-like turrets and views of the Hudson River—sounds familiar—but also with long porches that wrapped around most of the lower floor *and* with views of the Catskills Mountains.[10] Let the one-upmanship begin!

Elizabeth Schermerhorn Jones was not the lone Jones in on the whole trendsetting standard bearer act. Seventeen years earlier, in 1836, deep in the thicket of the Jones family tree,[11] a distant relative named David S. Jones had retired to his farm in Massapequa and proceeded to build what was considered not just the finest mansion on Long Island at the time but also the largest trout preserve in the world. Then, sixteen years *after* Wyndclyffe was finished, Mary Mason Jones—the daughter of Chemical Bank's John Mason, and the grand dame of the Manhattan social scene — built a large marble mansion on 57th Street in Manhattan.[12]

It was a decision that captured the attention of New York high society, and that many today believe was equally responsible for the phenomenon of keeping up with the Joneses, because at the time no one who was anyone was living within twenty blocks of that area. It was completely undeveloped.[13] But Mary Mason Jones suspected that would change, and she was right. Prominent families not only started building around 57th Street, they also built in the same style, matching her opulence. Eventually there would be enough of them that the houses on that stretch came to be called "Marble Row." Mary Mason Jones basically made the entire city of New York keep up with her by playing on the insecurity and envy of its prominent wealthy families, dragging development of Manhattan above Midtown in the process.[14] The mountain had come to Mohammed.

....

[10] The mansion was torn down in 1940, but the land it was on came to be called Astor Courts and it was where Chelsea Clinton got married in 2010.

[11] It's so hard to keep up with all these Joneses.

[12] In the late 1830s and '40s, Mary Mason Jones lived at 734 Broadway with her husband Isaac Jones, while her two sisters owned the adjoining homes on either side of them. When the drawing rooms of all three homes were opened, they had the longest ballroom in the city.

[13] This would be around the time the grid for Manhattan laid out by the 1811 Commissioners' Plan was spottily filling up with incoming residents. 🔊

[14] Edith Wharton memorialized Mary Mason Jones, her great aunt, in her 1920 Pulitzer Prize-winning novel *The Age of Innocence* as Mrs. Manson Mingott.

A SONG AS OLD AS TIME

We tend to think of keeping up with the Joneses as a distinctly American phenomenon. The phrase started in America with Pop Momand's comic strip. It was arguably inspired by a storied American family. And it has persisted, if not flourished, into present-day thanks to Americans' glowing reputation for buying crud we don't need in order to impress people we don't like. The truth is, though, that this kind of behavior has been going on everywhere for millennia, for as long as people have been using possessions as a measure of wealth and status.[15]

The Egyptians probably did it. (C'mon, did the Great Pyramid of Giza really need to be *that* great?) 🎙️ The Romans definitely did it. "[H]ow much do we acquire simply because our neighbors have acquired such things, or because most men possess them," the famous Stoic philosopher Seneca wrote in his *Letters from a Stoic* in the first century CE. 🎙️ And the Europeans did it in the decades leading up to the Industrial Revolution, which is when pretty much everyone agrees the seeds of conspicuous consumption were planted that would sprout as consumerism during the Industrial Revolution and then blossom into what we now call "keeping up with the Joneses" during the Gilded Age.[16]

One historian from Cambridge, Sheilagh Ogilvie, has gone so far as to call that period in the mid-1600s the "Industrious Revolution." Very catchy. She argues that was when households in some of the wealthier European countries like England and the Netherlands started buying lots of stuff which, back then, were considered luxury items almost by definition. This consumer behavior then trickled down to the poorer countries of Central Europe over the following decades as they tried to keep up with their rich rivals to the west. The explosion of consumerism, Ogilvie says, is what made the Industrial Revolution in Europe necessary. People needed to make more money to buy more stuff, and they needed to be able to produce that stuff faster and cheaper so more people could afford it and then show it off and make their neighbors super envious.

....

[15] In his essay "The Worst Mistake In the History of the Human Race," anthropologist Jared Diamond argues that humans' shift from hunting and gathering to agriculture beginning around 12,000 years ago created the possibility for surpluses, initially in the form of crops, which formed the basis for the eventual emergence of wealth, status, and, inevitably, materialism.

[16] We just realized "keeping up with the Joneses" is a metonym. It's the name of the comic strip and it's the term for conspicuous consumption as a method of social competition with neighbors and peers.

KEEPING UP WITH THE CLAUDIUSES

Presto-change-o, the factory system of manufacturing gets developed and mass production begins. Large swaths of European peoples who now have a taste for this new "more and better" thing immigrate to America. Being a fairly new country, these hoity-toity[17] immigrants recognize that the States offer an opportunity for upward social mobility that doesn't exist in the more highly class-stratified countries of Europe. This process of industrialization and economization repeats itself on American shores, beginning in earnest in the early nineteenth century and culminating with the Second Industrial Revolution, built around the rise of bulk steel production, starting around 1850. It would be the industries that grew up out of this period—steel, oil, railroads, shipping—that propelled robber barons like the Vanderbilts, the Morgans, the Rockefellers, and the Carnegies to the top of New York high society; not just keeping up with the real-life Joneses, but supplanting them ass over teakettle onto their surprised faces.

....

[17] Not to be confused with hoi polloi, which is the opposite of hoity-toity.

Japanese Joneses?

While the phrase "keeping up with the Joneses" typically refers to behavior among individual consumers and households, the Japanese have their own version, *yokonarabi*, which also has a corollary that is deeply ingrained into Japanese business culture.

Yoko meaning "beside" or "alongside" and *narabi* meaning "line up" or "in line with," when combined, refer to a cultural tendency for copying the behavior of others in a peer group or an industry as a way to fit in or even to compete. That could mean buying the latest designer labels or all the newest tech gadgets right when they come out; in the case of business, it could mean doing exactly what your competition is doing, all the way from market strategy to product design, for no other reason than if they're doing it, then you should do it too.

At the core of yokonarabi, particularly as it relates to business, is something very similar to the honor-based motivations we talked about in chapter 15 that drove Japanese soldiers in World War II toward *kamikaze* and *banzai* instead of surrender. As one consulting firm put it: "It involves doing something not because you yourself think it's a good idea, but rather because you want to avoid any negative perception from not doing what others are doing."

MONEY CAN'T BUY HAPPINESS, UNLESS . . .

You may have noticed by now that, interesting as it is, "keeping up with the Joneses" is kind of a bummer. Here we are, talking about a phenomenon that likely took its inspiration from millionaires competing with other millionaires, and took its name from a cartoon about a family that was never comfortable in their own skin. It's a phenomenon that, in modern times, is generally harmless within the domain of upper-middle class suburbia,[18] where people have the luxury of disposable income to pursue luxury in the form of largely disposable goods, while poorer, lower income families feel

---

[18] Financially harmless, perhaps. Psychologically, that's another story.

compelled to go into credit card debt up to their eyeballs just to have a chance of staying in the game. And what, exactly, is the point of the game anyway? When you take a step back from the whole thing it's hard not to wonder, *why isn't anyone satisfied? Why do we all seem so unhappy? Why isn't a million dollars, or a billion dollars, or one home, or two cars, or a good job, OR EACH OTHER, enough?*

It turns out there's some science that explains all this, for the richer and the poorer. In a 2010 study titled "Money and Happiness," three UK psychology researchers found that the best predictor of overall life satisfaction for the participants in their study wasn't raw income, but income relative to those around them or those like them. You could make $500,000 a year, but if Ken and Karen across the street make $1.5 million and Biff and Muffy next door make $2 million and everyone you know your age is making a million dollars, then it is very likely that you will be appreciably less happy than if they all made less than you.

On the other side of the coin, according to a pair of researchers from Boston College and the Sorbonne, if you are a "bottom-tier consumer" (their words, not ours) your life satisfaction increases as your material possessions increase, but only to a point, and only to the extent that the increase closes the gap between what you have and what the people above you have. That sense of satisfaction begins to dull and the drive toward greater conspicuous consumption—toward keeping up with the Joneses—reignites when you realize that all this new stuff vaulted you over other bottom-tier consumers and set you up to get ahead of middle-tier consumers if you keep going.[19]

Basically, the value of money and stuff is not absolute. It's relative. And neither will buy you happiness unless it means you have more of either than most of the people around you. This is what keeping up with the Joneses is about: the human tendency toward social competition through conspicuous consumption; the pursuit of happiness at the expense of friends, family, neighbors, and colleagues. This is not to say that each of us is doomed to a life of envy and relentless, exhausting pursuit. It's quite possible to not pay attention to what others have—to some degree—but, as you might imagine, that mindset tends to be found most frequently among the people who already have the most. In other words, the Joneses.

....

[19] All of this ties in pretty well with our episode "Do objects or experiences make us happier?" If you don't feel like listening, the answer to that question is experiences. 🎧

CHAPTER

25

DOG
SMELLS
CANINE SCENTS AND SENSE-ABILITY

One of the more underappreciated elements of director Christopher Nolan's dreamscape movie, *Inception,* is the way he depicts how action in the waking world can affect events in the dream world. A character is asleep inside a building that is under attack in the waking world, for example, and in the dream world everything starts crumbling around him.

We've probably all experienced a version of this in our own lives, even if we didn't realize it at the time. Next time you have a bad cold that makes it hard to breathe, don't be surprised if you wake up with a fright from a roller coaster 🎧 dream or a falling dream, right at the start of the big drop, trying to catch your breath—that's how your lungs gasping for air in the waking world could translate in the dream world. Inception!

Not all real-world intrusions into our dreams are so dramatic or traumatic, however. Some are also delicious. Maybe you've had this dream: you're hungry. The mouth-watering smell of something salty and savory and warm is overwhelming your olfactory senses. You move toward it, but it seems to be eluding you, teasing you, until finally you see it. In your mind's eye it looks like a tray of nachos. Or maybe your grandma's Frito Pie. The next thing you know, you're eating. One bite, then another. Suddenly, you begin to pick up steam, shoveling the food into your mouth. No, wait. Actually, someone is shoving it down your throat—it's like you're being waterboarded with a Fritos firehose!

And that's when you wake up . . . to find your sleeping dog's out-stretched paws in your face and their paw pads smelling distinctly like corn chips. If you don't own a dog, or if you are a monster who doesn't allow your dog to sleep with you,[1] this type of experience is likely quite foreign to you. Rest assured, it happens every day to permissive dog owners around the world and it smells yummy, which may be a big part of the reason dog owners don't do anything about it when they probably should.

----

[1] Or if you're just a grown-up with good discipline and better hygiene.

FRITO FEET, QUITE THE COMBO

This phenomenon of a dog's paws smelling like corn chips is most popularly known as Frito Feet (or Toes). And while it would be comforting to believe that it only happens when the magical Corn Fairy sprinkles her special corn dust on all the good dogs each night, the reality is much mustier. That corn chip smell results from an accumulation of yeast and bacteria suspended within the moisture that gets caught up in the crevices between the pads of a dog's paws. How's that for a buzz kill?

The problem—and to be sure it can become a problem—starts with the fact that dogs only sweat where they don't have fur, so basically their noses and the bottoms of their paws.[2] And for some breeds, on their little pink "pig bellies." Then, when you take the ol' girl out for a walk, those sweaty pads inevitably come in contact with standing water, soil, 🛈 and all manner of waste, each one a thriving breeding ground for a variety of bacteria and naturally occurring yeasts.. Once the bacteria and yeast are squeezed up between your dog's sweaty toes, they've found the perfect place to breed. It's dark, warm, damp, and protected by a carpeted canopy of fur. And, importantly, the area typically goes undisturbed so the microbes can get down to business consuming dead skin and other miniscule detritus. As they do their dirty business they release volatile gases as a byproduct. It is those gases, not the bacteria or yeast themselves, which are largely responsible for the smells that are produced. It all depends on the recipe—what is being digested, what kind of bacterium is doing the digesting, and what byproducts that digestion produces. In the right combination and proportions, that process can produce the unusual Frito Feet smell that has you rummaging through the kitchen cupboards looking for chips after your dog has had a good scratch sitting next to you.

As you might imagine, then, not just any bacteria can produce Frito Feet. Just as merlot and cabernet franc grapes are blended to produce many amazing Right Bank bordeaux wines,[3] or sodium and chloride ions bind to make salt, or cookies and cream combine to make, well, cookies 'n' cream, only bacteria from the *Proteus* and *Pseudomonas* families combine to make your dog's feet smell like Fritos. Both very common, *Proteus* bacteria appear in decomposing animal matter and all those fun places where feces is found: intestines, manure, soil, and plants that have come in contact with animals.

------

[2] The sweat produced in the paws and nose are largely meant to keep those areas from drying out and to release pheromones that act as chemical messengers to other animals (more on that later in the chapter). This kind of sweating does not help dogs regulate their temperature, however. For that, they turn to panting, which evaporates heat through their breath and cools them. They also use conduction to lower their temperature, like lying on a cool floor. That's why so many dogs like to chill out in the kitchen or the bathroom. It's not because they're obsessed with food or poop, though both those things are true for many dogs. It's because those two rooms often have the coolest floors in the house.

[3] Bordeaux has two major vineyard regions: the area south of the Garonne River, which is called the Left Bank, and the area north of the Dordogne River, called the Right Bank. Left Bank bordeaux are also blended wines, but cabernet sauvignon grapes are predominant, whereas with Right Bank it's merlot. Also, don't forget to swirl this footnote around in the bottom of your glass before you drink it up.

They are known to cause urinary tract infections in both dogs *and* humans and tend to produce a sweet odor as they decompose. *Pseudomonas* bacteria, on the other hand, are generally harmless to healthy humans but are often the culprit with nasty skin and ear infections in dogs. They are commonly found in water, soil, and plants all over the world and tend to smell more on the fruity side.[4] Together these two particular strains of bacteria cook up quite a corny treat in your dog's fuzzy feet. How's that for a song lyric?

STUFF YOU SHOULD KNOW . . .
About Fritos

Fritos, which is the Spanish word for *fried* (this is relevant, give us a second), were "invented" by Charles Elmer Doolin in his mother's kitchen in San Antonio, Texas, in 1932. *Invented* is in quotes because it's probably more accurate to say Doolin white-labeled them when he bought a corn chip business for $100 from a local soccer[5] coach named Gustavo Olguin, who was looking to return to Oaxaca where he was from.[6] The deal included Olguin's corn chip recipe, for which he used *masa*, the potato ricer he used to process the masa, and all his retail accounts—one of which, it seems likely, is where Doolin was first introduced to these delicious chips. Doolin was a hustler and the consummate salesman, and by the time he passed away in 1959 Fritos were everywhere, including Disneyland's own Mexican restaurant called Casa de Fritos.

Which has to make you wonder: assuming dogs have had paws that smelled like corn chips since before the Great Depression, what did they call that smell before Fritos existed? As the chips spread across America, do you think when people opened their first bag they said, "Omigosh, these chips smell like my dog's feet!" Hey, maybe that's why Fritos are shaped like a dog's toenails!

---

[4] *Pseudomonas aeruginosa,* which is among the most prevalent and most studied of the pseudomonas species, has been known to smell like grape juice when it infects burn patients.

[5] Futbol

[6] Jeez, Oaxaca is really bringing it on the artisanal front. First it's mezcal and weaving, as we saw in chapter 5, now it's the best corn chips ever. What *can't* Oaxacans do?

Now, this isn't necessarily a bad thing, despite our tendency to worry any time Latin medical terms get thrown around about someone we love, including our four-legged family members. Dogs' paws are always going to smell, and to an extent this particular corn chip smell is as natural and normal as, say, your own B.O., but if you want to keep it under control the best thing you can do is to commit to regular paw maintenance cleanings and to make sure you wipe down and dry off your dog's feet any time they go splish-splash through a muddy mudhole.

You should only be concerned about Frito Feet, veterinarians say, when either the smell or your dog's licking and chewing become excessive. That is often an indication of a bacterial infection—Funky Frito Feet, one might say—at which point it is probably time to bribe your dog into the backseat of the car with treats and take them on a ride to the veterinary clinic for a date with the doctor and a personalized fitting for a cone of shame.

EVEN PUPPY'S BREATH IS CUTE

You can think of Frito Feet as perhaps something of an acquired taste among discerning dog lovers, but another smell associated with dogs—puppy breath—is, if we're daring to present opinion as fact in a book of facts, universally loved by every single human on Earth. Even cat people. Puppy breath is truly the stuff of legends. It's hard to accurately describe as it's a smell unlike any other, so comparisons are kind of useless.[7] Regardless of its undefinability, people love it. But why exactly? Why do so many people love that smell so much? Just like with Frito Feet, the answer lies with bacteria, though for the opposite reason. Whereas the presence of bacteria is what's responsible for the smell emanating from our dogs' feet, its *absence* is what appears to explain much about puppy breath's sweet smell.

----

[7] For the record, Chuck's wife Emilie always says it smells like toast. Many a stranger's puppies have been accosted while she yells "Gimme some of that toast!" Confusion typically abounds.

It makes sense when you think about it. Puppies, by virtue of their newness, have not yet had a chance to get into the bacteria-laden stuff that produces horrible breath in older dogs. Kind of like human babies. Filthy chew toys, bones, old shoes, sticks, chunks of kibble, hunks of poop. All the things that, if they aren't cleaned out from a dog's mouth sufficiently, create plaque, which makes bad breath, which sends our heads snapping back after one big whiff.

A Puppy PSA is No Sweat

A dog experiences a hot day differently than we do. It might feel nice out because there's a pleasant breeze, but that breeze is only pleasant to us because it's evaporating the sweat from the glands all over our bodies. Dogs don't have that luxury, however, because dogs don't sweat. They don't get the sweat-wicking experience of a cool breeze on a hot day; to them it's just hot out. Things can become even more dangerous for a dog when the heat combines with high humidity. The humidity prevents efficient heat transfer at their mouth through panting, which can set them up for heat stroke. What does all of this mean? Never exercise your dog in the heat of the afternoon, even when it feels nice out to you. Take them out quickly to do their business and then bring them back inside to resume their position on the kitchen floor or the bathroom floor. Start thinking like a dog and your dog will thank you for it.

In those first few months, puppies are basically pristine. The normal bacteria found in their mouths stays relatively balanced as their baby teeth come in and then, a couple months later, they start losing those tiny little razor blades as their adult teeth push through. At the same time, their gastrointestinal tracts haven't been adulterated either because their diets have consisted almost exclusively of their mother's milk.

Interestingly, some believe that it's wholly the mother's milk, that sweet life-giving nectar of the doggie gods, that explains puppy breath. But that sweet smell tends to persist past the weaning stage, so that can't be the whole answer. It's much more likely, according to what we've managed to cobble together from the vets who found time to write about this stuff, that all the changes going on in a puppy's body (mouth included) during its first six months of life, combined with limited exposure to plaque-producing pathogens, and of course mama's milk, explain why puppy kisses are the absolute best.

THE NOSE KNOWS NO LIMITS

Interestingly, researchers have found that all of the scents produced by bacteria, including Frito Feet and grown-up dog breath, don't just smell to us; they're "smelled" by bacteria as well. What we sense as a smell is, in other words, a chemical message that conveys some meaning and may produce a response. Poop smell, for example, generally carries the message that it comes from some kind of poopy pathogen and we should, therefore, move along and not hang around said poop.

So long as an organism has some way to detect that chemical message, it may respond to it too. This extends to bacteria as well. As a byproduct of their defense against antibiotics, bacteria often produce ammonia. Some recent research has found that through something called *bacterial olfaction,* other bacteria—even ones living a universe away within entirely separate petri dishes nearby—sense the ammonia and respond to it as if it's a distress signal or a warning and reduce the permeability of their own cell membranes, which will prevent antibiotics from getting through.

The idea of bacterial olfaction is pretty neat, to be sure, but it pales in comparison to the astounding interestingness of dogs' ability to smell.

We've talked about dog olfaction in plenty of episodes, probably the most in-depth in our "How the Beagle Brigade Works" episode. 🎙 But it's one of our favorite things to talk about, and this just wouldn't be a bona fide *Stuff You Should Know* book without some dog smell discussion.

Because dogs primarily navigate through the world with their highly attuned sense of smell, an average-sized dog's brain is only ten percent the size of a human's brain, but the part responsible for processing smell is forty times bigger. They have anywhere from twenty-five to sixty times more scent glands than we do, which makes their sense of smell 10,000 to 100,000 times better than ours.[8] They even have a second olfactory system, called the *vomeronasal organ* (or Jacobsen's organ), which allows them to pick up pheromones. Then on top of all that, their noses are perpetually wet to make collecting scent particles easier, and they have horizontal slits on the bottom edge of each nostril to let them exhale out the sides without obstructing the inhale of fresh air (and scents) up the center. That's some serious double duty and gives them the ability to continually sniff, which is basically the canine version of Miles Davis' circular breathing and just as cool.

And that's just dogs in general. We must also mention the scent hounds, whose big snouts and large nasal cavities make them the Dyson dual cyclone vacuum cleaners of smell collection. These are typically the breeds with big floppy ears (yes they are!) that help to brush additional scent particles up toward their noses. They are exceptionally good at picking up scents in all kinds of environments: across flowing water; within large mounds of rubble; inside the human body (in the case of cancer-detecting dogs); even in gas tanks, as was the case with one drug-sniffing dog that found a bunch of marijuana submerged in a truck's full gas tank. Some can actually detect certain scents in parts per *trillion*, which, according to one dog cognition researcher, would be like detecting a half-teaspoon of sugar in an Olympic-sized swimming pool.[9]

The top dog among all scent hounds is the bloodhound. This adorable, lumbering, wrinkly-skinned, droopy-faced pooch boasts up to 300 million scent receptors and is so reliable that evidence collected as a result of its tracking ability has been admitted in court.[10] That's not a joke. Like the basset hound, which is second in sniffing prowess, it also has a large flap of loose skin around its neck, called a "dewlap," that traps scent particles near

---

[8] Dogs have between 125 and 300 million scent receptors, depending on the breed. How that translates to a sense of smell that is 10,000 times stronger instead of twenty-five times (humans have a pitiful 5 to 6 million scent receptors), we have no idea, but them's the numbers.

[9] This is akin to humans' own superability to detect a few parts per trillion of petrichor, the smell made just before it rains, like we talked about in our Short Stuff episode on that very subject.

[10] Whether this should be the case is debatable. Dog-scenting evidence is considered by many to be junk science, perpetrated by nefarious handlers who subtly guide their dogs toward a conclusion that supports who they (or those who have hired them) think is guilty. You might say it's like phrenology of the nose.

its snout so it doesn't lose track of what it's trying to find.[11] A bit of advice: if you ever get tossed in prison 🔊 and harbor delusions of escaping one day, make sure you're in a place that doesn't keep bloodhounds onsite so you at least have a puncher's chance of making it out of the county. That's how mythically powerful the bloodhound's sense of smell is.

A Criminal Defense Attorney's Guide to Inducing a False Positive from the World's Best Scent-Detecting Dogs
(*If the Crime Scene Is the Bedroom of a Filthy Teenage Boy*)

SCENT RECEPTORS	DOG	BACTERIA FAMILY	WHAT WE SMELL
300 million	Bloodhound	*Staphylococcus*	Dirty sneakers
230 million	Basset hound	*Nocardia*	Musty basement
225 million	Beagle	*Candida*	Yeast
125 million	Dachshund	*Haemophilus*	Wet fur
5 million	the Bounty Hunter	*Corynebacterium*	Fruit

Sense of smell is not the only place where dogs show exceptional ability above and beyond human beings, though it is definitely the most impressive. Dogs can see better in low light, like at sunrise and sunset, and they can track moving objects much better. They can hear much better too, even though they're born deaf and stay that way for about their first month of life. Once mature, however, they can hear four times as far as the average human and at a much higher pitch as well. None of which seems to make one bit of difference when you yell at them to get their paws out of your face after they've woken you up from the most delicious dream about Frito pie.

....

[11] When he was a kid, Chuck had a basset hound whose ears were so big the dog would step on them while walking.

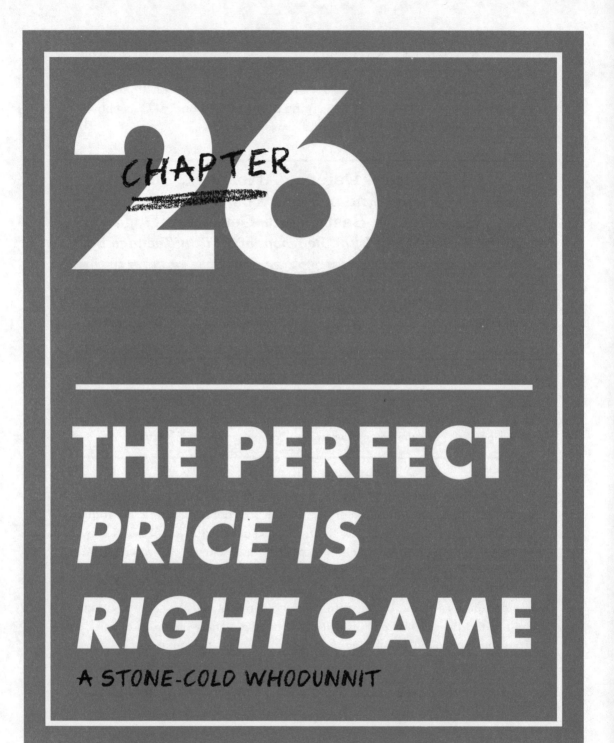

CHAPTER
26

THE PERFECT
PRICE IS
RIGHT GAME

A STONE-COLD WHODUNNIT

At the heart of every conspiracy theory is an asymmetry involving the acquisition of information and the ease of understanding it. Rocket science, astrophysics, advanced math—these are not easy subjects to study. The government lies and hides things from us—that is a concept that is very easy to understand. Put those two things together in the right proportions and, boom, you get things like the flat earth theory or the moon landing conspiracy. 🎙

Yet even for those of us who are not particularly conspiratorially minded, when we watch things like SpaceX's Falcon 9 rocket land itself back on a pad in the middle of the ocean, or we see moving images of the big blue marble[1] rolling beneath the International Space Station, 🎙 our immediate response is often some kind of expression of doubt. *Incredible! Unbelievable!* We don't mean it that way, obviously, but it says something about us that when we see something special, we tend to use words that literally imply that what we are seeing with our own eyes is *not to be believed*.

That's more or less what happened on September 22, 2008, when a retired weatherman from Las Vegas named Terry Kniess went on *The Price Is Right* (TPIR) game show and won both showcases in the Showcase Showdown finale by guessing the price of his showcase to the dollar. "Right on the nose," the show's new host, Drew Carey, told Kniess as he looked around in gape-jawed surprise and the studio audience went wild. A perfect

----

[1] "The Blue Marble" is the name of the famous image of Earth taken in December 1972 by astronaut Harrison Schmitt aboard the Apollo 17 spacecraft and which has, over time, become a metonym for Earth itself.

bid in the Showcase Showdown hadn't happened since 1972 or '73, Carey announced to the audience as he wrapped up the show, with a look on his face like he just found out the pet population was actually being controlled with euthanasia instead of sterilization.[2] Carey was wrong about the last time this happened, though. It hadn't. Ever. Terry Kniess was the first in the history of the show.

THE BID

Kniess's showcase was a fairly typical complement of prizes for the show, which had been on for thirty-six years[3] at that point: a karaoke machine, a regulation pool table, and a telescoping travel trailer. It was originally supposed to be his opponent Sharon's showcase, but as first to bid she was able to exercise her prerogative to pass the showcase on to Kniess and wait for the second showcase, which she did after getting confirmation on the length of the trailer—seventeen feet.

When it was time for Kniess to bid he looked out into the audience, which is standard practice for TPIR contestants, who normally come to tapings with friends or family. It's typical for a contestant to search out their people in the audience, try to make out what they're shouting, then scan the crowd for confirmation or for other suggestions before offering an answer. Kniess did none of that. He looked straight down to his right in the very front row where his wife Linda was seated, looked intently at her without breaking his gaze, and then, as Carey bantered with Sharon—"if it had been an eighteen-foot trailer she might have bid on it, but it was only a seventeen fo-"—he turned and blurted out, "23,743!" No preamble, no equivocation. Not even the word "dollars," just the number.

....

[2] Sometime between 1979 and 1981, the original host of *The Price Is Right*, Bob Barker, an animal rights crusader and strict vegetarian, started signing off every episode with the line "Help control the pet population—have your pet spayed or neutered." Drew Carey continued the tradition when he took over for Bob Barker in 2007.

[3] *The Price Is Right* first ran from 1956 to 1965, when it was hosted by Bill Cullen and traveled from NBC to ABC mid-series. The show was revamped in 1972 on CBS (that's a network hat trick), with Bob Barker as host, as part of the Great Game Show Revival that followed the Quiz Show Scandals of the '50s, which nearly killed off the format. We talked about all this stuff in "SYSK Live: How Game Shows Work." 🎙

"23,743 dollars, wow!" Carey said. "That was a very exact bid." If he only knew. And he would, in about three minutes' time, after Sharon bid on a quartet of vacations[4] and the show went to a commercial break.

Historically, TPIR has always tried to film to time—that means shooting a sixty-minute show in sixty minutes. On this day, when the cameras went off, they stayed off for a good fifteen minutes, which is an eternity when you're trying to film to time with a live studio audience *and* you tape multiple episodes a day. Carey walked off stage and was met by long-time TPIR producer Kathy Greco, who is the one who broke the news: Kniess had hit the number exactly. They were both in complete disbelief.

To hear Carey talk about it, which he did on the podcast of fellow actor and comedian Kevin Pollack,[5] it was like he went through all five stages of grief in the fifteen minutes they were off air:

> DENIAL: **No way!**
>
> ANGER: **Eff this guy, he's obviously cheating and messing with the show!**
>
> BARGAINING: **Is this possible? Could this even happen?**
>
> DEPRESSION: **This is it, they're shutting down the show, I'm out of a job.**
>
> ACCEPTANCE: **Screw it, they're never gonna air this episode anyway.**

Episode 4524K did air, three months later, on December 16, 2008. Loyal viewers of the show loved the perfect bid—there are clips of the episode all over YouTube, many posted the day after it aired—but they did not love Drew Carey's muted reaction to Kniess's incredible, unbelievable win. They roasted him in the comments sections and in TPIR fan forums. They thought he should have been more excited and congratulatory the way Bob

---

[4] One of those vacations was to Chicago, except the accommodations were set fifteen miles outside of town at a hotel by O'Hare Airport, which meant what they were really offering the "winner" was a two-way trip along the road to perdition that is the Kennedy Expressway into downtown Chicago. For shame, *The Price Is Right*, for shame!

[5] Little-known fact: Kevin Pollack is a *Stuff You Should Know* fan, and you can hear him in an episode of ours, "Live in L.A.: How Rodney Dangerfield Worked," when he brought us water on stage after one of us said we were thirsty. 🎧

Barker would have been. A supposition that Barker confirmed in a 2010 *Esquire* article about the incident: "Oh, I would have run with that, you bet," Barker said. Carey wasn't so sanguine about the whole thing. And he wasn't particularly interested in what the hardcore fans had to say, either, because he initially thought Kniess had cheated and that those same fans were partly (or mostly) to blame.

So what happened? We'll find out, but first a word from our sponsor: dramatic tension.

I'M SENSING A PATTERN HERE

In our "SYSK Live: How Game Shows Work" episode we talked about a man named Michael Larson, who in 1984 went on a game show called *Press Your Luck* and pressed his way to $104,950 in cash and two vacations. The year prior, Larson had taken to recording the newly premiered game show on his VCR—which was unusual in itself, since not that many people had

VCRs in 1983—and he noticed a pattern in the eighteen-square rectangular game board. Two squares, which he labeled #4 and #8, not only never showed a Whammy (a character that could wipe out all your winnings) but also held big cash prizes that often came with an extra spin. If you landed on one of those two squares consistently, you could basically play forever and win as much as you wanted, which is more or less what Larson did.

Twenty-four years later, whether they knew it or not, Terry and Linda Kniess took a page from the Michael Larson playbook. In the late spring of 2008, the Kniesses found themselves despondent and in need of a new lease on life after they put their beloved Maltese to sleep.[6] So when a friend of theirs returned from a really fun taping of TPIR in Los Angeles and told them all about it, Terry and Linda decided that dedicating themselves to the show would be just the thing. They planned to go to a taping when filming resumed in the early fall and hoped, as is the hope of any TPIR fan, that one of them would get called to "come on down." The show fit their mental makeups. Linda was great with numbers, while Terry had distinguished himself through his proclivity for pattern recognition, first as an Emmy-winning weatherman, then in retirement as a surveillance expert at Circus, Circus casino. 🎧 As a weatherman, he always seemed to know when the rain was coming when others were not so sure. As casino security, he was always able to catch the cheaters and card counters when others just saw someone on a lucky streak.

Recording the show in the morning and then watching it together before bed, eventually Terry picked up on a pattern—or maybe the better way to think about it is as a tendency. The show regularly used the same prizes with the same prices, over and over. He first noticed it, he told *Esquire*, when he saw the Big Green Egg smoker show up in multiple episodes at the same price: $1,175. It was an innocuous pattern, as most patterns are, because it was most likely a product of comfort and familiarity, not intention. That's just what happens when you do something long enough: whether it's producing a daytime game show for thirty-six years, or commuting to the same job every day for twenty years, or getting ready for school every morning. Eventually you begin to repeat yourself and you don't even notice, though others might. It's human nature.

....

[6] Forever :(

Just as our brains are wired to find energy-saving shortcuts, like by repeating our behaviors, our brains are also wired to recognize patterns. It's how serial killers find their victims and how law enforcement find serial killers, for example. Both rely on the human tendency to do what worked the last time, to go where they are most comfortable, to return to the familiar. Another word to describe this is "habit." Habits are learned behavioral patterns that become automatic with time and repetition when they prove efficient or effective, and the incentive to do something different isn't strong enough to get the person to change.

TPIR producers had *a habit* of using the same prizes over and over again because it was efficient (they had a fixed prize budget) and effective (the show was immensely popular, and no one seemed to mind). From the day Terry Kniess picked up on their habit and noticed the repetition, he and Linda started tracking prices assiduously. Terry spotted the pattern; Linda remembered the numbers. That seemed to be their system, and it was going to be their edge. It was the same kind of edge Terry had busted card-counters for in his post-retirement career at the casino. It wasn't illegal or fraudulent, *per se*, but it was against the spirit of the game for sure, which usually meant you'd be asked to leave and never come back if you were caught. The benefit of *The Price Is Right*, of course, is that shouting out numbers to your confederates to give them an advantage was encouraged. It's part of the game! All that loudness and chatter really whips viewers into a froth and adds to the excitement. If one of them were to get on the show, Terry and Linda thought, how could they possibly lose?

C-O-N-SPIRACY, MY BROTHER

The first episode of *The Price Is Right*'s thirty-seventh season premiered on September 22, 2008. It was the same day Terry and Linda Kniess stood in line at three in the morning, hoping to get good seats and get picked. This was only Drew Carey's second season as host. At the end of the previous season, the show's first without the iconic Bob Barker, they fired Barker's long-time producer, Roger Dobkowitz, who'd been with the show for thirty-five years, since right out of college. Dobkowitz was a superfan

favorite.[7] He was known for greeting people waiting in line outside CBS Television City[8] studios, taking pictures with them, as well as making contestant selections from the pre-show interviews. Loyal fans were furious at his firing, and they blamed Drew.

Drew knew this from the previous two months of filming, and he suspected that a particular group of superfans was also getting inside knowledge from show staff.[9] They seemed to know stuff they shouldn't have known. And on this taping day, it seemed as if they were weaponizing it, because Terry Kniess's showcase win wasn't an isolated incident. He got onstage from Contestant's Row earlier in the show with *another* exact bid. This one for, wouldn't you know, the Big Green Egg smoker: $1,175. Convenient, no? Not only that, everyone else was winning that day as well.

....

[7]   Wouldn't one have to be a superfan to have a favorite producer on a game show?

[8]   Television City is in the heart of West Hollywood, taking up a huge lot on the southeast corner of Fairfax Ave and Beverly Blvd adjacent to the Original Farmers Market and The Grove outdoor mall, both of which are known for B-list celebrity spotting and horrible parking.

[9]   You could make the case one would have to be a super*duper*fan to get insider info about one's favorite game show.

The first contestant off Contestant's Row, a young guy named David Jahns, won a car in a game called "Any Number." The last two numbers he picked, 1 and 8, came directly from the audience. Drew Carey even mentioned it. "Literally everyone in the crowd . . . is holding up the number one," he said. Then when the 8 secured Jahns's victory, Carey shouted, "You got it! The crowd gets you a car!" After Jahns, who bear-hugged Carey and lifted him off the ground in celebration, a chiropractic student named Zachary Brantner won a digital camera and $2,000. Then it was Terry Kniess, who actually *lost* his pricing game. After Kniess, it was Sharon Floyd, who he'd eventually face in the Showcase Showdown. She won a car too, in a game called "One Away" in which a wrong price is displayed, and the contestant has to change each number by 1, either up or down. She got it exactly right. After Sharon, it was Julie Jenkins, who played for an entertainment center in a game called "Pick A Number" where she changed her guess at the very last moment . . . and won. It seemed like every contestant —except for Terry Kniess, ironically enough—was nailing it.

STUFF YOU SHOULD KNOW . . .
About Taxes

Everything you win in an American game show—whether it's cash, a vacation, or a physical object—is considered ordinary income and is subject to both federal income tax up to 37 percent and to state income tax if you live in a state that has it. This often throws game show contestants for a loop and makes winning bittersweet. As a result, it is very common for winners to sell their prizes in order to cover the tax liability. David Jahns planned on selling the boat and the car he won for that reason. And the Kniesses sold all three prizes from Terry's showcase to pay the taxes on those and the vacations he won from Sharon's showcase. Smartly, they took the vacations.

It's not just winnings that are taxable either. Giveaways are subject to gift tax, which Oprah Winfrey's audience found out in 2010 when she gave everyone a car. The show paid for the registration and sales tax, but they didn't pick up the tab on the gift tax, which was $7,000. It left a number of audience members more than a little upset.

They say freedom isn't free, well apparently free isn't free either, whether it's game shows or talk shows, winnings or giveaways.

To long-time show staff, it reminded them of some of the TPIR episodes from the nineties when they'd have two or three people make perfect bids from Contestant's Row and then nail pricing games up onstage. Except all those shows had one thing in common: a superfan in the audience named Theodore Slauson, who had managed to memorize hundreds, if not thousands, of prices over the years and would shout numbers out to any contestant willing to listen to him.

As the new host, Drew Carey suffered from that informational asymmetry we talked about in the beginning. It was impossible for him to have his arms wrapped around thirty-six years of institutional knowledge. That's why this rash of winners didn't remind him of anything, and why it was much easier for him to wrap his mind around the idea that what he was witnessing from the stage of the Bob Barker Studio that day didn't feel right. It felt less like a great day of TV and more like a cabal of TPIR fanatics—teeth aching to drip with his blood, eyes ablaze with a thousand fires of hatred—were trying to get the show shut down or him fired by fixing the games. All, Carey reasoned to himself, as revenge for Roger Dobkowitz's firing, which Carey insists he had nothing to do with. That's why when the crowd was losing its collective mind and Terry Kniess was racing over to his wife Linda to celebrate as the credits rolled, Drew Carey looked like he'd seen a ghost. His producer Kathy Greco saw something else, or should we say *someone* else. It was Theodore Slauson. He was in the audience that day, seated right next to Linda Kniess.

WHAT ABOUT TED?

Ted Slauson was a *huge The Price Is Right* fan.[10] He fell in love with the show in the early seventies when, as one of six kids with only one TV in the house and only four channels to watch, *The Price Is Right* was one of the few shows they could all agree on. Slauson had a gift for numbers not unlike Linda Kniess; he would eventually become a math specialist for a standardized testing company. One day he noticed that in early episodes of the show there was an item that kept showing up with the same exact price. It was an avocado green refrigerator-freezer "from world-famous Amana" that was

----

[10] Dare we say superduperüberfan? Yes.

always priced at $789.[11] And just like for Terry Kniess, this discovery set him on a course to start tracking prices.

That was where the similarities ended between the men, however. For Slauson this was no four-month summer lark to distract from the unfortunate loss of a beloved pet, like it was for Terry and Linda Kniess. It became almost a vocation for him. He built massive spreadsheets filled with all sorts of prize and pricing data. He built a TPIR computer game. He started attending tapings on an annual basis, hoping to get chosen but enjoying being part of the crowd, shouting suggestions and being right way more than he was ever wrong.

At one taping in the early nineties he even got the attention of Bob Barker from the stage, when he helped not one but two contestants in the same episode. Slauson had grown frustrated with contestants on Contestant's Row not heeding his advice in his previous visits, so this time, on the very first item up for bid, in the quiet pause between the announcer Rod Roddy describing the item and Bob Barker cueing the first contestant to bid, Slauson shouted out the price: "$1,250!"

Everyone laughed. Barker told Slauson to stand up as he revealed the price of the item. "The actual retail price . . . is $1,250," Barker announced. The crowd went wild. And when the contestant—who actually listened to Slauson and won—made it up onstage, he told Barker that he owed Slauson.

At the commercial break after that game, according to Slauson in an amazingly entertaining 2017 documentary called *Perfect Bid: The Contestant Who Knew Too Much*, another contestant on Contestant's Row, an attractive woman named Susan, turned around and asked Slauson to help her. After a miscommunication on the next item up for bid, he ended up giving her the exact price of the following item, and Susan made it onstage, much to the delight of Bob Barker and the entire studio audience, who turned the whole exchange into what feels today, when you watch it back, like an awkward, slightly creepy, very public first date.

Regardless, that was two perfect guesses out of three for Ted Slauson, and it would go like that for the rest of the taping and in almost every other

---

[11] Amana appliances were originally created by a company formed by members of the Amana Colonies, a self-sufficient Christian group in Iowa who produced everything from beer to clocks to refrigerator-freezers.

taping he attended.[12] It even got to the point that on one of his annual visits to Television City, Kathy Greco planted her friend Pam, who happened to be the secretary of the show's legendary creator Mark Goodson, next to Slauson to see if he had smuggled in pricing sheets with him, which were strictly *verboten*. He had not. Slauson was just that good.

Slauson stopped attending TPIR tapings after he was *finally* selected as a contestant in 1992. The show rules back then stated that once you'd been on the show you could never get back on again. And if he never had a shot at getting onstage again, Slauson's thinking went, what was the point of going? Eventually, producers changed that rule (they would settle on a ten-year exclusion period) and when Slauson learned about the change it reignited his interest in attending show tapings, which sent him on a collision course with the Kniesses in the front row of Bob Barker Studio on September 22, 2008.

THE REAL CONSPIRACY

This, it seems, is where the seeds of a conspiracy really lay. Not with a vengeful group of blue-haired Barker lovers, as Drew Carey hypothesized, but with two middle-aged white guys, each claiming to have mastered *The Price Is Right* by identifying a prize pattern and tracking historical pricing. One of the men, Kniess, says in not so many words that he did it all by himself with a little help from his wife and a little bit of luck. The other man, Slauson, makes the case that not only did he help Kniess by giving his wife Linda the exact price of her husband's showcase, but he helped others that day as well.

Ah, a delicious mystery is afoot! Who do we believe? It's hard to know for certain; they both seem like nice fellas, but here is your choice. On the one hand is a math genius who knows how to write computer programs and build Excel tables. On the other hand is a meteorologist from Sin City with an intimate understanding of gaming cheaters. As one of the many *Stuff You Should Know* mottos says, you're usually better off going with the guy who has all the spreadsheets.

---

[12] He attended thirty-seven tapings when it was all said and done.

This is how the two men explain what happened: Slauson says that he knew the price of the karaoke machine was $1,000 and that the pool table was $2,800. The trailer was a little trickier, though, because there were two versions—a seventeen-foot model and a twenty-foot model—and the prices varied accordingly. Once Terry's opponent in the Showcase Showdown confirmed that it was the seventeen-foot model, he remembered the price from his database, did the math in his head, and gave it to Linda. $23,743.

In an interview with a Las Vegas radio station a few days after his episode aired, Terry Kniess explained that *he* knew the karaoke machine was $1,000; he knew the pool table was "about $3,000"; and he knew that "the rule of thumb with boats and campers" was $1,000 a foot. The thing is, he thought the announcer said the trailer was nineteen feet (even though no such model existed), which put him at $23,000. Then standing there, staring at his wife, the number "743" just fell out of his mouth. He would later explain to *Esquire* magazine that he picked 743 because that was his and Linda's PIN number (who has a three-digit PIN?), which was a combination of their wedding date (April 7th—sure, if you use European dating conventions) and his wife's birth month (uh-huh, okay).

Kniess acknowledged in the radio interview that he'd met Slauson waiting in line earlier that morning—he called him "the guy sitting next to me who'd been there thirty-three times"—and they'd played pricing games while they waited, but he never used Theodore Slauson's name and he never even suggested that he got help from him. Kniess had done his homework, he said, and had benefited from a little luck and good fortune along the way.

GOOD LUCK IS HARD WORK

If we take these men at their word—which (despite our parenthetical commentary on Terry Kniess's story just now) we are inclined to do, since both could easily be telling the truth—what jumps out at us is that in recognizing a pattern in TPIR prizes, both Kniess and Slauson recognized an opportunity that set them on their respective paths, as it did for Michael Larson and

Press Your Luck. But that was only the spark, the inspiration, the beginning of the journey. What made them successful was good old-fashioned hard work. Larson practiced for weeks perfecting the timing of his buzzer pressing in order to nail squares #4 and #8 on the *Press Your Luck* board. Kniess and his wife studied the show every day for four months. Slauson practiced with his database of prices so much that in the days before he departed for Los Angeles to attend the September 28 taping, he could make it through 1,000 prices in less than an hour with blistering accuracy. That is to say, they did the work.

And still, hard work wasn't enough for either Slauson or Kniess. When Slauson made his one appearance as a contestant his pricing knowledge got him off Contestant's Row and through the "Punch a Bunch" game, but none of that was any help when he had to spin the Big Wheel, the buzzsaw of fate that stands between every winning contestant and the Showcase Showdown. Slauson spun twice and accumulated just fifty-five cents. He was easily beaten by the next contestant up, who amassed seventy cents and was the one to move on.[13] Terry Kniess faced the same challenge, and yet he managed to make it through with a spin of ninety cents.

We look at that moment differently. One of us (the bearded one) sees it as a simple matter of alternately being the victim or the beneficiary of random chance. You spin the wheel, it lands where it lands, *que sera sera*. The other sees the spinning of the wheel as something of a metaphor for fate and good fortune—in other words, for luck. Maybe you can chalk it up to statistics, or maybe there's something to cause and effect that we don't yet understand. Either way, it appears that some of us have it, whatever "it" is, and some of us don't. And who has it or doesn't changes as fast as the numbers on the Big Wheel as they go by after a good pull.

---

[13] Probably having put in basically zero work aside from showing up at a TPIR taping on a whim while vacationing in Los Angeles. Such is life sometimes.

CHAPTER

27

CHILD
PRODIGIES

PRECOCIOUS MIMICS OR
TINY GENIUSES?

In a perfect world, every discussion of child prodigies would begin with *The Royal Tenenbaums* and its three young geniuses.

There's Chas, the brilliant business mind; Margot, the award-winning playwright; and Richie, the tennis phenom. Sadly, these are fictional characters, so a real conversation about prodigies should probably start with Wolfgang Amadeus Mozart.

Little Wolfie began playing the harpsichord at three years old, when most kids are just learning to wipe their own behinds (if you're lucky). By five, he was writing music. By seven, he was touring with his his older sister, Maria Anna.[1] By his teenage years, he'd written numerous concertos and symphonies that are still being performed today. Along with the Spanish painter Pablo Picasso, who could draw before he could talk and the enigmatic American chess world champion Bobby Fischer, who became a grandmaster at fifteen years old, Mozart is considered the epitome of the child prodigy.

But when you dig into the history of child prodigies, what you realize is that these great historical figures are anything but exemplars. They are the exceptions to the exceptional.

WHAT IS A PRODIGY?

In America at least, nowhere is the race to keep up with the Joneses (or the Smiths, if you'll recall from chapter 24) more pronounced than in the competition between parents to prove how advanced their children are

> Ethan knew his ABCs by the time he started kindergarten.
> **My Madison read the entire Harry Potter series by the time she was six.**
> Our little Violet read Baudelaire in French when she was five.

These hypothetical advanced children would never be considered prodigies, much to the chagrin of their parents, because it isn't about being ahead of your peers: it's about not having any peers at all. To be a child prodigy, according to the literature, is to meaningfully display talent or ability in preadolescence that meets or exceeds adult levels of expertise.

---

[1] Many historians believe Maria Anna was nearly as talented as her younger brother, if not equally so, but once she reached "marrying age" in 1769 her father refused to allow her to tour anymore. She stayed back at their home in Salzburg, Austria, while her brother continued playing for audiences throughout Europe, adding to the acclaim that they'd first built together.

That is the main difference between *proficiency* and *prodigy*. Prodigies are doing something as kids that most adults couldn't do. And yet that only touches on the output of the prodigy—it doesn't get to the heart of what makes one. According to experts in the field, child prodigies possess a few distinguishing characteristics: they have incredible working memories; they have exceptional focus and attention to detail; and they have what Boston College psychology professor Ellen Winner calls a "rage to master," which is sort of like a combination of obsession and perfectionism. It's also a great album title. Together, these traits allow a child prodigy to hold large, complex concepts in their minds, break them down into their component parts, and work on each piece incessantly until the whole thing is perfect.

Like Priyanshi Somani, from Gujarat, India, who won the Mental Calculation World Cup as an eleven-year-old by solving for the square roots of ten six-digit numbers in less than seven minutes. NBD.

Or like Taylor Wilson, who built a bomb at the age of ten and a fusor as a fourteen-year-old,[2] then designed an underground molten salt reactor that he presented at the TED Conference in 2013 as a nineteen-year-old. Whew!

For many kids like Somani and Wilson, the pursuit of excellence and expertise becomes all consuming. They will forgo nearly everything that interests other kids their age—playing video games, watching TV—in order to spend more time engaging with their obsession. Parents of prodigies report having to drag their children away from their keyboards, their musical instruments, their work benches, just to make sure they do the most basic things, like eat or bathe or go to school.

WHAT MAKES A PRODIGY?

Very little is understood about the biological basis of prodigies, but it appears that the cerebellum plays a big role in making a prodigy possible. If the brain was like a mullet haircut, the cerebrum would be the business in the front and the cerebellum would be the party in the rear.

---

[2] A fusor is a device that creates nuclear fusion. The most common type was invented by Philo T. Farnsworth, who is most famous for having invented the electric television—a design he came up with at almost the exact same age as Wilson when he made his fusor.

Located in the hindbrain—at the bottom, connected to the brain stem—
the cerebellum makes up only ten percent of the brain's overall size[3] but
contains fifty percent of its total neurons, which means there's a lot going
on back there. Typically we've thought of it as being responsible for fine
motor skills and for coordinating voluntary movements that are controlled
by the cerebrum, which is also responsible for intelligence and memory.
But research in recent decades has shown that the cerebellum doesn't just
coordinate physical movement; it coordinates cognitive processes as well. It
has evolved that way over the last million years or so, during which time the
cerebellum has tripled in size and developed intricate circuit-type connections to the cerebrum (called the cerebro-cerebellar system) that allow the
cerebellum to increase the performance of particular skills that reside in the
cerebrum, provided those skills are exercised.

This brings up the age-old "nature versus nurture" argument. Are child
prodigies born or made? If obsession and focus and practice are essential
elements of prodigy behavior, then surely prodigies are made, right? It's true
that Mozart played three hours a day from the time he was very young; that

....

[3] In Latin, *cerebellum* means "little brain."

Picasso drew and painted and sketched and sculpted incessantly; that Tiger Woods was at the course with his father Earl every day; that the Williams sisters practiced multiple hours every day for their entire childhoods. But none of that explains why Picasso's first word was "pencil," or how Tiger Woods could hit an entire bucket of balls at a driving range at eighteen months old, or how Mozart played the harpsichord at three, or how the Williams sisters gravitated to tennis as four-year-olds.

Clearly, as it is every time the nature versus nurture question gets raised, the answer is both. Child prodigies are naturally gifted and innately interested children who are nurtured by parents, mentors, and coaches to indulge their obsessions and to practice as much as they need to in order to get better and achieve whatever goals they have set for themselves. Some parents will homeschool their kids to give them more practice time; others will move their entire family so their kids can be around the best. Richard Williams did both. He homeschooled Venus and Serena until they went to high school and he moved them from California to Florida when Venus was ten and Serena was nine so they could train at a prestigious tennis academy.

That said, to the extent that you can help to make a child prodigy, you can also break one. For every Tiger Woods there is a Todd Marinovich. For every Venus and Serena Williams there is a Jennifer Capriati. Both Marinovich and Capriati were considered prodigies in their respective sports—football and tennis—as young kids and were pushed, some would say bullied, by overbearing fathers until they washed out or burned out. Both had much shorter careers than anyone expected; both had trouble with drugs and run-ins with the law during and after their playing days. Any innate talent or interest that Marinovich and Capriati had for their sports was seemingly corrupted by the self-interest of parents who pushed their kids to practice more in pursuit of their own goals rather than their kids'.

IT'S HARD OUT HERE
FOR A KID

The struggle for child prodigies begins much earlier than adulthood. It starts in childhood with making friends. While most prodigies don't mind being alone and often enjoy spending long hours by themselves perfecting their talents, eventually everyone wants a friend. Except when you're a kid, friendships are based on simple things you have in common with the people around you. But if you're not around many people, and you're most interested in nuclear fusion or mastering Beethoven's "Hammerklavier,"[4] the pickings for friends are going to be slim.

The real test for child prodigies, though—perhaps the only one they will ever struggle to pass—is when they age out of the prodigy label. "Most prodigies do not make the leap in early adulthood from mastery to major creative discoveries," Helen Winner said. That's the real reason why the conversation around child prodigies should begin with *The Royal Tenenbaums* and not Mozart or Picasso or Bobby Fischer. Those were true geniuses who reimagined and revolutionized the disciplines they worked in. Music, painting, and chess were never the same. The Tenenbaum kids, while not exactly mediocre, turned into a collective mess, which is far more representative of the arc of child prodigies than the achievement of great wealth or acclaim.

It's this inability to bridge the gap from child prodigy to adult creative genius that is hardest of all for child prodigies to manage. What makes it so hard, according to experts like Winner, is that for years child prodigies are exalted for their ability to do things at an adult level of expertise. Except it's always in a field of study that already exists. And then, when they cannot transcend that field, either by revolutionizing it or inventing a whole new one with their work, they by definition cease to be all that special once they become adults. They get *jobs*, and they become more or less just like everyone around them. They have peers; they are no longer peer*less*.

To be fair, most child prodigies don't fall off a cliff or become a mess like the Tenenbaum kids when this regression to reality occurs. They lead fairly normal, productive lives, working successfully in fields they've had a lifelong talent in and passion for. And there are worse fates to befall young geniuses, let's be clear. They could end up hosting a general interest podcast and wake up every morning asking themselves the same question: "I memorized all those Trivial Pursuit cards as a kid for THIS?" No one in their right mind would want *that* life!

....

4 Composed between 1817 and 1818, the sonata is considered Beethoven's most technically difficult piece of music to perform.

Stuff You Should Know

PODCAST EPISODES

A decade-plus of researching and talking about anything and everything that has piqued our interest informs so much of what has gone into this book. That fact is in evidence here in the podcast episode appendix, which is, functionally speaking, an audio bibliography (the title we considered assigning to this section if it were not both so fancy and so schmancy). The episodes listed beneath each chapter are the ones referenced throughout the book with the little red microphone icon (This one: 🎙) These podcasts, and all the rest, are available at www.iheart.com/podcast.

STUFF YOU SHOULD KNOW

This certifies that _____ is the owner of 100 [ONE HUNDRED] percent of responsibility for entry into a demolition derby of any size, in any geography, whether officially sanctioned by the International Order of Crashing Into Stuff or informally organized by amateur collision enthusiasts (otherwise known as "a rampage"). Owner hereby indemnifies Josh Clark, Charles W. "Chuck" Bryant, their successors, heirs, families, and anyone they've ever met, the *Stuff You Should Know* podcast, and Flatiron Books from the consequences of Owner's questionable decision making. Further to the rights and privileges that accrue herein, responsibility and its associated value is wholly transferable in the event the original bearer of this certificate shares *Stuff You Should Know: An Incomplete Compendium of Mostly Interesting Things* with a friend or loved one and that person gets it in their head to strap on a helmet, take all the glass out of their car, and drive it into other cars over and over again. Such indemnity shall never, ever be void anywhere in the universe, in perpetuity, until the end of time or the heat death of the universe, whichever comes last.

Josh Clark	Charles W. "Chuck" Bryant	Pierre Andre

STUFF YOU SHOULD KNOW

DATE

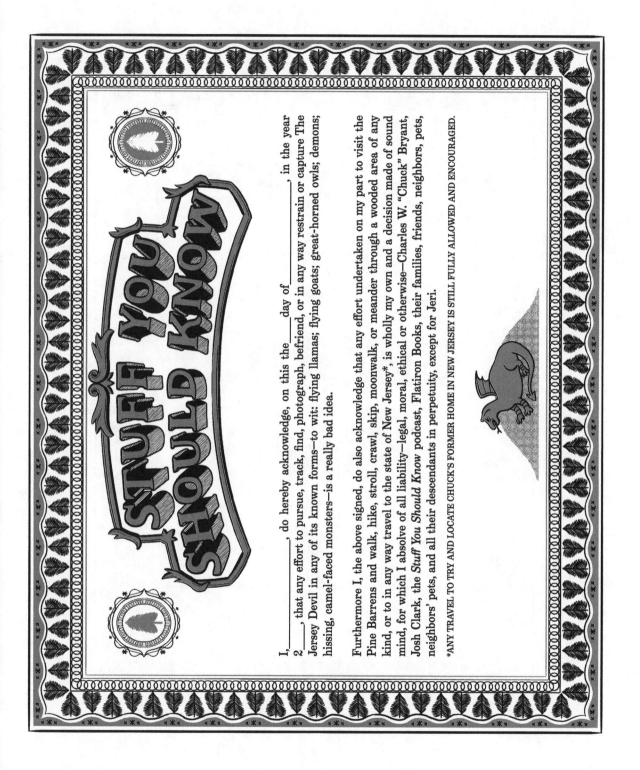

STUFF YOU SHOULD KNOW

I, _____, do hereby acknowledge, on this the _____ day of _____, in the year _____, that any effort to pursue, track, find, photograph, befriend, or in any way restrain or capture The Jersey Devil in any of its known forms—to wit: flying llamas; flying goats; great-horned owls; demons; hissing, camel-faced monsters—is a really bad idea.

Furthermore I, the above signed, do also acknowledge that any effort undertaken on my part to visit the Pine Barrens and walk, hike, stroll, crawl, skip, moonwalk, or meander through a wooded area of any kind, or to in any way travel to the state of New Jersey*, is wholly my own and a decision made of sound mind, for which I absolve of all liability—legal, moral, ethical or otherwise—Charles W. "Chuck" Bryant, Josh Clark, the *Stuff You Should Know* podcast, Flatiron Books, their families, friends, neighbors, pets, neighbors' pets, and all their descendants in perpetuity, except for Jeri.

*ANY TRAVEL TO TRY AND LOCATE CHUCK'S FORMER HOME IN NEW JERSEY IS STILL FULLY ALLOWED AND ENCOURAGED.

STUFF
YOU
SHOULD
KNOW

DATE

ABOUT
iHeartMedia

iHeartMedia is the number one audio company in the United States, reaching nine out of ten Americans every month—and with a quarter of a billion monthly listeners, it has a greater reach than any other media company in the United States. The company's leading position in audio extends across multiple platforms, including more than 850 live broadcast stations in over 160 markets nationwide; its iHeartRadio digital service available across more than 250 platforms and 2,000 devices; its influencers; social media; branded iconic live music events; other digital products and newsletters; and podcasts as the number one commercial podcast publisher. iHeartMedia also leads the audio industry in analytics, targeting, and attribution for its marketing partners with its SmartAudio product, using data from its massive consumer base. Visit iHeartMedia.com for more company information.

ABOUT THE AUTHOR
JOSH CLARK

Josh Clark has been writing since childhood, but *An Incomplete Compendium* is his first book. In 2008, he transitioned from writing for a living to speaking when he started making podcasts, including SYSK and his ten-part series *The End of the World*. He's enjoyed being back to writing.

When he's not working, Josh likes to do things that have nothing to do with deadlines or computers—riding bikes with his wife, Umi, and their daughter with four legs, Momo; working outdoors, digging and chopping and the like; and mixing up world-class cocktails.

Josh's home is wherever Umi and Momo are, mostly between Florida's Space Coast and Atlanta.

ABOUT THE AUTHOR
CHUCK BRYANT

Chuck never imagined he'd make his career as a professional talker and imitation comedian. He figured he'd be a teacher, and weirdly, he's also that. In addition to SYSK, he hosts his beloved *Movie Crush* and works in podcast development.

At home in Atlanta, he hangs out with his wife, Emilie; daughter, Ruby; and their cats and dogs, mostly laughing and being as silly as possible. He also plays guitar and sings in his old man band, El Cheapo, with his dear friends Eddie, Jim, and Chris, at various neighborhood festivals and basements. He enjoys big California red wines and is no stranger to a nice bottle of gin.